LIVING BEYOND BELIEF

HOW TO DITCH THE LIFE YOUR MIND CREATED AND START LIVING THE ONE YOUR SOUL INTENDED

JAIA LEE

LIVING BEYOND BELIEF: HOW TO DITCH THE LIFE YOUR MIND
CREATED AND START LIVING THE ONE YOUR SOUL INTENDED
PUBLISHED BY BRIDGEWAY BOOKS
PO Box 80107
Austin, Texas 78758

For more information about our books, please write to us, call
512.478.2028, or visit our website at www.bookpros.com.

Library of Congress Control Number: 2006927583

ISBN-13: 978-1-933538-59-4
ISBN-10: 1-933538-59-7

For information:
Beyond Belief Publishing
1223 Wilshire Blvd #475
Santa Monica, CA 90403
www.livingbeyondbelief.com
(Formerly published by iuniverse, ISBN : 0-595-27702-0 pbk, and ISBN: 0-595-65706-0
cloth)

This book is simply the author's experience and view, and is not meant
to replace medical treatment or advice that you feel is in alignment with your
present journey. So please always listen to and trust your own guidance.

Table of Contents

For Ariel

*Thank you for reminding me of who I am and
what really matters in life …*

Acknowledgments

I need to be mindful here or this section could become larger than the book. First off, I want to thank all of those people throughout history who have influenced me so profoundly over the years by asking deeper questions—of themselves and of the nature of reality. Thank you to everyone who has helped with this book, or anyone who has played a part in my life, including the ones who continue to play a part on the other side of the veil. I hold you all in my heart. You know who you are and how much you mean to me.

A special thanks to my mom and dad, to my "angel mom," Thalia, to my sister Lisa, and to my Oma, for just being who you are, and for contributing to who I am today. I would also like to thank the staff and faculty of the University of Santa Monica; to Drs. Ron and Mary Hulnick, to the unique and visionary psychology program, without which this book may never have been written; and to the class of 2002 for their continued love, support, and inspiration. A special thank you to the Agape International Spiritual Center for being the answer to a prayer in the way of spiritual community. A heartfelt thanks to all those wonderful souls who choose to participate in the unique dynamic and rich flavor of Agape, and a thank you to the Agape center itself for being an all-around fun place to hang out and grow. There's only one thing better than being in Heaven, and that's being in Heaven with other people.

A very special thank you to Reverend Dr. Michael Beckwith for "saying it out loud" and, by example, giving me the courage to do the same.

Above all, I wish to thank this indescribable essence for gracing me with this message and this Life. Even though there is ample use of the word "I" in this book, I carry no illusions that I, alone, did any of this. On a personal level, not only would I not have been able to write this book, I would never in a million years have such stories to tell. Before I became aware of what Life really was, the only story I had to tell was one of constant suffering and confusion. Whenever I forget what Life Is and Who I Am, I find myself back in that same state.

Everything that is good in me is God in me.

Everything.

Addendum

It has happened many times before and during the writing of this book that something I believed to be fresh and original has actually been coined by someone else. Some believe this is only the subconscious mind at work, digging up long-forgotten words heard or read long ago. I have many times had a "new" idea, coined a "new" word, or wrote an "original" phrase, only to read or hear it later—sometimes only hours later, sometimes years later.

When I first came to what I consider to be my spiritual home, Agape, the Rev. Dr. Michael Beckwith began a Wednesday night service by making the statement, "Life is Good." It was somewhat of a signature statement and my mouth almost dropped open since this had been something I had said on a regular basis for years. I had made a hand-made a plate carrying those words, created post-it notes, drawings, and poems. And when I use that phrase (or some of the many others which I found out later to be not as "original" as I had thought), I find I am not just using these same words, but the vibration of the insight which came with the words.

After my daughter had been out of the school system for a time, I began having insights into why the system—traditional education in general—fails our children at such a fundamental level, and why my daughter's natural enthusiasm for learning and for life seemed to shrink a little more with each successive year she spent in school. I had read books on homeschooling but had come to realize that once we have the thought that we need to learn something, we place it outside of ourselves and make learning into anything other than what it actually is. I also came to the conclusion that any type of forced learning created apathy and resentment and an energetic vibration of imprisonment. I'm sure things I read and studied helped to open my mind to these concepts, but it was only when I saw it in operation, in my daughter's life and in mine, that I was able to really experience the theoretical results firsthand. I felt like I had tapped into one of the biggest secrets of the world. Something that had the potential to free people from their negative beliefs about their own level of intelligence and break deeply held unconscious patterns of aversion to learning. I thought of how valuable it would be to get this message out into the world, only to discover later there was an entire movement called unschooling.

Since we are One, a scientifically "proven" quantum theory, and common knowledge to the spiritually discerning, in Reality everything comes from the same Source. This Source will be referred to many times throughout the book as the Soul, the Heart, the Universe, Spirit, Good, Life, Love, God. It would only make sense that we catch similar ideas, even while we are in different locations, given this paradigm of Oneness.

Some phrases in this book are ones I have heard before and have used wholly intentionally, since I have heard them in so many venues by so many different people. I either have no idea who originally uttered those words, or they are phrases that are commonplace to the English speaking westerner. There are many ideas and phrases I believe at this time to be wholly unique, but, as I've seen before, that could change.

I know that I have been greatly influenced and inspired by many great thinkers, visionaries, and artists—those who lived centuries ago and those around today—and I would only expect that each influence is a thread which has been woven into the fabric of my individual conscious memory as well as existing in the collective. I have tried to give credit where credit is due and apologize for any omissions.

When I was growing up, my younger sister would sometimes use my ideas and I would become agitated, thinking, "Hey, that was my idea."

But, that was when I was a child.

I am in no way advocating consciously using others' ideas to prosper or to not give credit when it is known, but I've come upon a place where getting the message out is much more important than getting credit for it, and it is more apparent every day that even my so called original ideas do not originate from my individual mind, but from the One Mind of all Creation. The real gift is in the inspiration, in the wisdom, in the sharing, in the freedom, and in the incredible potential these ideas have to alter the course of human history. Not in the personal recognition.

Besides, there's much, much more where that came from.

Life

is

Infinite.

Introduction

It was the summer of '96. At the time, I was one hundred pounds overweight, severely depressed, engulfed in various addictions, and involved in an eleven-year relationship tinged with abuse on every level.

Then one day *everything* changed.

The change came as the result of crisis, as most initial transformation usually does. There are only so many times we can press the snooze button on our universal alarm clocks. Eventually, we have to wake up.

Even with over fifteen years of an obsessive interest in, and study of, metaphysics, philosophy, and psychology, nothing I had read could have ever prepared me for what happened. It was as if I had woken up in an entirely different world—a world where worry, fear, and pain simply didn't exist; a world where everything was so brilliantly and remarkably perfect. During this time I was so happy to simply be alive, I cried tears of joy upon waking every morning.

At first the change was only internal, but soon my outer experience began to reflect this inner shift. People I had known were openly shocked when they saw me weeks later, saying I looked ten years younger. I soon left the relationship, released the weight, let the addictions go, and realized financial independence. These outer changes happened with relative ease, and I began to experience firsthand the incredible power of consciousness and its ability to affect physical-world reality. More meaningful than any outward manifestation, though, was the inner change. For the first time in my life, I was genuinely happy and at peace.

The initial shift was so enormous I didn't know quite what to make of it, and quite honestly, I didn't really care to. There was such an overwhelming sense that everything was perfect just as it was. It didn't matter what I thought about anything. It didn't even matter what I did. Everything was in order. It always had been, and it always would be. It was so clear that everything—absolutely everything, no matter what it looked like—was in complete and utter harmony. After several months this awareness began to fade, but an opening had occurred, and through practice, focused intention, and Grace, it continues to open in new and beautiful ways today. Once you've walked, you will never be satisfied with crawling again. You become aware that you are capable of more than you ever dreamed of and are willing to do whatever you can to remain in that awakened state of flow and freedom.

I suspect the intention of this book was for me to share my personal experience of this inner shift in awareness and to share what happened as I continued to experiment with different metaphysical principles, just as any scientist might report findings of the experiments they had conducted. Many of the initial openings were a complete shock to me, and it was only upon reflection that I began to piece together what may have actually happened.

Some concepts, ideas, phrases, or even grammatical phrasing in the book might not sit well in the mind. The tendency of the conditioned mind is to try and understand everything from its paradigm of reality in order to figure out how to fit any new information into that paradigm, in order to remain in control. In order to not have to change. The intention of this book is not to feed the mind more information or to tell you exactly "how to" as the title might imply, but to provide a space for you to become more aware of what and who you think you are in order to realize you're not that at all. There is no strategic ordering of chapters, or a system to learn and live from. This book will give you nothing to believe in. It was written in order for you to escape from any form of mental imprisonment and to hear the voice of your own heart. You don't necessarily hear the voice of your heart by listening to others tell you how to do it; you hear it by others speaking from theirs.

In many ways the book wrote itself, so much so that it's impossible to really take credit for it. I had actually intended to write a book on peace, but just couldn't get it started. Then one morning, while on a walk, I had stopped to sit on a bench when the poem at the end of the first chapter came to me. I walked back home and began to write.

As I wrote, I had no idea what was coming next, and for a long time I had no idea what the book was really even about. In fact, I still have trouble answering the question, "What is your book about?" since it wasn't written with a specific idea in mind. Even though I answer that question a number of ways, in all honesty, it's not really "about" anything, I simply wrote what was on my heart and shared my experience. I found that whenever I had the discipline to show up at the keyboard, the words were always there as if by appointment.

There was only one exception. Midway through the chapter on patience, everything dried up. It felt as if I had been stood up by the universe, by my muse, and I began to wonder if she had taken her business elsewhere.

A week or two later, though, out of the blue, the memory of a speech by the science fiction author Tad Williams, which I had heard a few years before, came to me. The experience he spoke of was a mirror of my own and couldn't have been more perfect for the chapter at hand. The book had become much more than a project or an artistic endeavor. It seems when we give ourselves fully to the creative process, it becomes an entity in itself—our mentor, our teacher, our healer—and allows us a glimpse into, or a path to, our true nature, our true desires, our true life.

Writing this book has reminded me that to be engrossed and engaged in the process of creating is one of the most gratifying aspects of being alive. When you lose yourself in the act of creating, rather than thinking about producing an end product, you are met by the powers of Creation. The end product, even though it may be quite magnificent in itself, will only ever be an afterthought of that blissful and intimate interaction with the Universe—a Universe which is Self-aware and alive with limitless possibilities.

And, this model of creation is not reserved for the ones we have deemed the artists of the world; it is a model of how we are to live our daily lives.

We are to lose ourselves in the act of living, rather than struggling to force an idea we have into existence. As we surrender our personal agenda, the agenda of the Soul can emerge. This way of life isn't easy by anyone's standards, but in the end it leads to experiences that exceed our beliefs, exceed our expectations, and is at times so magnificent, exceeds even our comprehension.

Through our schooling and cultural conditioning, we have been taught to live through our personal intellects, our rational minds, our physical senses, and/or our personal goals. But this way of living can take us only so far. It cannot take us into the realm of the Heart. Into the realm of Heaven on Earth.

It cannot comprehend the desires of the Soul. If we aren't actively questioning the limiting beliefs we have taken on and become willing to let go of them, we can very well produce a life that we would want to ditch. But before we start carrying out plans to ditch that life, we have to understand to a certain degree how that life materialized in the first place. If we don't, we may be tempted to just shuffle the cards, deal ourselves an entirely new hand, and in the end find ourselves to be in the same situation, surrounded by the same issues, and living a life lacking true fulfillment. We may fail to realize that there may be something inherently wrong with the deck itself. If each suit in the deck were a different body of awareness, we would find a physical body, a mental body, an emotional body, and a spiritual body.

If we failed to acknowledge any one of these bodies, we wouldn't be playing with a full deck, so to speak, which would invariably lead to a sense of something being a little off. Even though all of these bodies are important, they are not equal. Real transformation comes through the revelation of the Spiritual Self, of the unmanifest possibility, as our True Self. When we come to this realization, we begin to identify less with these other bodies and come to understand that they do not exist for a purpose of their own and are only a reflection of consciousness. In Reality they are only tools for the Soul to know and experience Itself as Itself while in a physical body.

They exist to support the Life Our Soul intended.

When I say we can ditch the "life" our mind created, it is with the understanding that in this context, the words "god" or "self" or "love" are interchangeable with life. We have to leave behind the ideas we have about these things and begin to see there is an Essence, a Truth, a Reality, which exists beyond our personal mental conditioned concepts. An entirely different kind of life is waiting for us when we become willing to seek a new understanding of, and relationship with, these things themselves, as opposed to continually experiencing our conditioned mind's ideas *about them.*

Right now we are all being invited into this new way of living and being. At this point, "invited" may be too soft a word. "Initiated" is more reflective of the nature of the process that asks us to step aside and pay attention. It goes beyond belief. In other words, it goes beyond merely co-creating positive experiences with our personal intention, engaging a limited awareness of possibilities. It goes to the next step, beyond manipulation, even positive manipulation, and into a deeper realization of the truth that "Heaven" is Here Now.

Instead of planning our lives, we have to open ourselves to the Plan. This takes a trust and a faith that may feel severely unnatural to the part of us that experiences our lives—and ourselves—as something fixed and solid. It feels extremely threatening to the part of us that carries a fixed idea of what is good and tries to control our lives based on that limited perspective. In this endeavor to truly live, we find that living really has nothing to do with a fixed idea.

In its very essence, it is a walk with the unknown. It is a dance with a force that is alive with possibilities, with a rhythm, a beat, a cadence all its own. To align oneself with this natural force and allow Its direction to become our direction is the current invitation to us all. We may choose to decline the invitation and continue to attend the parties of our personal creation, but sooner or later, as the call gets stronger, we will eventually need to find a new way. The pain associated with being out of alignment with our true nature, with Our Selves, will continue to bring us to our knees until we can begin to listen and act upon that inner voice—without reservation.

And to, eventually, no longer hear a voice, but become it. To hold hands and dance with the mystery until the notion of a mystery falls away and all there is left is…*nothing.*

And in the nothing…*everything.*

To have a relationship with that which can never be fully known or understood by our intellect seems to be the ultimate folly, but in truth it is the only worthwhile endeavor. It is only through this sort of relationship that we come to really know and experience the Authentic Self and Real Life, which is far greater than anything we could have ever imagined, thought possible, or, sometimes, at least in the beginning, even thought we wanted.

This is an ancient model, in the sense that this way of life has been talked about, and lived, by the mystics, sages, and prophets throughout history. It is a new model, because instead of talking about these ancient prophets, instead of merely worshiping spiritual masters who lived in other times and seeing them as chosen and special, when we actually practice what they taught, we find ourselves beginning to have the kinds of experiences they talked about.

It is a new model, because we live in different times than these mystics did, with many more possibilities available to us through technology and other means. It is new because this knowledge is now available to just about anyone who chooses to study it, rather than being available only to a select religious initiates and officials, or secret sects. It is new because when we experience this life for ourselves, we find it to be so astonishing, so different from anything we could have ever possibly imagined that a part of us can't help but feel we have discovered something new.

"How could they not have told us it was *this good?!*" we think.

Ah, but they did.

Yet until we begin to experience the intricate web of the Universe working its wonders through us, those prophets and spiritual masters will remain enigmas to us, rather than fellow human beings who walked the earth just as we do now. They will remain the chosen few who were fortunate enough to tap into a secret, inexhaustible, mystical well which seemed to immunize them from the usual ravages and sufferings of a typical human incarnation, instead of ones who consistently practiced spiritual teachings and through their practice came to know their true nature and the true nature of Life.

This is an incredible time in history to be alive on planet earth. There are tremendous challenges facing the planet, carrying with them the potential for transformation on a massive scale. There are people across the globe who are already living in the world described above, a world where heaven isn't somewhere you go when you die, but is discovered right here on earth through a state of consciousness: A world where miracles happen continuously; where joy is not dependent upon outer circumstances; and where peace resides in spite of the fact that many are still dreaming war.

There are some people, right now, who are waking up in this new world for the first time.

There are others still, who may have been woken by their universal alarm clocks and have decided that it's finally time to go to work—working not merely for money or external recognition, but on behalf of their Soul. Working to know themselves on deeper and deeper levels. Working to seek a deeper meaning of, and deeper joy in their existence. Working to discover what on earth they are really doing here. And, in the end, not really "working to" at all, but *living* to, *inspired* to, *loving* to!

If the alarm was loud enough, they may have decided that today was the day to put some of their fears—masked as hate, cynicism, or indifference—aside, and to begin to reflect on the possibility of a different type of life than they had previously imagined.

Maybe peace really *is* possible. Maybe unconditional love *does* exist. Maybe life *doesn't* have to be a struggle.

And, maybe after a time, after peeking out from the covers and deeming these ideas too silly, too wishy-washy, too irrational, too unbelievable, or too unsettling, they'll hit the snooze button once again and settle back down into sleep.

No worries.

There's no way to disable the universal alarm clock. The alarm will continue to go off on national levels as well as personal levels, as these are only reflections of each other. The good news is that eventually we'll all wake up. The bad news is that until we do, the nightmares will continue....

The Child
Innocence Regained

So when did you forget?
The game isn't over yet
When did you stop playing?
If you choose to stifle
and keep your Self bridled,
It's only Joy you're delaying

The wise ones all know
to posses that glow
One must become like a child
It's somewhat tragic
to cut off the magic
That remains within all the while

So just let yourself go
and always know
That Heaven is at hand
When you can smile
and just play a while,
Life becomes more than you planned

One day I discovered that I had spent the better part of my life try-ing to fit myself into a world I had never even fully believed in.

I hadn't done a particularly good job of it, either.

Basking in various addictions from my early teen years, flailing about in dead-end jobs, carrying one hundred extra pounds of weight, spending eleven years in a limiting, and at times nightmarish, relationship and marriage, having no real friends to speak of and no real peace of mind to speak of either.

Life pretty much sucked a whole lot of the time.

I couldn't figure out what on earth I was doing here, but I just knew there must be some reason for the whole ruckus.

Then, just as I was resigning myself to a monotonous and tired existence, believing there was nothing more, the hand of destiny dealt a card and my daughter came into my life. It was through reading books on parenting that I began to understand the basis of psychological conditioning on a deep level—deeper than I ever had before. I began to personally relate my past experience to current behaviors and see how the words from those closest to me had infiltrated my heart and mind, and how brilliantly I, usually unconsciously, tended to fulfill their prophecy.

Some things that had never made sense suddenly began to. The process led me to wonder: What would happen if, from the beginning, we treated our children as if they had their own answers? As if they knew themselves? What if we didn't assume they were sinful by nature?

And, by God, what would happen if we started doing this for ourselves?

Stepping Outside the Box

As children we know certain things. We just know. It is a seed of knowing planted by the hands of heaven into the rich soil of our soul. We know that life is miraculous and brilliant. That a magical adventure is encased in every moment.

We know this.

Then the world—full of well intentioned people, for the most part—convinces us that we've got it all wrong and, lucky for us, they can teach us how it really is.

The world is not a magical place, they say. You can't just play all day. You have to watch out. Be careful.

Be *quiet.*

See that box over there? See if you can shove yourself into that.

What, you don't fit? Well, we can just shave off a few parts…there. That's better.

What? You say it's cramped in there? You can't breathe very well? Don't worry, you'll get used to it. You won't need too much oxygen. It doesn't take much to go to a school that only asks you to parrot back facts with no meaningful context, or to a job that doesn't truly engage you, or challenge you to use your inherent talents. It takes even less to stare at a screen for hours at a time, conditioning you to a life of economic enslavement. Heck, you certainly won't need too much oxygen for brainpower, since the media and others will be doing most of your thinking for you.

It may sound a bit harsh, but if we truly think about it, this is the process that many of us went through as we were "socialized" into a world big on fear and conformity and one lacking in vision, inspiration, and real freedom.

It may have been done with a smile and a bribe, or it might have been done with a scowl and a smack. In a way, it doesn't even matter how it was done. In the long run, the result was the same. We ended up sacrificing who we were in order to fit into a limited system.

Into a box.

Into an identity that didn't really have a whole lot to do with who we really were or why we were really here.

An identity that didn't acknowledge our inherent talents and gifts, and that certainly didn't accommodate the great and magnificent Life that lived within us.

And that We lived within.

If we found ourselves in this situation as a child we may not have had much of an alternative. As an adult we do.

An entirely different world of possibilities exists for us when we step outside the box. But, it does take a few things in order to become free of this self-imposed confinement. First, it takes the awareness of the walls that currently surround us. We get so used to these walls we may not even notice them anymore. There are physical walls, which consist of an over-identification with our physical bodies and the material world. There are mental walls, which include our current BS, or belief system. There are emotional walls, which house unhealed and/or "stuck" energy. Then there are spiritual walls, which are sometimes never even felt or acknowledged, as many of us may never make it past our religious BS and into a personal relationship with Spirit, which transcends our thoughts about It completely.

It takes courage to look at the walls that have been erected around our being. It takes courage to break out of the box we rely on to protect us from the world around us, and ironically, to protect us from the inherent genius within.

It takes courage to speak up. To be great. To leave behind a limited idea of what our parents thought we should be. To go beyond what the conditioned mind has formerly identified as "itself."

The adult in us may be able to justify the surrounding walls indefinitely, while the Child within never stops dreaming of escape. Never completely forgets the magical world that once existed. We may begin to wonder how we got so far away from that child who knew he had all of his answers. From that little girl who wasn't afraid of speaking up and asking for what she needed, when she needed it. How could we have wandered so far from that Divine Child who was at home in the world around her? From that little boy who held no fear in his heart and was free to love, unabashedly and unconditionally?

From the time we get here, we are told "how things are" in one way or another. On a rudimental physical level alone they are helpful. We learn to not walk across a busy street. Or to drink Draino. But there are other levels that the adults around us were no longer able to see. In this process, we may have come to feel that our own ideas were silly or that we were incapable of thinking for ourselves. It may also have been insinuated by those around us that thinking for oneself could lead to dire consequences.

From the Newtonian constructed model of the world, we operate in a paradigm in which we assume that we are merely a bag of bones with a brain. An empty slate. This paradigm puts information outside of us, as something separate from us, and fails to acknowledge the innate wisdom that rests within our being. We are led to believe that there are others out there with the answers to our problems; made to think that if someone has some letters behind their name, they must know more than we do; that if someone has some years under their belt, they are automatically in a position to know what is best for us. Ridiculous.

During different stages and circumstances, you may feel pulled to research alternate theories, immerse yourself in subjects that interest you and gather information from varied sources in order to have a broad base of knowledge and opinions to draw from.

And while you may want to politely acknowledge others' good intentions as they try to help you (as well as gratefully acknowledge information and guidance that truly serves you), when you discover your Self, you find, in turn, the answers to your questions discovering You. Answers begin to come to you that you could never have thought of "yourself." And from sources you never would have dreamed possible.

This doesn't mean you, as a rule, shut yourself off to feedback and outer information, it's just that the bottom line no longer lies with anyone or anything else. You find the only real authority on your life is You. Your Self. The Love that simply Is.

You know what you are interested in. *You* know what you love. *You* know what your next step is. *You* know what is best for you, and who is best for you. *You* know your strengths and your current areas of growth.

Unless…

Unless you don't think you do. Unless you have listened to others tell you how to "do" life and how to "do" yourself until the whole thing has become such an incredibly jumbled mess that you forget where the ideas about yourself began—and who, in essence, You really are.

One day, you may have climbed into the box thinking, "I'll just climb in for today, just to make things a little easier." Then the next day you may have climbed in again, noticing how much smoother the day went when you did. No one yelled at you. Or laughed at you.

Or worse.

So you continued to climb in, even though you noticed that it was a little boring in there and you certainly couldn't see much.

By climbing in the box, you lost your enthusiasm as well as your perspective.

You may have wondered why this made the adults around you so happy. One day you may have decided it was too much trouble to get out. "Oh, I'll get out tomorrow," you thought. And as the days went on, and as the expectations mounted around you, there finally came the day when you completely forgot that you ever climbed into a box in the first place. Reminders of a world outside didn't excite you anymore, but actually threaten your sense of safety and security. You forget all about that magical world alive with limitless possibilities.

And then you do what anyone would do. You begin helping others climb into boxes so that they will be as comfortable as you are.

And maybe, so that you won't feel so alone.

The Child as Teacher

Typically, children are thought of as inferior. Childish. In need of instruction.

How much of that belief alone limits our children's potential?

What if, instead, we believed them to be wise and knowing? Closer to the mysteries of life, if you will. What if we could humble ourselves enough to see that we had just as much to learn as we had to teach? Maybe more to learn.

Maybe much more.

How might these beliefs effect our interactions with our children, which in turn would effect their interactions with themselves?

When my daughter entered kindergarten, one of the first things they did was test for aptitude. She scored very high in many areas, including a seventh-grade comprehension level. Different teachers told me she was the most amazing child, as she was extremely outspoken, yet at the same time respectful and courteous. Parents and teachers alike began asking me what I had done.

Heck, in a way, I was just as surprised as anyone else. The answer that I heard from within was, "I just loved her." At the time I thought that I might be blanking on an answer because I really didn't know. I knew that I hadn't really done anything and was a little surprised by the question.

I now see that "doing nothing" was quite possibly the answer. Not a doing "nothing" kind of doing nothing, but rather not doing things that would inhibit the natural flow and rhythm of growth. By giving her the space to be, to explore, to discover. By not making her wrong for her feelings. By listening to her ideas and thoughts about the world without needing to immediately correct those that weren't "right" according to the general consensus. By not dealing merely with a negative behavior, as much as discern the cause of it in order to have understanding and compassion. By carrying a deep inner conviction in my heart—a *knowing*—that there was never, anything, ever wrong with her. By carrying a deep trust in Life and Its Self-organizing principle and by continuing to ask the question again and again and again: what would serve her on a Soul level?

During this process I began to witness a strength within her, a positively indomitable Spirit, that I, without resorting to physical punishment or drugs, simply did not have the power to control. And, after a time I realized I no longer had the desire to control it anyways, since when I was able to just trust what was happening and let it run its course, astonishing things would transpire—"lessons" I never could have created on my own.

I didn't have a vested interest in her intelligence, and even though I had noticed it was quite amazing, I was never much interested in making her smart. In fact, I guess I wasn't interested in *making* her anything. I realize now, if I did anything at all, I paid attention. I listened. Sometimes for things she was unable to express. To the unspoken language that said, "I'm overwhelmed and tired; please help me calm myself," that lay just beneath a crying, screaming, very angry three-year-old's voice, informing me she was running away. As best I could, I listened.

Some part of me knew she was a genius even before she was born, and I probably tended to treat her like one. I don't want to be misunderstood here, though. Part of me knew she was a genius because *every child is*. There is no child on this planet, no being on this planet for that matter, who does not carry a seed of genius within. A seed, that when nurtured, grows into a special and unique way of being in the world. A seed of genius that is part of the whole and contributes to the whole; recognizing genius as the unique pattern of magnificence that rests within every being on the planet.

Instead of trying to influence or manipulate a child into a simpleminded idea of genius, what we really need to do is engage the genius that is already there. There are many definitions of genius, and if you think about it, a high score on an intelligence test is probably one of the least remarkable. The Mind, this Higher Mind, this Divine Intelligence, this Genius, can do so much more than solve problems. It can see the world in new and interesting ways and put things together that, before that moment, seemed to have no relation. It can create out of thin air. By having my daughter in my life, I began to remember I was here to do so much more than solve problems. Here to do so much more than just make it through another day.

We took weekly trips to the local library from the time she was six months old simply because it was a joy reading to her. It was a joy having her in my life. It was fascinating to watch her process the world around her. I would often put myself in her shoes and think how a certain situation might look if I had never experienced it before. Just by being in her presence, I began to remember things I had forgotten after all those years of worksheets. To-do lists. Worrying.

One day, when she was around a year old, my daughter helped me to see a butterfly. This might sound a little odd, but to this day it has remained one of the greatest gifts she has ever given me. She saw the butterfly and was at first a little shocked, then slowly became absolutely enraptured, shouting in delight and joy and amazement. If I had never seen a butterfly before, I thought, how would I experience it?

In that moment, something happened.

I remembered.

I began to feel the wonder and beauty of life creep back into my awareness. I had forgotten what a miracle Life really was.

I began to remember all of the questions I had been told weren't important. They may not have been important, but they were mine.

And, I have come to realize, *that is the important part.*

Sometimes, through a fear of "spoiling" our kids, we end up creating an individual who becomes completely cut off from their true being. The child has to manufacture a false sense of identity in order to live up to our ideas of what they 'should' be. We may forget that each child is an individual, with individual needs and challenges, gifts and callings. Different levels of sensitivities. Unique ways of learning and processing the world around them. We may begin with an image of what we believe a child should be and proceed to mold and sculpt, crimp and cut, until the final product barely resembles the original.

We might end up realizing our fear of spoiling them, just not in the way we had originally thought. And we may come to realize that we don't just do this with our children.

Thinking vs. More of the Same

So, how do we get beyond the limited ideas we hold of our children, or of ourselves, in order to see and experience what is actually there? Does this mean that we offer no guidance or instruction to our children?

Yes and no.

The conditioned mind, or limited self, which imagines us separate from Life and Love, would do well to keep a lid on most of its so-called guidance because most of this guidance would merely be projection. Projection can be defined as the tendency of this limited self to project things, or to see things, that it is unable to see in itself onto a world that it imagines to exist independent of itself. These projections originate from the limited self's recorded past experience, where unhealed childhood wounds and fears reside and where a very limited idea of life dwells. From that space, a cycle of shaming, threatening, judging, and bribing occurs. In that paradigm, the seeds of fear, limitation, doubt, and indifference are planted into the fertile minds of children, much in the same way they were planted in ours. And so this germination goes: generation after generation after generation.

We would do well to instruct and guide from the beautiful flower of our being, as opposed to guiding from those overgrown weeds of fear and judgment. We would also do well to protect our children. Not so much from the world, but rather from our limited consciousness, which imagines a world where protection is needed. Protect them from a limited awareness that lives in a state of fear and separation. From all of the simple-minded, conditioned, and fixed views of reality; and all of the wretched ideas this conditioned mind might carry about the "right" way to raise a child. Protect them from the idea that there is anything other than Love.

We can either raise a child or train a child. Raising insinuates elevation. Raising them up in the awareness of Who they really are. Raising them to be the divine creators they are. Or, we can train them to jump through hoops and how to fit themselves, come hell or high water, into a highly mechanical, heartless, soulless way of life.

When we are truly inspired and in a state of creative flow, we do have answers. We do have brilliant ideas. We do create the space for insights and revelations and for miracles to occur. We provide teachings that lead to greater awareness and freedom for others. This instruction doesn't come from our personal point of view, though. It doesn't come from our conditioned mind. It comes from a greater perspective. It comes from Good. From God. From Love. From Our Own Self. From the One Self.

Instead of merely relying on some sort of guidebook to teach others what we have been taught, in the exact manner we have been taught, we come to rely on a consciousness of infinite possibilities. We bring our Authentic Self, our unique way of expressing, to the subject at hand; and in that bringing, we bring the space for true learning to occur. We don't feel a desire to tell people what to think, but we know that it is in everyone's best interest, including our own, to become more and more aware of *how* we think. And of "who" exactly is doing the thinking.

Without a set system to measure everything against, there is no underlying agenda to try and prove something or convince others that it's "our way or the highway." From this inspired place, we transcend the concepts of right and wrong, good and bad, and we find that in this space there is room to actually investigate. To actually explore. To actually think. The conditioned mind, which can only see things through its own filters of belief, takes leave in order for inspired thought to take root.

When you give yourself permission to think for yourself, thinking becomes an even greater priority than what you are thinking about. In this paradigm, it is not only important that we get a "right" answer (because from this perspective, in a sense, there is no one right answer), but that the answer comes from a place of beauty, from a place of enthusiasm, from a creative process of thought which can include sound logical, critical, as well as intuitive thought processes. This is a distinction many times not even acknowledged in a typical school setting.

It's not that we wouldn't want to teach concepts, such as, *c-a-t spells cat*—since we have agreed that this set of letters, formed in this particular way, represents a certain type of creature on the planet—it's just that we don't get caught up in mistaking the physical world for Reality, and realize that most of the people on the planet don't identify that same creature as a *c-a-t*. We also acknowledge that memorization and regurgitation of agreed-upon facts is one of the more remedial and lower functioning levels of the brain; and we don't pigeonhole our children, or ourselves, into such a limited paradigm of learning.

Another thing not generally acknowledged or talked about in a typical school setting is ethics. Ethics are not rules dictated by an authority outside of yourself, but something you develop through the wisdom of the heart. Ethics transcend human law and function in accordance with your current understanding of the inherent Oneness of Creation. True ethical development never comes by merely following someone else's directions—otherwise, behavior would change according to the direction of whomever one is following. This direction will ultimately be motivated by fear, not Love. Fear of what the rule-maker will do if they find out the rules have been violated.

Fear of what our family and friends will do if we start to question the unspoken agreements. Fear of what "life" will do to us if we step over that line.

Fear of living.

Fear of loving.

We aren't typically taught how to make decisions based upon what is important to us and why; to really think about what it is we want and why it is we want it; and then to continually get outside of our personal agenda and perspective altogether to see if there may be something else for us to consider. But many times we are taught how to become quite adept at playing a lifetime game of Simon Says.

Whenever a child, or the Child within, asks why, and an impatient, tired, burned-out, or overwhelmed caregiver (which we can all be at certain times) makes the child feel like a nuisance or a burden for asking, the message is transmitted that asking questions is troublemaking business.

Actually, asking questions *is* troublemaking business for the status quo, for business as usual, for a constructed reality we imagine to be real, or for the best or *only* possibility.

Good questions inspire change. Real thinking leads to good questions. Good questions cause one to consider different possibilities and to reexamine the current modus operandi. Memorizing someone else's answers without a larger, holistic perspective does not lead to thinking, critical or otherwise. It leads to more of the same. More of the same always leads to more of the same.

Depending on where we are coming from (i.e., what intention we are holding), more of the same will ultimately lead us to greater levels of freedom, creativity, and contribution to the evolution of life on this planet; or, alternatively, to more apathy, confusion and suffering; and possibly, eventually, off the edge of a cliff.

How many times today have we heard that unconditioned Mind within? Was a question raised? Did It have a suggestion, or urge us in a direction that didn't quite fit in with our current beliefs about reality or what is possible? Didn't fit in with the program?

Were we willing to listen, to explore, or did we immediately shut the lid to the box?

Remaining open can be a daunting endeavor. It's so easy to get stuck in what we think is right. Letting go of beliefs and opinions that are keeping us stuck in the box can be tremendously challenging, and if we have come to completely identify with them—imagining those thoughts to be who we are—it can be damn near impossible.

Beyond the "Shoulds"

You find that when you are living beyond belief, there are no predetermined rules. Every situation is unique. Every child is different. And, invariably, it comes down to the underlying intention we have for our children who are really just mirrors of ourselves and for ourselves. Are we trying to fit them into our society's idea of what it is to be happy and successful, or are we allowing them their individual, unique life process? Are we trying to mold them into some unnatural idea of happy and good (and quiet), sometimes even to the point of drugging them? (Are there ways we do this to ourselves?) In many ways, it is much easier to simply play the authoritarian role than to allow our children to have their own ideas and opinions.

One day when my daughter and I were at odds, I thought, *Hey, who taught you to think for yourself?* Then, in typical Homer Simpson fashion, immediately responded with, *"D'oh!"*

A Child could go through his or her entire childhood and never really be seen for who he or she is, but only for what they are supposed to be according to someone else's definition of good. Only then, when they are fitting nicely into that idea, are they given positive acknowledgment. To most, this is an absolutely justifiable parenting strategy; but in the long term, it produces disastrous results, since the discovery process is the very thing needed to bring out the genius within.

You have to color outside the lines to be a great artist. You have to fail hundreds, if not thousands, of experiments to discover anything of real significance. What the conditioned mind usually does is stop that organic process in its tracks in order to maintain the illusion of control; and the joy, the discovery, the unique gift, gets replaced by the idea of what is acceptable.

Life becomes stifled.

Beliefs are formed about behavior. We end up living at the effect of a dead and lifeless belief system, rather than the First Cause, fully alive, Self-aware, unlimited, creative Beingness *We* truly *Are*.

If we could only love our children more than we love the idea we have about our children and how they should be.

Then, maybe, we could love ourselves more than we love the idea we have about ourselves and how we should be.

Then, by chance, maybe by some miracle, we could come to love Life more than we love our idea about what Life is and how It should be.

Ah, what a miraculous Life that would be!

What Do We Really Learn at School?

When my daughter had finished second grade, I was guided to remove her from school, a proposition to which she happily agreed. I had no idea how to go about teaching her at home, but I knew it was what I needed to do. It took me on a journey I was completely unprepared for and absolutely destined to undertake. It was like opening a can of worms, as I began to question all of the beliefs I had about learning. I began to wonder if learning was really something that occurred in a special room, age-segregated, community-segregated, with bribery, coercion, manipulation, and competition as motivating factors. In the end, who and what does that really serve? We all chime in and say, "Our children, of course."

But does it really? Where does that bottom line actually rest? Where does that intention really lie? With an exciting exploration of the world and themselves? A thought provoking adventure of juxtaposed ideas and concepts, or a competition for tax dollars through test scores? Have our children merely become pawns in our childish pursuit of competition and greed?

There is an episode of the PBS show *Nova* on the subject of creativity, which I happened to see soon after my daughter was born. In that episode, a typical art lesson was documented, with a distinct finished product on display for the children to copy. The narrator made a comment that has stuck with me to this day. He said something to the effect of: If we took the best minds in the world today and asked them to devise a plan that would cut our children off from their creative selves, we couldn't possibly be doing a better job.

After my daughter and I began to remove ourselves from the matrix of compulsory education, I began to see that the same implication lies with learning in a traditional classroom.

We couldn't be doing a better job of cutting our children off from their innate curiosity and capacity for internal motivation to learn and grow than by drowning them with unrelated, irrelevant facts and to-do lists.

We couldn't be doing a better job of building a life of stress than by constantly testing and grading (judging) our kids.

We couldn't be doing a better job of conditioning people to a life of apathy than by having them spend hours and months and years on tasks that have absolutely no meaning and no relevance for them on a personal level. Or by or conditioning them to live for the future by forcing them to do things in which they have no interest in, talent for, or desire for, in order to (supposedly) get to do something else (better) later on.

We couldn't be doing a better job of creating people who are emotionally unbalanced and immature than by expecting them to keep a lid on their personal lives and feelings; or by treating their feelings as aberrations and interruptions rather than valid and informative, and actually quite mandatory, in order to learn how to relate to themselves and others.

We couldn't be doing a better job of conditioning people to a life shaped by external motivation and competition than by dangling the rewards of a high grade and by pitting them against one another for the attention or acknowledgment of the teacher.

We couldn't be doing a better job of conditioning people to see themselves and their lives as fragmented and compartmentalized than by teaching subjects in a dissociated fashion, as opposed to demonstrating the interrelatedness and interconnectedness of all subjects and their enhancement of, and dependence upon, one another.

We couldn't be doing a better job of creating feelings of unworthiness and incompetence than by limiting most instruction to a logical/rational/lecture mode, forgetting that there are many forms of intelligence and many ways of learning (including auditory, visual, kinesthetic, interpersonal, intrapersonal, musical, and intuitive), and that different people excel in different areas and learn by different means. Or by concocting an imaginary level of competency for every age frame, as if they were robots instead of unique beings with individual time frames and abilities.

We couldn't be doing a better job of entrenching ourselves further into this paradigm and becoming lulled into a false sense of security, when we learn to fit nicely into it. This paradigm is born of fear, and tells us that life will not provide us the basic instructions and lessons when we are fully engaged in it. It is a paradigm that says Life can be improved upon. In this paradigm we need to make up irrelevant tasks, goals, and rules to distance and distract ourselves from Life's real lessons and opportunities as they present themselves. If we begin simply to pay attention, we are able to see the relevant lessons and opportunities for learning on the physical, mental, emotional, and spiritual planes of our being. We are able to see where our attention is, where our energy is, where our love is, and where our growth is, as well as what is really important to us. We are also able to more easily see what is merely keeping us occupied and stuck in our current modus operandi—while the life of our Soul is held at bay.

There are alternative schools, which attempt to serve the unique genius of the individual child, as opposed to a blank slate or an empty bucket; and while there may be a strong academic focus in these schools, they focus just as strongly on the love of learning. Each child has the freedom to learn about things he or she is interested in and to develop their own curriculum and projects. Along with the opportunity to interact with adults who are not burdened with the prospect of having a standardized test to teach to, an environment is created which has the potential to inspire a lifelong love of learning and growing, not a sense of dread and aversion to it.

This is not to say that there aren't wonderful teachers working in the trenches of the government system who refuse to teach to the test, who are inspired to go beyond what is expected, and who, instead of becoming shining examples for their peers, are many times resented for raising the bar. It's not a pleasant thing when you can only experience the raising of the bar as being forced to jump higher, rather than being excited by the possibilities and inspired and motivated to rise to new levels yourself. But in a sense, how can one be blamed when they imagine themselves to be as mediocre and unimaginative as the system they came through?

Even though there are individuals within the system choosing creativity, enthusiasm, and excellence, the system itself is a problem because its underlying intention is to prepare people to get a job, not to bring out the genius from within. These are completely different intentions. The underlying intention isn't to foster a level of self-awareness and competence, or to explore values and meaning, or to introduce varying opinions and theories which allow students to think critically and independently while gaining the insight and wisdom to live an adventurous, pioneering, and magnificent life. It is, instead, a fixed, manufactured system, whereby individuals are measured against that system and judged by how well they can memorize and ultimately fit into it. Much like our current society.

News at 11. Test at 12.

We have all been schooled into a very narrow-minded and limited idea of ourselves and of life. We have had to shrink down the vision of what is possible for us, based on other people's opinions. Unless our calling in life happens to be highly academic, we leave school many times having no idea of what we are really capable of. We are usually asked to memorize theories presented as facts, or to memorize facts that have no relevance or meaning in our lives, and are then reprimanded if we don't do this well. I wonder where we could possibly have gotten the notion that life is a struggle, that learning is boring and hard, or that we have to spend our lives doing something we don't really enjoy?

Well, of course we have to work for a living. That's just the way it is.

Or is it?

When we understand the psychological theory of conditioning and realize that a limiting belief can be formed and may play itself out in a person's life indefinitely—after *only one experience*, if that experience is emotionally charged—can we even begin to imagine the conditioning which occurs after weeks and months and years of living in this fashion? In fact, we might not even see it for the prison that it is, since it is so deeply ingrained in our belief system as a necessary aspect of life. When it comes down to it, though, coercion is coercion is coercion, no matter how nicely it is packaged or how many rational reasons there may be for forcing someone to do something a certain way.

If we truly want freedom, we have to be willing to let everyone have it, regardless of age or rank—and to be *trusted* with it. Maybe we don't trust our young people with freedom because deep down we know we're not doing the greatest jobs with it ourselves.

Probably the most damaging aspect of school is the distinction made between work and play. If you come to believe that work or learning is hard, boring, and monotonous—and only after working are you allowed to play—you have cut yourself off from the essence of life itself.

When you look at people who have made notable contributions to the planet, who have lived passionately, and who, upon exiting this life left no question in one's mind that they had lived up to the life their Soul intended, it is clear they did not see work as something to be done in order to get somewhere else or to do something else. It was part of who they were. Their work was a significant part of their life, their joy, and their being. Cutting our children off from their true loves and interests to serve a system for the sake of itself, or to be productive for the sake of productivity, is destructive not only to the souls of our children, but to the soul of humanity. And, I dare say is affecting the very future of the planet.

It doesn't take a rocket scientist to see the unspoken beliefs we have taken on and the effects they have had on us, but it does take courage to talk about it, to see that a different way is possible, and to get off our hineys and take action.

There is a bumper sticker designed by a statewide homeschooling group that reads: "Trust the Children." I know, to the rational and conditioned mind, this sounds crazy.

"What? We're supposed to just let them do whatever they want? Trust them to learn on their own? If we let them do whatever they want, they wouldn't learn anything!"

That "If we let them do whatever they want, they wouldn't learn anything" is a nice theory, and it holds up so well because, for the most part, it's never truly been tested. We are surrounded by evidence that we need to manipulate and bribe children to learn; however, this "evidence" comes only after we have all but destroyed their natural impulse to discover new things by imposing our will upon them and by forcing them to learn who, what, where, when, and why we tell them.

Is it any wonder many of us come to resent learning? Or that we, as adults, lose our ability to think for ourselves?

My God, when were we ever given the chance to practice?!

In the end, everything comes down to a case of mistaken identity. If you really knew who you were, the jig would be up. You would realize you aren't really here to "learn" anything, but only to create and explore and love. From this perspective you would tap into your true potential and begin to live a life beyond your wildest imaginings. You would step out of a paradigm where learning is hard work; out of an environment where people are putting their energies into what you should be doing, as opposed to what you're sincerely interested in doing; and you would be free to explore what you love. In an atmosphere of love and inspiration, learning becomes as natural and effortless as breathing.

Beyond the Textbook Brain

A few years back, I had the opportunity to visit a plastination lab while taking a behavioral neuroscience class at a community college. Plastination is where cadavers are transformed into plastic-like substances, dissected, and sent to medical schools around the country for study purposes. Our professor thought it would be a wonderful experience for us, and, after the initial horrifying shock, it turned out to be just that. The man who dissected the brains gave our class a presentation. He said something that truly astounded me: the sizes and locations of the parts of the brain were always different from person to person—so much so, in fact, that there really was no such thing as a textbook brain.

No such thing as a textbook brain?

After studying the brain for a little while and coming to understand how a brain injury or diseases in different areas of the brain affected people emotionally, physically, and intellectually, this was fascinating to me. I wondered how different all of our brains are when we are born and how much of an impact that has on our ability to process the world around us. I wondered if, and how, an individual might be naturally predisposed to a certain way of processing the world, and why on a Soul level his may have been chosen. I wondered if our outer experiences and our choices of focus in certain areas could actually affect the formation and size of the different structures of our brain. (This is a yes, by the way.)

How could a system that sets a standard—and measures everyone against that standard—be of any substantial value to the individual? If such a standard wasn't of value to the individual, how could that in turn affect the whole of society? If the system isn't set up to promote each person's potential and unique contributions to the whole, what is the system's purpose?

The assumption here may be that if we set up a system to honor the individual, we would have a society full of egomaniacs only looking out for themselves. In truth, though, in order to give and love unconditionally, to live a life of service to humanity, to live the life your Soul intended, you first have to know your Soul, your Self, which calls for "selfish" stages of individuation.

In this stage of development we learn boundaries and learn to say no. We come to understand and use our personal power in the world. Some call these stages "terrible," but if we were never given permission to say no when we were young, we might find ourselves consistently betraying our Souls when we are older with a yes simply to be nice. A yes simply with the intention to be nice rarely does anything to honor the Self, the Soul, or Life, and actually does much more to put us out of alignment with it.

Labeling children negatively when they are unable to excel in a traditional school environment can create a weakened sense of self that lasts a lifetime. Labeling children as exemplary when they do fit into the system can be just as damaging, because they might not actually have learned anything more than how to use their inherent abilities to play a system. They may have also learned that they must perform to feel good about themselves. True self-esteem comes not from proving yourself but from knowing yourself—knowing yourself on a deep level and appreciating who you are.

If we appreciate ourselves for who we are, as opposed to appreciating ourselves for what we do based on someone else's idea of what is good, our performance in the world will come from an inspired and healthy place, rather than from one that is subconsciously seeking the approval and attention of others.

Many of the great minds, from Einstein to Blake, Twain to Krishnamurti, Tolstoy to Russell, have been very critical of traditional schooling. If you read the letters and essays written by these extraordinary thinkers, they all subscribe to the notion that their success was not the result of their schooling, but actually came in spite of it.

The world is an absolutely fascinating place. If you ponder the galaxies and the intricate workings of the universe, the cycles of history, the great literary works across the ages, the mind-blowing technological advances, the subtle and distinct flavors of every dish imaginable, the exotic lands and people too numerous to comprehend, there is so much—so much!—to keep us absolutely enthralled every moment of our existence. What could possibly be so powerful as to destroy this natural inquisitiveness? Subjects so rich with promise are put into a format unpalatable to even the hungriest of minds. Children are then subjected to punishment and even drugs if they do not cooperate with this most unnatural and degrading of situations. The most important lessons any of us learn are ones that are impossible to measure with a standardized test.

What is this system really teaching our children?

What did it teach us as we were growing up?

One alternative learning concept is a holistic theory. By focusing on a single area or subject, one can glean a tremendous amount of knowledge. Using banking as an example, you might learn basic math and accounting, but that is only scratching the surface. Business, marketing, human relations, history, psychology, social science, geography, reading, writing, architecture, currency, and language are all a part of banking. Even the spiritual concept of money as being another form of energy is part of banking. This wouldn't come from a banking curriculum, but from the student's natural interest in the subject. When you fully engage yourself in any subject, you learn many things on many different levels. You find the Universe supporting your efforts with synchronicities and surprises at every turn. You find one interest leads naturally to another, and then to another. True learning is incredibly fun and exciting and, ultimately, even much more productive. The challenges that arise during times of inspiration are not seen as problems, but as unique—even auspicious—opportunities to expand to new levels.

In Heaven, the curriculum is developed in the Here and Now, as one is engaged in Life. The curriculum is flexible and changes according to the moment. There is no need to force anyone to do anything because the inner force is honored and trusted.

Many times, education is seen as a ticket to a good life, but the ticket may come with a greater price than ever before imagined. It may come with an idea that learning is something to hurry up and get over with in order to do something else.

Our charge, the only thing we really need to do, is listen for the clues our children give us. What do they love? What are they so curious about that we couldn't stop them from learning if we wanted to? We can seek out resources such as community classes, mentors, books, and activities to help them reach greater levels of mastery and fulfill their natural hunger for knowledge when our resources or interest levels in those areas are limited. This not only lets our children be themselves in environments they love and are excited about, it also builds community and lets the mentors gain by contributing to the life of a child who is truly interested in something they themselves are passionate about.

We may also find that we often become aware of these resources at the perfect time and in the perfect way. Things we could have never possibly arranged on our own come into being, and the Soul is free to attract exactly what it needs to continue its journey. Everyone grows together, and we all become more. We all become greater versions of ourselves.

Why *wouldn't* we do this?

It does take a heck of a lot more creativity and flexibility. It also takes a lot more trust and faith in learning as an inherent, natural dynamic as opposed to something we do or make happen for someone else. It takes courage to go beyond the belief that if something isn't learned in a particular time frame or in a particular way, it never will be learned. We will see that things may be learned effortlessly when the internal motivation is present and the brain has been allowed to more fully develop in order to freely accommodate and effectively interpret facts and information.

It takes effort on our behalf to tap into our own genius and our own true loves, since we teach more by example than by anything else, and if we're not honoring our own Soul's calling, we wouldn't even know how to begin to help others honor theirs. It takes patience to resist our own conditioning, which prompts us to dig up the planted seed every day, by obsessively testing our children instead of letting them come into their own and bloom naturally. It takes boldness and a vision that most people are not open to. It's so much easier not to rock the boat, completely ignoring the fact that the boat itself is sinking quicker than the Titanic.

Become as a Child

Without the qualities of innocence and trust, we don't stand a chance to enter those gates of heaven. Without these qualities, we will continue to live from the patterns of fear and suspicion that have been set in us. Without being deeply engaged in curiosity and wonder, we may never come upon our own questions and may spend our entire lives occupied with activities and distractions that bring us no true sense of fulfillment and meaning. No understanding and experience of who we really are at the depth of our being. Without flexibility, we may become too attached to a specific idea or outcome and forget that we are not here to force anything, but to simply allow the splendor that already Is.

Only those who have become like children can enter that kingdom of Heaven.

It's our seriousness that gets us stuck. It's our lack of flexibility that leads to a stagnant life. If only we could remember to have some fun, stay light-hearted, dance, laugh, and play.

Different parenting strategies, which mirror how we "parent" ourselves, could be argued for eternity, but some questions to ask ourselves are: Is what I am doing working? What does "working" mean? Is it working at the expense of what we truly value and love? Are we happy? Are we free to express who we are? Are we learning and growing in a supportive and resourceful environment? Are we free to discover who we are, and to make "mistakes"? How do we treat each other when we do make "mistakes"? Are our needs honored and respected? Is Love present?

A lot of the time the questions are of a different nature and, in turn, produce an entirely different result in the long run. Is everyone acting the way I think they should be acting? How can I make someone else do what I want? How can I make the other person into who I want them to be?

We may have so fully bought into limiting beliefs about what children are, and about what we were when we were young, that we completely lose track, completely forget, or completely abandon the awesome potential that lives within us. We fully expect children to act childish. We may even set them up to do so. Most of the time we are so busy projecting unhealed issues and ridiculous expectations of the conditioned mind onto our children and the world that we wouldn't know what to do if we were no longer able to relate to them in that manner.

We fully expect ourselves to be only human, however that may translate in our individual lives. We constantly set ourselves up to prove that we are only human. We are so busy projecting small ideas, small concepts, and limiting ideas onto ourselves that we wouldn't know what to do if we stopped relating to ourselves in this manner!

All of the suffering we experience in this world comes from the fact that we have forgotten who we are and what we are capable of. And unconsciously of course, we make darn well sure our kids forget who they are too. I guess things just wouldn't be the same if we didn't. Sentimentalists we are. Gluttons for punishment.

But…things are changing.

Nothing can stop the evolution of Life, and we are on the brink of something truly astounding. The systems that do not reflect and honor Life are already beginning to collapse and will continue to do so, while those that do will absolutely, positively, begin to thrive.

It is time for us to take the hand of that Child and to let them lead us back into a world of infinite possibilities, of miracles, of true living.

As a species, and as the ones responsible for the welfare of the planet, at this point in time can we really afford anything else?

Today,
in the early morning
On a bench overlooking the ocean
I sat as a Child.

The scene whisked my senses
like a blender on high speed
Drew me in
like a rope tugging on a mighty bull

I had forgotten
the world was so rich with wonder

Had forgotten how a small black bird
with beady yellow eyes
could take you into his world
while making his morning rounds
And how I could feel such love for this fellow soul
sharing its time on the planet with me, however brief
and seemingly inconsequential
the encounter

I had forgotten eternity was to be found in the moment

Or how each wave broke with its own story to tell

I had forgotten that each leaf
has a name,
and that if you just listen,
they will begin to tell you theirs

I had,
in all of my attempts to belong,
to fit into someone else's idea of myself,
forgotten what it felt like
to be alive …

Re-Birth

Death as an Aspect of Life

A small, delicate flower
fresh from the bloom
Came into a world
where the rule was gloom

Knowing there was more
than what it had been told
It fought to find its own way
and not to be sold

From a cold winter's frost
to a harsh desert heat
Finally it died
No choice but retreat

But below that rich earth
all was not lost
A small tiny seed
had survived the great frost

Through only great trials
and a death to endure
Came a flower much stronger
more beautiful and pure

So when all you can see
is destruction and doom
Know there is a new you
waiting to bloom

As we are ushered into a highly materialistic understanding of the world, we are taught to identify our life in terms of the years we have been on the planet, and from that perspective, when the body dies, our life is over. We spend a lot of our time worrying about and protecting this body of ours, this "life" of ours, as if keeping the physical body alive for the longest time possible was the ultimate goal.

What if, in the greatest of ironies, dying was actually the goal? Of course, we're not talking about the death of the physical body here.

If you think about it, there's really not too much challenge in that. There are many steep cliffs, poisons, and an array of weapons that could accomplish that task fairly easily. It wouldn't take too much creativity or, in the end, even effort to accomplish, and you'd probably be more than a little ticked at yourself once you got to the other side and realized that it's pretty much the same deal, only you didn't have a body to work with anymore.

No, that's not the type of demise we're talking about.

What we're talking about is the death of the conditioned part of our minds that holds us hostage in a limited and narrow viewpoint. We're talking about doing away with limiting mental concepts that keep us from seeing the world from a more expansive perspective. About "offing" the deluded parts of ourselves that keep us from seeing who we actually are, and, in turn, from expressing what we have come to this world to express.

To die to the limiting ideas and beliefs that hold us back from living fully is actually the greatest thing we could ever hope for. It is truly ironic that the death we fear, the very thing we pray with all of our might to be shielded from, is actually a gateway to a new level of freedom. There seems to be a strong connection between how we view death in our society and the fear and resistance to the necessary changes and transformations we need to make as individuals—and as a collective species—to evolve into our next level of awareness and living. In our rigid material view of the world, we have come to view our physical death as a defeat, a great embarrassment, or a horrific tragedy, rather than a natural occurrence on the material plane. In the physical dimension, forms of life are ever changing. Constantly shifting. In the spiritual dimension, however, Life is eternal.

We don't need to wait until we physically die to go to "heaven." When our conditioned mind takes a leave of absence, we realize that Heaven is already Here. That it always has been Here. That there is actually nowhere we could have ever gone to escape it. That there is absolutely no place on this planet (or any other planet or dimension, for that matter), we ever need to get to, as there is really never anywhere else we could ever be than Here. Now.

Heaven.

We have to understand that this thing we call the mind, in addition to serving as an information sorter and a time and space organizer, also serves as an incredibly diligent gatekeeper, standing in the way of the revelation that everything we will ever want, need, or desire is already here. That we don't need to *do* anything.

Well.

Except allow something that seems incredibly real to us, something that seems as if *it is us*, to die. That's all.

A resistance to death is ingrained deeply in our minds since our culture's scientific view of the world tells us that indeed death is the end. Our physical senses tell us death is the end. All outward indications would seem to point to the fact that a person who has died is indeed "gone." The mystics, prophets, shamans, and seers from across the ages have known this to be utter nonsense.

We are eternal.

We don't die.

We transform, we change, we move on to different ways of being and operating, but to think we just end someday, never to be again, is a myth. Our physical bodies will most likely die at some point, and, depending on their condition, we may be more than a little relieved to be free of them. But, our Spiritual Essence, our Soul, is Eternal. In Truth, there is no death. In God, there is no death. In Love, there is no death. In Heaven, there is no death. In the awareness of our true nature, there is no death.

But, in the awareness of ourselves as "only human," earthbound citizens, living through and depending upon the physical senses alone, there is.

What can make it hard to initially explore whether there might be more to this whole death thing is the fear of going against the general opinion. We want to be… normal. We want to fit in. The ridicule of the mass majority is often too much for us to take because it usually includes the mass majority of our friends and family. If we understand that we don't really ever die, that we simply go on to the next phase of life, it is impossible to experience someone else as "gone" when they leave the physical plane. The more aware we are of our eternal nature, the less we will identify others as merely human and instead see them as Eternal Spiritual Beingness. While we may mourn the loss of their physical presence and a physical relationship, we wouldn't mourn the loss of the relationship itself, since it would continue on another level.

The less we identify with our physical bodies, with our physical incarnation, the less we will mourn because we will no longer experience a loss.

This is not due to denial, an unhealthy detachment, or fear of intimacy, but an overwhelming awareness of who We really Are and what Life really Is.

Truly there is no loss in the Mind of God.

The good news is, droves of people are experiencing a gnawing sense that there is more, that something is missing, and they are realizing that this something will never be alleviated by more general opinion, thoughts, and relationships (i.e., rational, Newtonian, physical world perspectives). The truth is, the only thing that will stop that gnawing permanently is the realization of the Authentic Self, the Essential Self, the God Self, through the continuous death of limiting beliefs and identities that have been formed from a limited awareness of reality.

Questions Worth Asking

The very first questions we probably asked ourselves when we found ourselves in this life experience must have been something to the effect of *Who am I?* and *What am I doing here?*

Even though we may not have been able to articulate those questions, they probably hung in the air like a familiar fragrance—one you noticed frequently but couldn't quite grasp. They stood in the room like the proverbial pink elephant.

There has always been a feeling that encompassed my awareness ever since I can remember. An understanding that there was so much more going on here than I could see or understand.

Who am I? What am I doing here?

This seems to be the core of all suffering on the planet. We don't know who we are, and we don't know what we're doing here.

When we begin to find the answers to these questions for ourselves, everything changes. The real problem begins when we stop asking these questions. We have either been given an answer based on a limited understanding of Life or we have been told that the questions themselves don't really matter. We may have stopped asking after reaching a certain conclusion—forgetting that as we are constantly discovering new dimensions of ourselves—and as we find new and expanding areas to play in, experiment with, and grow in, our answers expand as well. We might have been satisfied with the answers we received from our parents or caregivers, our teachers or the "experts" who explained our existence, and never even ventured into the mysterious sea of real thinking.

But really…what's the real scoop? Why are we here? *What in the world are we doing here?!*

It might seem pointless to ask questions which can seemingly never be answered, but in asking limited questions we can only receive limited answers, which in turn leads us to believe in, and experience, a very limited universe. We become conditioned by classrooms that put teachers in front with the answers and students on the other end of the room to memorize those agreed-upon answers. What an utter bore to think we exist in a world where all of the answers have already been discovered! To think that mere facts and words are the only suitable answers to questions! What a chore to be searching for something outside of yourself that already exists within you!

It has been said that the mind is a fire to be lit, not a bucket to be filled. We need to engage ourselves with questions that make us truly think. Questions that engage the Soul, not bury it in a mindless sea of physical world facts. If we look to the universe, to the stars and the galaxies, to the natural world around us, and see ourselves as part of this awesome creation, we will understand to what extent we are created in the image and likeness of an Infinite Awareness. An Infinite Intelligence. We will see that the dimensions of the cosmos are dimensions within our own consciousness and that we are a storehouse of outrageous potential. We will come to understand that the questions *Who am I?* and *What am I doing here?* can never fully be answered because Life is progressive. Whatever we might say in response to that question today will not be the same as our answer next year, next month, or sometimes even the next day when we are consistently focused on growing and becoming more aware of what is really going on.

Paradoxically, just as the answers are always changing on the physical level, there is no more to become in the dimension of the Soul. Nowhere to grow. The Soul just Is, so We just Are. The answer has always been the same in that dimension, in that awareness, and it will always be the same. When we realize that part of Us, We realize that we are one and the same with that Universal Presence.

Some call this realization "enlightenment," but it doesn't matter what you call it. We realize that what we have up until that time thought of as "God" was indeed only a thought we had about it. We realize it is not some force outside of us that we need to be in good favor with in order to gain its love. It is not a vision, or a passing insight. It is not a mental concept at all, but a profound realization that changes everything. It just Is, and when you realize that, there is no mistake in your mind.

You know.

You feel you have found the secret of existence, because you have realized You Are existence Itself. In that Love, in that total saturation and realization of the Spirit as You, of the Spirit as a free unbounded unconditioned potential, the question has been answered.

And then again, it hasn't.

We would be remiss to assume we have no more inner work to do after we have touched this realm. In a way, it is only the beginning, as we experience ourselves in the present moment and must continue to do the work to remain conscious. We have to continue to release limiting ideas and ways of being; continue to Live no matter what thoughts and energy may be passing through our awareness.

It's very tempting to imagine that we are totally "done" after we have discovered this dimension of ourselves and of life. The ego, or conditioned mind, may want to take over the experience and imagine itself to be the key to salvation for others, and forget that its only job is to be a vehicle for the divine energies and ideas to flow through it. Without continually seeking to become a purer channel, we may begin sidestepping issues that surface and start imagining other people or circumstances to be the source of our frustration, since we believe ourselves to be "enlightened."

We need to be clear on what is really happening and check where our intention—and our attention—is throughout the day. Who am I when I am standing in that long checkout line? Who am I when I believe someone is acting unkind to me? Who am I choosing to be in that moment? Who am I then? Who am I now? *Right now?*

Who do I imagine myself to be?

Although it is quite easy to be loving when people are being loving to us, the questions of real substance are, how loving can we be when we believe someone is treating us horribly and we are experiencing things as not going our way? These situations give us valuable insight into where we actually are in our ability to be unconditionally trusting and loving, as opposed to where we believe ourselves to be. These are situations where we need to be in touch with our true being in order to express loving because there is no pat formula. There are no simple answers to what Love would do in any given circumstance, and when we rely on a formula we are in our minds trying to figure it out rather than being a space for Love to express. As they say, location is everything. Love does not reside in the conditioned mind. If we only have an *idea* about what love would do, we can get stuck in our heads indefinitely and try to use the intellect to solve problems. We might not be progressing spiritually, since we are not developing the strength of the Soul by listening to the Wisdom of the Heart, but rather relying on fixed ideas about what is right or good.

To be loving in the face of unloving behavior doesn't mean we play a spiritual martyr and become a victim to another's unconscious behaviors only to prove ourselves more aware and enlightened. The loving thing to do may be to not allow the behavior. Or, it might be to allow it, and remain "in love" during the process. It may be to allow the behavior and match the energy and create a temporary boundary in consciousness or on the physical plane—if we are at a place where boundaries will serve us and the other as well.

The action we take is not so much the issue. We are all taught such a superficial way of living. It doesn't mean that the action doesn't matter. That is not true either. What matters is the energy in which the action is performed. This matters just as much if not more than the action itself. The real questions become: *Is the underlying energy of the action Loving?* Is there a purity of love in my intention, or do I want to prove something, to be right, or to get even? Are my actions coming from fear, from a small-minded and restricted sense of possibility, or from the ever-expanding, ever-extending hand of Love?

What Do We Really Need to Protect Ourselves From?

On another level entirely, in an "Ultimate Truth" kind of way, Love is all there is and is always the motivating dynamic. If we are living in the illusion of fear, we naturally want to protect ourselves and others, fully believing this protection to be a loving action and fully justifying doing whatever we believe necessary in order to "protect."

It is out of our lack of awareness that we believe we are not protected.

When we are living life from the perspective of the physical senses and the material world, it may appear at times that we are not protected; but from an eternal perspective, we were never born and can never die. While this idea of not dying, of eternal life, may be a comforting thought to the ego, it is not written to comfort the ego. It is written to inspire awakening and to coax the ego into loosening the grip on what it considers to be real in order for us to see and experience Reality. From this view, this vista, this revelation that we are eternal, we see through the illusion of needing any type of protection whatsoever. In fact, from this state of mind, the idea seems quite silly.

This may sound ridiculous, insane even, to the conditioned mind, which can only experience the illusion of separation; but there is a Mind, an Intelligence, a Reality beyond what we would call reality— beyond what we can see and know with our human mind and human senses. When we begin seeing the world through that Mind, through God's eyes, we see miracles happening everywhere—not because things have changed in the world, but because our consciousness has. And, not even changed, but what is not real has simply been transcended to reveal What Is.

On an energetic level it makes perfect sense. When we believe we need to protect ourselves, we are subjected to living in that energetic. We will actually attract people and situations into our lives that we need to protect ourselves from. We then go on to form all kinds of theories, justifications—maybe even an entire BS—for our exclusionary treatment of others based on a consciousness of separation. As long as we are personally creating boundaries to protect ourselves, we will never experience true freedom. We will always have to be on guard, even if on a very subtle or unconscious level. When this happens, we have failed to realize that we are really only attempting to protect ourselves from our own limited consciousness, from a belief in good and evil. From a belief in sinners. From darkness. From hell.

From a world that exists outside of God.

In Truth, there is only One of us Here.

And We are Love.

When we truly give ourselves to Life, we will get messages to move ahead, move back, turn left, pull away, but it won't be an action based on a fear of being used or hurt, it will come from the guidance of the Soul.

It might appear in the world as the same action, but it will be coming from an entirely different energetic, which will create an entirely different result in the long run. It is a great paradox that when we know there is nothing we need protecting from, we find ourselves to be divinely protected. Not ego protected, but divinely protected. It is only our lack of understanding that appears to create a situation that we don't want.

In Truth all experiences come in service to our Self—in order for us to *be*—that we may wake up to our Selves. If we react to unfavorable situations from a place of fear or upset, from lower level or unhealed energy, we are just setting ourselves up for future upset, because we invariably get back the energy we put out. There is no judgment in this, so there is no reason to begin recounting failures and inwardly berating ourselves, as we might have been taught to do. This is not to promote guilt, but awareness. If we get caught in guilt then we are only adding more negative energy to the pool. It seems like a big ol' nightmare when we're trapped in it, because it is. It's not what is *Real*, but only a bad dream we have failed to wake up from.

If there is only love, forgiveness, peace, and gratitude to be given, that is what will be returned. Even when another energy is directed toward us, it will be unable to affect us. *Unable to effect us.* Maybe it will give us a new insight or occasion to offer another way of seeing, an opportunity to practice what we know, to forgive, love and heal, but it won't be able to upset us if we aren't carrying that corresponding vibration within us. The part of us that loves drama, that feeds and lives off of negative energy, is probably having a hissy fit reading that.

"Why, someone wouldn't even be human then! They'd be some cold, unfeeling, inhuman creature."

Actually, they would be allowing Love, Peace, Joy, and all of the other qualities of Spirit to live through them, to *Be* them. But that part in us reacts so fiercely because it knows there is no room for it to exist in that level of awareness. In that level of awareness, in those moments, we are no longer run by negative energy. We are run by Love. It doesn't mean that we won't feel negative energy from time to time, but it will become an energy we can consciously direct, learn from, and transcend. Not identify with.

When we continually hold the intention of being more loving and peaceful, the negative and manipulative ways of being that have existed within us know they're going down, and they don't like it. Not one bit. They know that to be "in the world, but not of it," something will have to die. In fact, it's not even accurate to say that they die. Nothing dies. In a higher level of consciousness, though, they simply don't exist. They may appear to die, but what has really happened is that your awareness has expanded, and that level of energy simply does not exist in that expanded state of awareness. They may still very well be existing in another dimension, but since your consciousness is not existing there anymore, you are no longer aware of them, no longer have to deal with them, and are no longer are limited by them.

When we experience life from the eternal part of ourselves, as opposed to our personal selves, we can begin to exist in a world independent of personal reaction and the effect of that reaction. We will be able to remain in a state of equanimity and peace regardless of outer circumstances. We will be able to demonstrate more fully what is most real about us as spiritual beings and generate numerous creative win/win experiences and solutions.

The Myth of Death as the End

Over the years, I've heard several opinions about whether past-life regression, a hypnosis-like technique used to recall past lives of one's particular soul, has any inherent value.

If one uses this tool to distract oneself from the work in our present lives, it may not prove beneficial. It can be tempting to use past-life regression as a distraction so we can simply entrench ourselves in another story. Even though I have had some very detailed "memories" surface during past-life regressions, I would no more want to identify with who I may have been in a previous life, than with who I have been in a previous year. We don't want to get trapped in any fixed identity, since it invariably ropes us into a limited idea of ourselves.

On the other hand, if you are directed to work in a particular area, you need to heed that inner calling. Many have had incredible physical healing and deep insight as a result of working with past lives. While I don't subscribe to seeking out others to tell you about your past lives, your future, or your inner terrain in general, these types of sessions can be used to confirm what you have already had insight about. If we begin to rely solely on the perceptions of others, we are once again subscribing to the paradigm that other people have our answers.

As channels of Spirit, we all have our filters. We may find certain people rubbing us a certain way without even knowing them. Since we all have our off-days, we need to thoroughly evaluate any information that comes to us before taking it to heart. Even if we do receive accurate information, or information which resonates deeply, we may still walk away with the feeling that our answers are "out there," especially if we depend on them exclusively. In the end, it's not about getting information, it is about waking up to what is Real.

Personally, the handful of past-life regressions I have participated in have helped me understand limiting patterns, provide explanations, and get glimpses of possibilities I had never before imagined. I never actively sought out a past-life session, but one came quite by accident, as these things usually do. I went with a friend to see a lecture by Dr. Brian Weiss, who works in the field of past-life regressions. After the lecture, Dr. Weiss facilitated a group session, which I entered into skeptically but emerged from transformed. I had found his book, *Many Lives, Many Masters*, very engaging and liked the fact that the whole thing came to him quite by accident. He had formerly been a very left-brained psychiatrist who decided one day to use hypnosis therapy with a patient after exhausting every other known treatment. Instead of going back to a childhood experience, she went into a vivid and detailed description of her own death as a grown woman. At first he was very skeptical, but he knew that something was happening when she began to give him detailed information about his son, who had died some years earlier. During this process, her chronic symptoms disappeared. Dr. Weiss gave up his very prestigious position as head of psychiatry at a major university in order to pursue this phenomenon, even though at first he was initially concerned about the potential reactions of his peers.

Dr. Weiss's case seems to be a great example of coming to live the life your Soul intended. The personality never would have given up such a comfortable and powerful position to pursue something so bizarre by western society's standards. He could have chosen to write the event off as a fluke or coincidence, as some of us do when we can't explain an occurrence, but he chose instead to research and experiment with it and to compile case after case of success stories. Dr. Weiss is currently Chairman Emeritus of Psychiatry at the Mount Sinai Medical Center in Miami, and since the initial writing of this book, he has moved into future progression therapy as well.

A great benefit of doing past or future life therapy is the ability to see, to actually experience, the big picture, and to be able to put things in the perspective of that big picture. If we're merely interpreting circumstances from a moment-to-moment existence in the frame of a single lifetime, something such as losing our car keys can seem like a traumatic experience. If our mind has been exposed to the realization and awareness of several lifetimes though, through the millennia, we can see the situation from that perspective. From that awareness, the experience becomes a very minor blip in the relative scheme of things, and it produces no more than a minor disturbance—or at most, a simple inquiry. If we believe and trust that everything happens for our good, and if we can be present to that state of awareness, we can even look for the opportunity in the situation.

In doing this work we can also more easily see ourselves in others. We can see people of different cultures, religions, and races knowing that we've probably "been there, done that," or, if we haven't, we will. Also, with this enlarged perspective of life, we might also be more willing to experiment with life and take greater risks in service to the Soul, as opposed to believing this is the only life we've got and being terrified of messing it up and ending up in an eternal southerly inferno. It also seems much easier, after experiencing other times, bodies, ways of being, and dimensions, to identify a body as a temporary garment rather than permanent attire.

One thing that strikes me about Dr. Weiss, besides his genuineness, is that he carries with him a tangible sense of peacefulness. There is a real freedom and peace that comes when you know you don't die— that nothing ever dies, and that death is really only a transition into a new phase of life.

Discovering Life in the Death Experience

When I was about nineteen, a time which I like to refer to as my past life, even though it was very much part of this lifetime, I was involved in weekend drug binges. Cocaine all weekend long—eight balls. I cringe just thinking about it. Underneath the cringe, though, is a deep appreciation for every experience from which invaluable perspectives, qualities, and lessons have revealed themselves.

The obvious jump may be to think I learned of the perils of drugs; that they are horrible, disgusting, and evil substances for all who use them. That's not what I learned.

I learned that the people who have the most judgment about drug users are probably using other substances, be it food, sex, TV, or addictive thoughts. All judgment is self-judgment. (More about that in projection.) I learned that there is a curiosity and courage in those who have used or use drugs that I almost admire. I know that may sound pretty radical, but it takes a certain chutzpa to experiment with your life, and if it were focused in a healthy way it could be generative rather than destructive. Most of all, through my use of drugs I learned that life doesn't end after we die. Not that I recommend drugs as a way to make this discovery! Not by any means.

I was in extreme emotional and spiritual pain and didn't have a lot of attachment to staying on the planet at the time. Even though I sometimes feel it's amazing I made it through those years alive, I wouldn't change the experience for the world…

My parents were out of town and had said it would be okay for my boyfriend, who later became my husband, and I to stay the night at their house. We had our sleeping bags laid out on the floor in the family room, ready to go to bed. We had been doing coke all afternoon, and drinking along with it as usual. After a while I began to feel very anxious. Something was wrong, but I couldn't put my finger on it. Extreme paranoia overcame me, and I thought I was going to lose it after a while. My partner wasn't feeling too great either, and he suggested we try to go to sleep. We both lay down and within minutes he nodded off. The feeling in me, though, was becoming more intense, and my heart was pounding so fast and so hard it felt like it was going to come out of my chest. I started to feel dizzy and kept changing positions to try to get to sleep.

I turned over on my stomach, and a second later I found myself floating over my body. I was suddenly overcome by the most intense feeling of love and bliss imaginable. It was not something I had ever come close to experiencing before. The thought in my mind was "I knew it, I knew it, I knew it!" I had always suspected there was more to the whole death thing, but the jury was still out. I wanted proof.

In that moment I knew that I had gotten it!

I bathed in this love, and saw all of the folly I had been involved in. How silly jealousy was! How could I be jealous of anyone when I am a Being of Pure Light made in Perfect Love?! I saw what an absurdity it was to pursue material possessions—not that they are bad in themselves, but that the pursuit of them is a folly because in truth they are just an illusion. From an Eternal, Spiritual perspective, the pursuit of material possessions is a meaningless activity.

It may be argued that we, as humans living on the earth plane, have to at least pursue material possessions to the extent we must provide for our basic needs. Obviously, we are not talking about physical survival here, but true revelations of *What Is* do not promote a balanced approach to things. They catapult one into an entirely different world and consciousness where not only do the old rules no longer apply, they no longer need to be applied.

I soon felt a motherly presence next to me as I continued to consciously exist in the space above my body. I didn't know who it was, only she was somehow communicating to me that I was being given a choice about whether to continue my life on earth. I was sure I wanted to leave, but something kept me from going in the direction I needed to go (which in the physical world was over by the stairway in the house). I hesitated and, in that moment, remembered that my boyfriend was lying there sleeping next to me. The moment I remembered him, I found myself back in my body. I had realized that my parents would be coming home early the next morning and that they would probably find us there before he woke up. I just couldn't do that to him. Or to them. It wasn't even something I thought about. Some choice, I thought later.

The whole experience seemed to take hours, but after coming back into my body I was sure that it had only been a second or two. My heart was still beating with incredible intensity, and I still sensed my anxiety in the background, but it just didn't seem to matter anymore.

I mean, what's the worst that could happen? I could die. Ha!

Even with the life-altering experience and the tangible awareness of another dimension of reality, which eliminated the fear of death and opened my consciousness to valuable insight, I was still entrenched in unconscious patterns of abuse that took years to get free of. The cocaine use did stop soon after that, though. Aside from that experience, we had gone to a friend's house one night and they had their eight-month-old baby there, sitting in a highchair at the table, while we did lines of cocaine. Having the baby there was extremely disturbing to me, and I suddenly realized that I might be a mom someday. I hadn't really, seriously, ever considered the possibility before. In my desperation, I had been praying for help (you know you're desperate when you consider yourself an atheist and you're praying), and if that wasn't the last time I did cocaine, it was one of the last.

Death as the Ultimate Gift

It has always seemed the greatest irony that the most horrific and painful experiences can be springboards into new ways of being for us. It is when we get to the end of our ropes that we have the opportunity to let go and, ultimately, find ourselves being carried to higher ground. It's the letting-go part that is always the most challenging—letting go of blame and judgment. Of fear. Fixed identities. Control

Our way.

Our plan.

Our life.

The truth is, the more we can let go, the freer we become.

Like Janis Joplin sang, "Freedom's just another word for nothing left to lose." For some of us it takes an absolute annihilation in order to awaken to a new dimension of ourselves and of life. Sometimes the annihilation leads to a prison of bitterness and resentment, instead of the bliss of freedom it has the potential to be. When we get to the end of our ropes and refuse to let go, we do much damage to ourselves. The people we perceive as the wrongdoers go about their business while we are left hanging on, day after day, to the rope of resentment. Unable to truly be free. Unable to truly fly. Unable to truly live.

All because...why? We want to be right? We want justice? They don't deserve our forgiveness? We'll show them, gosh darn it!

One of the things we forget in these times is that we are creative beings. Just because we have been "wronged" doesn't mean the Universe has suspended Its law. We are still creative beings. Our thoughts, words, and deeds still create the experience of the world we live in. The law is the same just as it was the day before we were wronged, and what we are putting out is what will return to us. We get more of what we choose to focus on. We really begin to see that we are never, ever really doing anything to anyone else, only to ourselves.

We might also fail to realize the astounding opportunity these incidents provide for us. It seems the worse the "wrong", the more rewarding it is for us to forgive. By forgiving, we can release negative patterns being played out because of the judgments we hold and move to an entirely new level of awareness and freedom.

In an expanded awareness—an awareness of our unbounded, unlimited Self and Life—we realize the error of believing anyone guilty of something we needed to forgive them for in the first place. We come to see that the true forgiveness work lies within ourselves. We have to forgive ourselves for misunderstanding and judging the true nature of our Selves, the true nature of Others, the true nature of Life.

It is indeed a great opportunity for us if we can stay conscious enough to remember to try it out. If we are still sleepwalking through certain areas of life and can only respond with a knee-jerk reaction, there is not much opportunity for us in that moment. Since we haven't transcended the world of cause and effect, and since thought is creative, the energy and thought we react with will produce a similar situation in the future. Then the next time, we will have another opportunity. Maybe then we will remain conscious and choose to act from a more conscious place.

Or maybe we won't. No worries. We will have unlimited opportunities.

As long as we keep putting out the energy to create the same scenario, we will have another opportunity. After awhile, we might get so sick of the whole deal, we'll have to do something completely different! We might even get so lucky as to reach the end of our rope and lose our precious grip ...

I had been with my husband for eleven years when I found out he had a girlfriend. It was literally one of those wake-up call moments that came when I picked up the phone to call my grandma one night. On the line was another woman's voice, and when I began questioning who it was, my husband came running into the house and tore the phone cord out of the wall. "She's just a friend," he blurted.

Did he think I was a total idiot?

Actually he did. It was just one of the many problems in the marriage. What I have come to understand, though, is that I agreed with him. He was only providing me with the opportunity to experience my current underlying, unconscious opinion of myself. No one could have treated me worse than I was treating myself. I now see all the ways I had burdened him with my love. I believed him to be totally responsible for my happiness and I was dependent on him for everything, as I believed myself and my own views to be worthless. I tried to make appointments for counseling, trips to a church, anything I could think of to change the situation. I was desperate. It was a few weeks later when I realized that things were not going to change. He wasn't following through on any promises. I was expected to just deal with the situation as it was.

One afternoon, in the spare bedroom of our house, I reached a point where I just couldn't take it anymore—not one more minute. Suicide was out of the question because of my daughter. Leaving her was out of the question. I didn't know what to do, but knew I needed to do something.

In utter frustration, I cried.

At first I cried for the current situation, but then I moved into a deeper space and it seemed I was crying for everything that had happened since I had come into this world: every moment of abuse, every incident of being used, every wrongdoing. I felt myself going into the darkest dark I had ever experienced. It was like going into a black hole. I didn't know how I would get out, but I just didn't care anymore. I went deeper and deeper into the feelings of despair. All of the loneliness. The sense of never really being appreciated. Never really being acknowledged or seen for who I was. The sadness. The pain. The frustration. The anger. The insanity. All of the feelings I had never allowed myself to fully feel. All of the things I had been in denial of.

There came a certain point where I knew I needed to stop. I knew that I really needed to stop. I actually had the sense that if I went any deeper, I would lose my mind.

I had come to the end of my rope.

And, in my desperation, in my utter resignation to this miserable existence called life, this chaotic, half-brained experiment full of disappointment and failure, I did the unthinkable.

I let go …

It's hard to put into words what happened next. There are no words, really. Language is so limited, especially in its ability to explain experiences that transcend the rational since language's very origin is, in fact, rational. The only way I can put it is: I realized who I was. For the first time in my life, *I knew who I was.* I woke up. I got it.

The big shebang.

The whole enchilada.

It was like waking up from a nightmare and realizing it had all been just a long, horrible, drawn-out dream.

There was a sudden and incredible appreciation for myself, for my being, and it had nothing to do with anything I had ever done— or not done, for that matter. I had compassion for every choice I had made out of ignorance and was able to see how I had not really chosen, but had just been living in reaction based on a very limited idea of who I was. I saw how I was treated in childhood, which had led me into a relationship where I was treated in much the same manner, just as many of us are. But I realized something else: I had a choice.

I had a choice.

Before that moment, I had lived in the land of excuses and guilt. I thought I was a certain way, that people were a certain way, that life was a certain way. I had been seeing the world in a very fixed way. But in that moment, I saw that everything was much more relative than I had ever, ever thought imaginable. And for the first time in my life, I had a choice, because I was *Here.*

There's no way I will ever be able to explain the enormity of the experience. I only know that something was so different, I didn't even feel like myself anymore. I felt as if I had been born again. I now see why traditional religious ceremonies have been developed, but also understand that a ceremonial enactment cannot make you of the

Spirit, it can only make you of the organization. To be truly born of the Spirit does not take a following of rules, but the willingness and courage to travel to the darkest regions of your soul in order to realize that in Truth there is no darkness. There is no evil. There is no other.

There is only Light. Only Love. Only One. There were no rules to follow during this experience, just my Spirit, my Soul, my Intuition, my Life.

The Spirit. *The* Soul. *The* Intuition. *The* Life. Same thing. Still the only things to follow. The only things to Be.

In fact, all the former rules seemed to fly directly out the window. Possibly, it was an experience coming from years of obsessively searching for my identity, of a focused and passionate, repeatedly asked question: *Who am I?*

During this experience there was even a "life review," which I didn't experience with the earlier drug induced near-death experience.

For a time after this experience, nothing changed on the outside. My husband at the time was still staying out late at night and sometimes not coming home at all, but it just didn't matter. I was so thrilled to be alive, so happy to be living on the planet, it just didn't matter anymore. I would wake up in the morning and tears of joy would stream down my face. I couldn't believe this was the same planet I had been on for the last thirty years. It was beautiful. It was glorious. It was Heaven. I had woken up in Heaven.

At the time, I was one hundred pounds overweight, and the weight began to drop off. I was living in the moment. I was free.

Well, almost.

A few weeks later, I met a man online in a computer chat room. I began talking to him on the phone on the nights that my husband was out. We started getting very close, talking for hours at a time. He was also in a very unhappy marriage. On one level, I didn't have a very good feeling about it. Technically, we were both still married, and I knew it was wrong; I had always told myself that I would never, ever do anything like that. But it wasn't like we were lovers, I reasoned. We were only talking on the phone, supporting each other. He would ask me over and over again if we could meet in person. I always told him no; it was out of the question, absolutely wrong. No way.

The weeks went by, with my husband coming home at night more and more infrequently and me wondering what in the world I was going to do. I remember telling my husband that I was going to find a boyfriend, since he had a girlfriend. "Who would want you?" he asked.

Looking back, I can see what an incredible support he was on a Soul level. He was making the whole thing way too easy.

The Dream

A month later, I realized I could not keep living like I was for much longer. On top of everything else, I was 'falling in love' with my friend on the phone. No one had ever talked to me like this before. We had much in common, and I began to look forward to our time talking more than anything else. For the first time in my life, I felt respected and appreciated. Adored, even. But the right-wrong arguments were raging on in my consciousness, and I went to bed one night begging for an answer. I wanted to meet my new friend more than anything, but I thought it was wrong. I wanted to get out of the marriage but felt a huge amount of guilt in regards to how it would affect our daughter. Also, it was "till death do us part." That was the promise. How could I not honor that promise? And how could something so wrong feel so incredibly right? Like nothing else ever had in my life? All of these questions whirled in my mind as I drifted off to sleep. A few hours later I had a dream that was to alter the course of my life...

Everything was white.

My grandfather, who had died a few years before, was lying down. A luminous glow radiated through everything. He got up from the bed and walked toward me, wearing a white gown. He looked like an angel. His face was so clear and bright that he seemed to be right in front of me. I asked him what I should do. I could feel my anxiety, my confusion, and I begged him to tell me what I should do.

"Just remember what I told you," he said, smiling.

I stood looking at him. I had never been close to my grandfather in this life. I had barely even known him growing up, as my grandparents had put most of their time and energy into their business and community involvement. I had gotten to know them better near the last years of their life, when my grandfather became ill with Parkinson's and Alzheimer's. I often visited him in the rest home, but by that time, he was no longer able to communicate through speech.

"What did you tell me?" I finally asked.

"You'll remember," he said with a radiant smile. He had the warmest glow about him. He was such a magnanimous spirit while he was here on earth, his presence would fill the entire room when he walked in, and I felt that same essence come from him in the dream. I was about to ask him again what it was, when something fell in the closet and woke me up. I rolled over on my side and thought about what he possibly could have told me. I must have stayed awake for at least an hour mulling over every moment I had spent with him and found nothing that could relate to my present situation. After a while, I fell back asleep. Upon waking the next morning, I had forgotten about the dream.

I went about my day and was exercising on a treadmill at home in the family room in the early afternoon. I was lost in the repetitive motion of my legs, thinking of nothing, when all of a sudden a memory of my grandfather shot into my head out of nowhere. Simultaneously, the memory of the previous night's dream and what he had told me came back to me. I literally fell on my knees sobbing. I had been given my answer.

The memory was of the very last words my grandfather had ever spoken to me. He had been brought to the rest home, and when I went to visit him the following week, his condition had worsened to the point that he wasn't able to speak. As I said before, my grandfather and I had never been very close, and on this particular visit he was very insistent on telling me something. I was having problems understanding him, and he even made a point of pulling me closer so that he could tell me directly in my ear. He was determined that I hear this message, but when I was finally able to understand what he was saying, it was so out of context that I brushed it off as coming from a mind with a weakened grip on reality. Now I know it was much more.

A raspy whisper of a voice said to me that day, two full years before the message would have any relevant meaning for me, "Sometimes opportunities only come around once, and if you don't take them, you'll regret it for the rest of your life."

I have to say there are a couple of things that are interesting about that statement.

For one, I know that it's not even true—not in Reality, because there are opportunities presenting themselves in every moment. The Universe is one of infinity, which includes infinite opportunity. The other thing is that if it hadn't been said in that particular way, with that intensity, it might not have moved me in the way that it did. It was true for me that day like nothing else. If I hadn't moved and acted right then, there was a very good chance I would have procrastinated further. Even though I know I would eventually have left the marriage, it could have very well been months or years, given the rational arguments that were keeping me there.

My grandfather has since come to me in other dreams, and though it may seem strange to say, we have a closer relationship now that he's on the other side. He's one of my angels, and I am honored and grateful that he is with me.

Only a few moments after that memory and realization, the phone rang. I was still on my knees crying and got up to answer it. It was my friend. One of the first things he said was, "Would you like to go see a movie with me tonight?" Without hesitating, I answered, "Yes."

We both sat in silence for a moment. It was a stunning silence and a stunning moment.

I was beginning to get used to them.

The Continual Cycle of Life

After that, things really began to move. I ended up leaving the marriage a few days later, and as I was driving away from the house, I felt the most incredible lightness come over me. It was as if a weight had been lifted off of my being, a weight I had always felt and had always carried until that day. One being that has always held a special place in my heart is Martin Luther King Jr. His words echoed in my head as tears of joy fell down my cheeks and I drove with my daughter to my grandma's house.

"Free at last, free at last! Thank God Almighty, we are free at last!"

There seem to be certain moments in which the Universe yells, "Jump!" and when we do, we find a whole new world rushing to greet us—just never quite in the manner we may have previously fantasized about. The lessons were and are endless. One of them being that my online friend was not the one I was destined to share my life with. This was a realization that came fairly quickly after I left the marriage. Ironically, after finding the answer to the question *Who am I?* I discovered I didn't have a clue as to who I was. How could I? I felt like I hadn't been in the picture for eons.

As we begin to get into the flow of real living, we continually find ourselves living in new worlds. It is just an illusion that there is an end point we get to. The Universe is in constant motion, flux, and growth. And sometimes, strangely enough, the next stage of growth is the stage of death, or transformation. There comes a time when some things need to die: old beliefs that keep us trapped in a world that we are outgrowing; old ways of doing things based on a limited idea of ourselves or others; relationships that do not support and encourage our growth; jobs that don't allow our greater capabilities and creativity to be expressed. This month's revelation becomes next year's history lesson when we are continuing to grow. And we have to remember that death, by its nature, can be painful. Birth can be painful as well.

The transition phase in labor is sometimes overwhelmingly painful. It helps to remember that we are in the process of birthing a new life, of waking up in an entirely new world, and that this is not a chronic pain that arises from ignoring the callings of our heart, but one that is actually part of the growth process itself.

Looking back, I never did hate my now ex-husband. It seems that when you become aware of who you really are, you simultaneously become aware of who everyone else is as well. There were those that tried to convince me that I should be angry or in some way make him pay, but I actually see him as one of the most important people on the planet to me. I would never have been able to get to a state of such desperation without his "help." I would not have seen how I had been a slave to my fear, to my childhood experience, to my beliefs, or to anything else other than the life my Soul intended.

On an ego level, he has been a formidable enemy; on a Soul level he has been my angel of transformation and awakening. There was a lot of anger that surfaced a few years after the divorce, and it was anger that began a long time before my ex-husband and I ever met. I realized how often I got to play the judge and jury in observing his behavior, how I got to play the saintly one, while in reality it was my choice to stay in the situation and play out the role of a victim. I had many excuses for why I couldn't leave, including fear for my safety, but in the end it turned out that's all that they were. Excuses.

When the Universe says jump—you jump.

I will always remain grateful to my ex-husband for helping me discover a strength within myself that I never knew existed, and I will always appreciate our path together even though his actions have tested me again and again. I have challenged myself to work on my reactions and to not go about my day or to sleep at night without finding a place for him in my heart. Sometimes I find myself severely challenged to get to this place and have to use every trick in the book. No matter how much time or effort it takes, though, it is always worth it.

This seems to be the truest work for anyone on the spiritual path. There's no need to condone actions which are out of alignment with a person's true nature, their true nature as a Divine and Sacred Spiritual Being; but if I can't find a place in my heart for my so-called enemies, I have no business helping others to find the peace with theirs.

Lip service is dead.

Practice is everything.

Practice doesn't make perfect, it reveals perfection. It reveals our true nature.

Life asks us for the humility and willingness to surrender to Love. To die to our selfish ideas and our sense of being separate from others. It asks us to enter into uncharted territory, into the no-man's land of our Soul, and realize fear and separation as an illusion.

And in return, as a reward, not a reward from a God outside of ourselves, but as a reward for being ourselves, our true Selves, we experience our true nature, which is unconditional love. We get to live in that environment. In the environment of unconditional love.

In Heaven. Not a bad deal at all.

Having your heart cracked wide open isn't such a bad deal either. You are able to see through the illusion and see that which cracked was never real in the first place. The truth is We are Love. When we make that discovery, we find that we have, in Truth, never been wronged, never been hurt, never even been touched by *anything anyone* has ever done to us

—or not done to us.

We come to see the perfection in the plan, the perfection in the annihilation, in the destruction, in the death and even though we may not wish it upon our proverbial worst enemy, there is a prayer of gratitude in our heart for that event that eclipses and encompasses all others. Because we have found that until we died we didn't even have a clue about what it meant to really live. We begin to experience life outside the relative bounds of good and evil; we stop measuring events and people against a set mental standard of right and wrong; and we begin to trust that everything that comes our way is in service to, and an opportunity for, our growth, our joy, our expression, and Our Life. We see that everything that happens in the world is an opportunity for Life to take on a greater expression and seek a grander vision.

And no matter how much it may hurt, no matter how wrong we may want to believe it is, we come to see that there is really only one thing going on. There has only ever been one thing going on. There will only ever be one thing going on.

Whether through pain, personal will, or surrender and trust
—it's only about Love.

And about letting go of anything that would have us believe otherwise.

Holding on to a rope of ideas
about how things should be.
Our
hands
stinging
and
burning
in our
re
sis
tan
ce
to
let
go.

In mindless effort
we hold on to a rope that, in turn,
holds us even tighter,
eventually becoming our noose.
Minute after minute
hour after hour
day after day
month after month
year after year
decade after decade
life after life
clinging to a rope of thoughts and ideas of how
"life should be"
"they should be"
"we should be"
while the angel
of peace
deep within us
whispers the same words
she has been whispering
since the beginning of time
only a thread beyond our perception
"… just let go …"

Purpose
What Am I Doing Here?

Once I had a dream
I knew that I was more,
But went back inside the cave
To hope was such a chore.

Once I had a dream
I was beginning to explore,
But sailing became too scary
And I cast the boat to shore.

Once I had a dream
Deep inside my very core,
I realize now it's something
I just cannot ignore.

True callings of the heart don't go away.

They may be sidestepped for a time. They may be ignored, denied, and even cursed at times, but they don't go away. It is no accident that you are on the planet at this time. Your Soul has chosen to be here. It is no accident that you are holding this book. Your Soul has chosen.

There is no such thing as a meaningless existence.

Unless you believe there is.

If you believe that life is a meaningless, random existence, then that very well could be your life experience. You are free to live your life out of that belief. No one can force you to believe anything you don't want to. You can get to the end of your life and look back over the whole of it and have a sense of something missing.

Only it might not be the vague uneasiness that captures you in the moments you aren't busy distracting or numbing yourself. It might not be a general sense of anxiety as you wake in the middle of the night, feeling something is off, nervously grasping in the dark for comfort. It could very well be an overpowering, overwhelming sense of failure as you realize you had never even come close to becoming the person you had the potential to be. What you came to do, never got done. A piece of the puzzle went missing. There was less beauty, less joy, less love, less life expressed on planet earth because you chose to hold back and believe in a meaningless existence. To doubt those inner callings.

We all have our reasons why we just can't do that thing we currently feel compelled to do. Sometimes it makes no sense. Maybe it doesn't fit into our ideas about who we are. We don't have the resources, the time, the right color shoes.

It's the strangest thing.

We all know what our next step is, and when we're not taking that step, we have a laundry list of reasons why we can't possibly do it. Or we conveniently forget that insight, that knowing, we previously touched upon. We throw up our hands and say we just don't know.

As we become more in touch with the larger part of ourselves and less prone to just want what we want when we want it, things begin to change. When less of our time is spent trying to satisfy personal desires, the messages become clearer. We are no longer fighting so hard for a limited version of ourselves, no longer attached to a particular outcome, and no longer kidding ourselves that our conditioned mind, our personality, our fixed idea of who we think we are, knows better. We become less afraid of what we might hear and more concerned about the chaos or deadening that comes when we don't listen to our still small voice, and we are able to hear with a depth and an accuracy that was not available to us at our previous level of consciousness or willingness.

Moving into the Unknown

My daughter and I were living in a nice mobile home park in Orange County, California, a few years back when I realized I needed to move. Things were shifting and changing, and I just wasn't comfortable there anymore. In October of 1999, I attended my first week-long spiritually oriented workshop out in the mountains of New Mexico, which included a firewalk. The firewalk is a ceremony used for thousands of years by people of varying cultures around the world and involves walking barefoot across hot coals with temperatures reaching 1200 degrees Fahrenheit. During that ceremony, as I stood in a circle with others around the fire, I suddenly felt as if there were invisible hands in back of me, pushing me toward the path of red-hot coals.

The only one who had walked so far was the instructor, and as I was making my way to the coals, I heard a voice from within saying, "Don't worry, this will be easy, you've done this many, many times before."

It was a very surreal experience.

As I walked across the coals, I was aware of many different worlds existing simultaneously. The feeling of expansion was mind-blowing. Time and space ceased to exist; yet I was extremely aware of my physical body, which felt as if it were walking across cold, crunchy leaves. There was no feeling of heat whatsoever. My paradigm of reality got a really good shaking, and I was later called to go through the training and become a facilitator of the ceremony myself.

This was my first experience of being immersed in the energy of a group that was holding a collective intention to heal and transform. It felt as if I spent the week in an entirely different world, and when I returned home I was surprised to find a letter from the owner of the mobile home park I was living in. The letter stated that my dog was too large and no longer welcome in the park. Since my dog was full-grown when we had moved in, and we had been there for over two years, I took it as another sign that it was time to move. There's nothing like a little extra nudge from the universe.

There's also nothing like being in open dialog with the universe, noticing and acting upon the signs and signals It is providing; in other words, being sensitive to what is being reflected from our inner terrain, rather than fighting against it and blaming others for what is showing up in our experience.

In a meditation one morning, I "knew" I needed to move to Santa Monica, with overwhelming certainty. I was planning to begin a Masters program there, but at that point had not even been accepted and even if I had, the courses were only one weekend a month, allowing people to commute from Europe and other parts of the world. I certainly had no reason to move there. I knew absolutely no one that lived there. I thought it was a crazy idea, but somewhere in me knew it was something else. So I remained open to the idea. Until, that is, I went up to look at a few places and saw the prices. Then I knew it was crazy! I decided to put the whole thing on hold while I bide my time and tried to figure out what to do.

That Thanksgiving, I had an opportunity to go to Germany with a friend and stay with him at his cousin's family's house. I was still questioning if Santa Monica was the place or if I should just try to find somewhere cheaper and closer to my old place. I was getting flak from my former husband and from others, and doubt began flooding my awareness. In Germany, my friend had an Aunt Monica who apparently had a falling out with the family. My friend had fond memories of her, though, and really wanted to see her. It was during a conversation at a kitchen table one morning in Hamburg that the world took on the quality of a *Twilight Zone* episode. Speaking no German, their conversation sounded oddly like:

"Blah, blah, blah, blah, Tanta Monica."

"Blah, blah, Tanta Monica."

"Tanta Monica blah, blah, blah."

"Yaaah."

"Blah, blah, blah, blah, blah, blah, blah, Tanta Monica."

"Yah. Santa Monica."

It was in that moment that I absolutely knew I was to move there!

To the rational mind this sounds insane. I understand. To my rational mind this sounds insane. But it has become the only way I make a real decision. It is the guidance that transcends the rational. It is beyond belief and beyond reason.

And it is magical.

I used to get confused when dealing with guidance and intuition, because in my mind there seemed to be some kind of subconscious categorizing of incoming information which only included two options: rational or irrational. One day I heard a new word, trans-rational, which transcends the rational since it exists in a different dimension and context than the rational or logical mind. It doesn't fit into the intellectual or logical mind's understanding and, since it doesn't, that mind is much more comfortable denying its existence by calling it simply irrational.

The truth is, when you make a decision from the rational mind, from the facts, from the material world, you have to live in that world and all that comes with it. When you make decisions based on the guidance of the Soul, which is in harmony with the Universal Whole, the laws of the material world no longer bind you. In fact, you are no longer bound by any law. You have transcended the law and live in Grace.

It needs to be said that sometimes this so-called intuitive guidance is our conditioned minds—our egos—wanting a certain outcome and choosing to see things a certain way. You can always find what you are looking for, so if there is any attachment to a particular outcome, following signs tends not to be the most reliable form of guidance.

In the particular case of my moving, there was no attachment to moving to Santa Monica, as I was getting a lot of negative feedback from most of the people around me, didn't know anyone there, and didn't have the resources. Even with all of the seeming obstacles, I came back home with a new commitment to move there. I made the forty-minute drive and registered with an apartment search service. I was still not able to see how I was going to afford to live there, but I knew Santa Monica was where I needed to be. During this time I remember walking down the street and, in a place of incredible frustration, looked to sky and said, "Hey, if you want me to move out there so bad, You need to do something!"

Even though we may look up to the sky in these moments, either out of habit, utter desperation or, for the artists in the house, a little dramatic effect and flair (hey, all the world is a stage, remember), we need to be reminded at times that the looking is only metaphorical. We may look to a "Higher power," to our "Higher Self," or seek "Higher ground," but while all of these indicate upwards to a "higher" vibration, in Reality everything is Here.

Paradoxically, even though everything is Here, Now, and even though we might have had a mind-blowing realization of this Truth, we have to be present to the energy that is in front of us in the moment. If we start putting rules on things, saying, "Well, I can no longer look up because that doesn't correlate with my recent insight," or, "I can no longer allow myself to feel this frustration because I am now enlightened," we're cutting ourselves off from the very energy we need to transcend the limiting conditions of the moment. We're no longer in the moment. No longer Here. We're off constructing new boxes in our minds.

Feeling frustrated, angry or fearful doesn't have anything to do with who We really are, but if these energies are directed consciously, as opposed to unconsciously released, they can add tremendous fuel to the fire of the Soul's purpose.

That moment of looking up to the sky was exactly what was called for, even though now I might do it a little differently.

Then again, I might not.

Ask and Ye Shall Receive

It was a week or so later when the phone rang while I was getting ready for the funeral of my mom's husband. They had only been married for a short time, and this man had had an incredibly positive impact on my mom—and she on him. I just loved him. I was struck when the voice on the other end of the line, my stockbroker and a friend of the family, offered his condolences and then asked if I remembered when he had told me there would probably be no more money coming from my grandparent's trust.

I remembered. The money that had initially come in was invested and being used to supply an income so that I could go to school and my daughter could stay home with me. It was very clear that I was not to use that principle to move. "Well, I was wrong," he said, and proceeded to tell me I had just inherited an amount even larger than the previous distribution. It took a while for the news to sink in, as there were other more important things to attend to that day. It was another experience that reminded me that money is great in that it provides opportunities for us and those around us, that it can be shared and have a positive impact when used constructively, but it is not the "be all and end all" that an economically based society wants us, or rather needs us, to believe.

I procrastinated for a few more weeks, until my place was just about sold and I didn't have a choice. In hindsight, it seems it was much less about procrastination and more about divine timing. I wasn't actively avoiding looking for a place, but I did keep wondering why I hadn't gotten around to doing it every time I thought about it. I was on the Internet one night looking at places and decided to put in a request for Santa Monica and the general amount I was willing to pay. I got a list back, got in touch with the broker, and we set a date to look at properties.

The broker was great. It turned out he worked for a company that was dedicated to service and gave ten percent of their income to different charities. I love it!

As we drove through Santa Monica and looked at the various

condos on the list, we simultaneously played games my daughter had invented with a few spare coins. It was a beautiful day and we were all having a great time. After awhile, the broker said, "Well, there's one more place I have to show you, but for the price, I wouldn't expect much."

I had been having so much fun playing, talking with the broker, and enjoying the day, I had forgotten that I really did need to find somewhere to live pretty quick, as my current place was in escrow at that point. When we came to the last condo, I thought it looked nice. As soon as the door opened and we walked in, it was another story. Brand new hardwood floors, new cabinets, brand new appliances, and the most incredible, wondrous feeling of being home. It felt like a dream, and in my mind all I could hear was, "This is it, this is it! This is the place!"

One of my only criteria had been that I was able to ride my bike to the beach from my house. At less than a mile away, this place was five times closer than my place in Orange County. The broker had a strange look on his face as he thumbed through his paperwork and made a phone call. He kept saying that he couldn't understand why they were selling it for such a low price, that maybe there was a mistake. It was then that I really knew it was my place. That's how these things happen. Unexplainable. Miraculous. When you're acting on the guidance of that still small voice, though, they become the order of the day.

The Universe conspires on your behalf when you act on Its behalf.

He made the call and found the price to be correct, but also found that three other offers had already been made. I drove back up the next morning, signed the offer, and was told to expect a call in a few hours to let me know if they had accepted. Since I was paying cash and paying the full asking price, which was still way below the market price in the area, he said it was pretty much a sure thing. I went about my day and by late afternoon realized I had never gotten a call from him. That evening I became a little anxious, thinking that something had gone wrong, and I picked up the phone to call him. I started to dial the number and realized that wasn't what I was being asked to do. I was being asked to surrender. Again.

Geez, how many times? I thought.

Then I remembered that no thing, person, or situation had any power over me unless I gave it that power, and that if something was truly mine, it would come to me. I had done all that I could, and if it wasn't truly mine, I wanted absolutely nothing to do with it. Surrender had always sounded like a wimpy, giving-up thing to me before, but I have since found it to be one of the most powerful acts a human being can demonstrate. To not have your happiness contingent upon anything outside of you is a freedom of such magnitude it is incomprehensible to those who haven't discovered its power.

The next morning, a call came in from my broker saying the offer had been accepted. He apologized for not calling the night before and mentioned something about a family problem, but that he still should have called and didn't really understand why he didn't. When he said that, I remember thinking, I know why. Then he mentioned we could do a two-week escrow. A two-week escrow!

It seems there is no formula, no set way to come into alignment with the Life Your Soul intended—to Live beyond belief—except to listen to Your Soul. To Your Higher Self. To the Wisdom of Your Heart. Your Angels. Your Guides. The Universe. To do this you have to throw out the rules. Put aside what you think you know. Get "out of your mind."

Whether the messages seem to be coming from within, or whether they are being projected and reflected in our life experience, it is the questions we are asking and what we are looking with that is important. Many times the messages we receive from the Soul field, from our greater Purpose, will have nothing to do with the wishes of the ego. Many times the messages will be in direct conflict with what the conditioned mind has been trained to want. One of the ways I pretty much know if it's guidance from my soul, as opposed to my ego playing the guide, is the ego's initial reaction to the guidance. When I hear it react with "That's crazy!" or "I can't do that!" or my personal favorite, "You must be joking!" I pretty much know I'm on the right track.

We beg and beseech the Universe for our next step, to know our purpose, for our soul mate to appear; and when they don't arrive in the package our ego had in mind, we dismiss them and go back to mental goal-setting and visualizing what our conditioned mind wants—forgetting our conditioned mind lives in a very small, very restricted, very limited world.

Living in a state of surrender can be a very difficult way to live, since the mind has such strong opinions of who we are and what we should be doing. It has been hypnotized so thoroughly, so systematically, to see the material, finite world as real. It thinks it knows what our purpose should be; what our soul mate should look like and be like; what We should be like.

The belief that we need to get a mental picture of what we want, to think up a goal or have someone else think one up for us, then proceed to personally create that mental idea, is so deeply embedded in our awareness that it can be extremely difficult to break the habit. When we create from the conditioned mind what we think *should* be, rather than what Already *Is*, we end up living out a limited idea of life rather than truly Living *Life*.

It must also be said that it is not just a different career or creative focus that makes such a difference. It is not so much the activity itself as it is the dimension in which you are living. You're not just being an accountant instead of a graphic designer or living in Phoenix instead of New York; you are living the life your Soul intended which puts you in the right place at the right time, and in a flow you could never have dreamed possible or created "yourself."

You can have fantastic and amazing success on the physical plane by getting an idea in your mind and creating that life using positive focus and action in the world, but that life will look nothing like the life your Soul intended. Deep down, there will still be a feeling of something being off. No matter how much worldly success. No matter how mighty your manifesting abilities become. There will be a feeling of it being off because it was created from a limited, linear perspective rather than from a field of Infinite Possibility. You are not here to live out your idea of a great life, but your true Life. The life your Soul intended when you took on this incarnation. A purpose that is beyond what your personality can dream up on its own.

In Reality, the life of God.

This life brings an incredible peace of mind and a harmonious, creative flow. You feel as if you are flowing in the great river of life. Your main focus is not figuring out or planning out what you need to do, but simply being yourself, paying attention, and listening for your next step—and most importantly, taking action on your next step when you become aware of it.

Guidance without action is worthless. It might almost be better if you don't get any guidance if you're not going to act on it. It is incredibly painful choosing to not follow what you have been guided to do. Resistance can be absolute hell.

There is no question, no doubt, in the moment when an insight or revelation comes. It all makes sense. We see it so clearly. Oh, it is so wonderful! We have been touched, we think—spoken to directly! Yes, this is the answer! Then the next day, or in some cases, the next minute, the mind and all of its limiting beliefs, comfort agendas, and cultural propaganda begin to infiltrate our awareness, causing us to question and doubt incessantly: Was that really guidance? Maybe it was just my ego. Besides, *I can't do that!*

How do you know if it is truly guidance or if you're just making something up? You don't. Not for sure, anyway. Especially if you return to your previous state of awareness. It would be nice if it were easy to be sure. Like anything else, it takes practice to discern the different ways of knowing within yourself and what those feel like. Many times the only way to find out if what you are "hearing" or "seeing" comes from the dimension of your Soul is to act on it and see what happens. In other words, just do it. If it is a major life change and you don't want to fully commit to taking action, at the very least, you can play the hot/cold game with the Universe.

When we were kids, my grandma Oma used to hide things for my sister and I to find. "You're warm…warmer…No, now you're colder…cold…Oh, you're getting warm again…warmer…hot… Hot!" she would cry out, as we moved closer to the hidden object.

The Universe seems to respond in this manner when we are out there asking for direction regarding our purpose, since all "It" is doing is reflecting greater or more advanced or more enlightened versions of ourselves back to us.

Go ahead and take a small step on something you feel you have been guided to do—just one small, little act. It doesn't have to be huge, maybe only a metaphorical step. If you take one step and it is in alignment with your Soul's desire, with your next area of growth, things will begin to happen.

You may just get a feeling of peace or wellbeing. You'll know when you're warmer and when you're colder when you start to really pay attention. Although many obstacles manifest, mirroring the conditioned mind's subconscious resistance, as well as unconscious and limiting beliefs, you will feel compelled to move forward anyhow.

The bottom line is that you need to listen to the wisdom of your heart. You eventually get to the point where you know. You understand that no one can give you the answer you seek. You must come to the answer yourself.

Sometimes you learn what something is by first experiencing what it isn't. This process usually involves making many, many "mistakes." Learning to recognize the voices that are not of the Soul is just as important as learning to recognize those that are.

It's good to keep in mind that mistakes are an unavoidable part of true living, and are actually a companion on the path to wisdom. If you haven't made some serious mistakes in your life, you're not really Living, you're merely surviving. Surviving may look good on paper, and it will look very good to the conditioned mind, but to the Soul it is a contrived, controlled, and meaningless existence. This is not to say that you want to incorporate mistake-making as a goal; but then again, if you have been conditioned to believe that making a mistake is a godforsaken sin and that idea is keeping you from taking action on behalf of your heart, it might not be a bad idea. Ultimately, you come to see the only real mistake is being afraid of making one and letting that fear run your life.

One morning, the message: "Write as if your life depended on it" came in while I was meditating. It was very clear and came through like a lightning bolt. I immediately questioned its validity, since it was different than the guidance I usually got. It was so commanding, I reasoned, it probably wasn't guidance, just my mind trying to "should" on me, as I've heard it said. I was journaling every morning, but I knew that wasn't the writing it was talking about. It was talking about a book and I knew it. The messages were coming in that it was time.

I had always loved to write. It was my first love, before anything else, and I had always gotten positive feedback for writing assignments throughout my school years. Something in me had always known I would someday write a book. Instead of starting the book, I spent a lot of time dealing with the creative energy that was trying to express. I ate when I wasn't hungry, swayed in and out of a relationship that my heart was telling me to end, and went about my day with a gnawing sense of something being off. I was doing many other things that were part of my path, but I knew that the writing was important and I chose to ignore the messages. One evening I walked into a liquor store to buy some wine (another former way of numbing/distracting myself) and, as if on automatic pilot, I walked right to the magazines. Right when I was thinking, "Why did I walk over here?" I noticed a copy of a magazine right smack in front of me whose cover read "Start Writing Now" in large, black, bold type. "Oh. Okay. That's right. I really need to do that more," I thought.

Upon reflection, I believe I wrote a poem that week. But the message wasn't to write a poem every once in a great while; it was to write as if my life depended on it. I finally understand as I sit and write this, as I have been writing every day for several weeks and am feeling like I haven't felt in years. I'm not writing to get published or even because I "should." I'm writing because I finally realize that I am a writer. That's what writers do. They write.

And my life, my connection to the Universe through a creative outlet, depends on me having the discipline to sit down and do it. Even when it starts coming out strange. To stick with it when it is ugly or brings up something that I'm not really sure I want to look at. It is really of no consequence or relevance at this point. I think back and wish I would have just started writing back then, but it's all part of the process. Each time I learn to listen a little better. Act a little quicker. And then there are times that I don't. Either way, it's not so horrible, I guess. It's all in service to learning and growing. Besides, what else is there to do?

The Importance of Sharing

As I sit and write, I am a little disconcerted about the number of intimate personal stories that are finding their way to the page. I am also beginning to see the real importance of sharing our stories of synchronicity and grace, transformation and healing. As a culture, we become our collective stories. We can turn on the TV and see endless stories on the news that provide ample evidence of our ability to completely forget our true identity as spiritual beings. Story after story, we become entrenched in a paradigm of fear and helplessness as we are shown a hostile and crazy world full of hostile and crazy people. These images become imprinted on our minds and play over and over, materializing in the collective experience again and again and again.

We need to relate the stories that point to our innate divinity, stories that demonstrate Life working its will through us in a way that is positive, progressive, and beyond what we once thought of as possible. It is not us saying, "Hey, look how great I am," but rather, "Hey, look how great We Are! Look how creative We Are! How Loving! Look how great Life Is!"

These kinds of stories jog our memories for similar experiences, which we may have forgotten about or brushed off as coincidence if we didn't have a context for them. Even for those who are outwardly skeptical, as I know I once was, and cannot relate with a personal experience of their own, the seed of what is possible has been planted and will someday bloom.

There is something almost haunting about stories of synchronicity and grace, of miraculous healing and transformation. They are haunting because some part of us instinctively knows that this is the kind of life we are meant to be living. The conditioned mind may instantly come up with justifications for not believing these types of stories, or that people with those kinds of experiences are different breed, or just lucky, but the truth is, we were all meant to live a life beyond belief. And, our Soul knows it.

As you begin to open to your Self, you may more frequently find yourself in higher states of consciousness and inwardly be having a magical love affair with Life. You may also feel you need to tone it down to fit in with others. But you'll find the more authentic you are in your love of Life, God, and your Self, the more authentic It gets with you. The more seriously you take It, the more seriously It takes you. The more interest you have in It, the more interest It has in you. And after a time you don't have to take it seriously, or even have any interest in it, because It has become You, and You have become It.

The more you can express what is in your heart, not as a rule or a mental agenda, but as a freedom to follow that inner direction and to share whatever you feel compelled to share in the moment, the more in tune you are with Its Grace and Its miraculous ways. The times you choose to hold back out of fear or habit, you are choosing a small life. You can feel the contraction, just as you can feel the expansion, in those times when you override the old patterns of withholding.

To share inspirational stories that reveal that Life does not reside in duality (and neither do We, actually); that suffering is a choice rather than a given; and to provide evidence of another way, is necessary to transform the current conditions in a world that has been perpetually created by relying on the physical senses alone for information and clinging to a negative focus. In sharing our stories of the mystery working its way through us in ways that are positive and progressive, fun and liberating, greater numbers of people will realize that true spirituality is not boring or restrictive, as their experience of a traditional organized religion and its rule following might have been, but in its essence, it is wildly adventurous and blissful. It's not something that happens in a special building on a particular day of the week, but in every corner of the universe, in every moment.

True spirituality does not restrict; it resurrects. It does not burden or inhibit; it frees the soul. It empowers people to live more fully than they ever dared. Quite possibly, part of the purpose of those who have come into Grace and experienced Real Life is to share those stories. I used to be incredibly cautious in sharing stories of a mystical or metaphysical nature; however, when I did share, most of the time I was met with similar stories from others who were equally hesitant about sharing in order not to appear strange or different. It's time for the lovers to come out of the closet—the lovers of Peace, of Joy, of Truth, of Beauty!

We are all heavily influenced by the collective "truth" we have agreed to. It seems that if there is ever a time to begin sharing, it would be now. We have to share those stories that speak of a compassionate, wise, and unconditionally loving God. A God that is not handing out goodies or punishments, but one that is only Good. One that is only Love. These kinds of stories bury an infantile and outdated image of a wrathful, jealous, and judgmental god, and reawakens the Truth.

God is Love.

It is only our lack of awareness, our fears, our negative beliefs, our limited sense perception, which create the experience of things we would call negative. Not Love. Not Life. Not God.

It has always been easier to pawn off our personal responsibility onto someone else, but once we realize the true joy and freedom that comes from a real relationship with the Divine, we do everything we can to remain conscious in order to maintain that relationship. There's just no comparison between walking through life as a victim and walking through conscious and fully alive. There's no comparison between living in a world you believe to be unsafe and cruel and one in which you understand and know to be friendly. And there's absolutely no comparison between believing in a god who is punitive and vengeful, and knowing God to be the most benevolent, indescribably beautiful, wise, and loving force in all of creation.

One morning I woke to find my eight-year-old daughter by my side in bed. "Mom," she said, "I have a theory of life."

"Oh, well, what's your theory, sweetie?" I asked her.

"Well, it's like, life is like a dream, and we just keep waking up in bigger and better ones."

I lay there for a long time pondering the simple wisdom of her morning insight.

And we think we have something to teach them.

To have the courage to walk through the screaming voices,
the insanity,
the haunting images of the past,

To come to know fear as just another emotion
that is powerless over me,
save the power I give it,

To entertain
and act on
a vision from my very Soul,

To build the most idealistic dreams of the heart
in the face of a culture,
and a part of myself,
that clings to an outdated paradigm and shouts, "Fool!" from
the safe and comfortable sidelines of Life,

To align with my True Nature
and develop my integrity to the point where there is no discrepancy

between my inner and outer voice,

To have the wisdom to remember,
especially in the critical moments,
that I and Thy are one,
and that what I do to others, I do to myself,

To be bold enough to sing the songs of my Soul,
and sing them true to the song,
without editing on others behalf,

To know
that when all is said and done,
there will be a peace in my heart,
a knowing in my Soul,
that I gave this Life thing my all.
And,
that I did it for Love.

Initiation
Purification of the Soul

Lost at sea
in a storm gone mad
Once I thought I knew
but wish I never had

Tortuous caverns
of unexplored thoughts
Old feelings, emotions
covered in rot

Loose cannons
of anger and hope
alternate
And I grope even further to imagine my fate

I don't know where I'm going
And yet I still try
Asking too many questions
Getting stuck in the "Why?"

To think with the mind
only tangles the web
instead I'll just Pray
and choose to be led

Let me relax, let me fall
into the great dance of Life
not to wish, not to plan
Just to love what is mine

There are times on the path that we can't anticipate even in our worst nightmares. We feel lost. Off course. Without a sail. Strange energies. Strange occurrences. Without anyone who can even begin to understand what we are going through, mainly because, for the most part, we have no idea ourselves.

Along with that profound sense of peace we formerly discovered, in periods of deep initiations, words and coherent thoughts seem to escape us as well.

We've all been taught that it is acceptable, even proper conduct, to mourn a loss in the physical world. Deaths, divorce, foreclosure, and bankruptcy all constitute respectable reasons to break down, lose it, need time to process and recuperate. But on the spiritual path, there are profound inner initiations that can make a bankruptcy look like a cakewalk.

When the very essence of who you think you are, your beliefs, your values, your entire identity, is being leveled, it might not be that easy to skip into work and perform forty hours a week. While initiation carries with it a negative connotation, what is actually happening is that you are being initiated into a new world. You have begun to get an inkling, maybe even a very large inkling, of why you're here, and in order for you to begin to fulfill that deep calling of the heart, your old idea of life and its current manifestation needs to break down. Belief structures that have no place in this new world will have to go. Habits that will never allow the fullness of the vision to manifest will need to fall away.

In these times of initiation, everything that has provided comfort in the past will lose its power to do so. This is where moderate addictions can get out of control, as the conditioned mind is trying desperately to stop the initiation process and to hold on to its own little creation, its own little illusion of life.

During this time, we may find we have become strangers in our own lives. My god, who decorated this house? Who are these people around me? And, for Pete's sake, why do I spend so much time staring at a box?

The resistance to going into this deeply terrifying abyss of the unknown (that which we have become to ourselves) may manifest as what the medical community refers to as depression. In our efforts to keep the ball rolling, no matter what may be going on, no matter how far away we may be from that deep calling, we may resort to modern ways of dealing with this spiritual crisis. One of them is Prozac. It is one of a number of chemicals or distractions we might use to keep lives the Soul wouldn't have chosen in a million years, and is begging us to get out of, running smoothly.

The word "smoothly " being relative of course.

People might mistakenly think that the spiritual path is a fluffy, feel-good route for wimps who can't handle the "real" world. I know that's what some people might think, because I used to be one of those people. If anyone comes into a real spiritual discipline and believes that though, they are in for a rude awakening. There is nothing soft and fluffy about one taking total responsibility for their reactions and actions in the world, realizing there is no one else to blame for anything going on in their life—or in the world, for that matter. It takes an amazing amount of courage and willingness to explore areas that most people choose not even to acknowledge. It takes courage to act on your inner guidance, especially when it doesn't fit into everyone else's program, including your own, and people you formerly catered to are not happy with you, to say the least. It takes everything you have to question the entirety of your existence and refuse to live your life according to anyone else's rule book. This is not to mention the many, many times during the process you may find yourself questioning your sanity.

Disease or Symptom?

The notion that depression (or some of the other diseases of the mind) is merely a chemical imbalance never sat well with me. I don't doubt the "scientific facts;" but would like to suggest that there may be more at work here than biology. I understand that there are people who would not be able to function in this culture without drugs; it's just that there might be a much greater possibility than "functioning in this culture." The drug itself is not the problem as much as the attitude our culture has around prescription drugs and the way they tend to be distributed like Pez. The way they are used as band-aids for the spiritual anemia from which our culture suffers.

The way the drug companies court doctors and give incentives and rewards for prescribing their drugs is also something to think about. Is the bottom line really our health or someone's financial gain? What may initially start as a good intention to help may eventually turn into quite something else, as the intention and bottom line change during the process.

One evening, a hearing was being televised on C-SPAN, which involved a group of individuals who were suing the manufacturer of the drug Ritalin. The prosecution presented a flyer as a piece of evidence. It turns out this flyer had been distributed to several schools informing them of the different goods the school would be able to purchase for each child who was prescribed Ritalin, since once diagnosed, the child would technically become "disabled" and worth more money to the school. For instance, for every five students diagnosed and prescribed, X amount of computers could be purchased. It was later discovered that the flyer had been distributed by an organization that was heavily supported and funded by the drug company in question.

With information like this coming to light, even though much of this type of information never seems to make it to the front page, it may be time to put the trust back into God, into Life, at least as much as we are putting it into a drug, a doctor, or a drug company. Taking spiritually based classes, spending hours in prayer and meditation, and taking good care of our body may take more time and energy initially, but once we make the discovery that the real power lies in our own consciousness, and work to (i.e., love to) keep that discovery new and alive within us every day, then the time, money, and energy we "save" can be astounding.

It would be wise to experiment with practitioners who help us become aware of and monitor our own health—mental, emotional, and physical—and assist us in "healing" ourselves, which ultimately translates to "knowing" ourselves. If we are in tune with the wisdom of our Hearts, we are led to alternate paths concerning our health that don't contain side effects and hidden financial agendas.

We have been programmed to be the quick-fix, band-aid consumer. There might be situations where drugs, prescription or otherwise, provide a reprieve from trauma, but unless we have the willingness, the courage, and the initiative to find another way to deal with the trauma, we may choose to use these drugs indefinitely.

We have to remember that everything is energy. What energy exactly do these drugs carry? How do they affect our ability to think clearly? They will almost surely affect our clarity of mind and sense of judgment. Many indigenous peoples used drugs to open their minds to other dimensions, to transcend the conditioned mind, and to catch insights from the spiritual dimension, but these drugs were never meant to be a permanent or daily solution.

I'm not talking about the use of drugs in the case of severe neurological damage (even though there have been cases of healing and reversal with alternative methods). What I am referring to here is the chronic emotional pain that is chronically dulled by the chemical. If only it were that easy to pop a magic pill and have everything be wonderful. Yes, it might take the sting off the cold, but there may be a gift in the cold that we will never get to discover as long as we're keeping it at bay.

If we convince ourselves of our inability to rise above the challenges that might momentarily overwhelm us, and if we buy further into the belief that we are weak, sinful, and damned (as opposed to understanding that We are Infinite and Eternal Love), then we might very well believe that our only solution is a chemical one.

We will never get to live in the world of Unconditional Love only because we don't really believe that world exists. Instead, we live in a world where we rely solely on our five senses for information and have totally forgotten who We are. Forgotten that we hold the power of the universe in the palms of our hands. Forgotten that in order to show our love, our devotion, and our gratitude to life, it is our charge to actually live it, not crawl through it.

We are powerful beyond measure. In fact, we are so powerful that if we continually think we are weak and hopeless, we will create the perfect image of a person who is weak and hopeless.

Damn, we're Good.

You may not be able to control what comes into your experience, but you do have the power to control your experience of the experience.

If the only answer we get in response to the question: *What is depression?* is that it is a chemical imbalance, it implies that we live in a meaningless, random, and unstable world.

Why are so many of us depressed? There's got to be a reason for it. I used to think I was born depressed. That it was just part of who I was, part of my genetic makeup. I chose not to share a lot when I was growing up. For some reason, I was able to discern that some of the experiences I was having, such as experiencing myself as the whole of the universe, or looking into the mirror at five and knowing that I was definitely not "five years old," were not for open conversation. I didn't know anyone who would understand, and I pretty much assumed there had been a mistake and I had been dropped off on the wrong planet. I always felt a little odd and strange, was debilitatingly shy, and I did my best to camouflage myself wherever I was. It's an interesting way to do life.

Actually, it's not doing life at all, it's doing camouflage, and my God, I have been a master at it! The only problem with the whole deal was that I still had a soul. I still had a Purpose. A reason for being on the planet, and I was beginning to realize it wasn't to camouflage myself in every environment I found myself in. Not that I was aware that I was camouflaging. I just thought I was born especially depressed and shy. I thought that I had forgotten to get in line when the social graces were being handed out, and that I had gained an extra hundred pounds because I was lazy. A freak of nature. A mistake. Real, exciting, fun, fulfilling lives were for special people. People who deserved it. People who were lucky. *Other* people.

But life is progressive. No matter how hard we try to hide who we are. No matter how much crud has been shoveled into our minds, at the core of our being, we are still our Selves. We are still a part of Creation. Part of the One. The Soul is still there, and intention is the fuel of the universe. It doesn't matter where you are, who you are, what you are. If you begin to start consciously questioning things and begin wondering if you are living the life your Soul intended, hang on—Mr. Toad's wild ride is about to begin.

Where Did I Go Wrong?

A few years back, when I was in the middle of a dark night of the Soul adventure, I was on a treadmill in the gym, listening to a cassette. The speaker was saying that in days gone by, the monks who had dedicated their lives to God would sometimes wait years before asking what their life purpose was, because they understood the magnitude and force of that question and knew that their lives would change drastically. My mouth literally dropped open and I almost fell off the damned treadmill. *Hey, why didn't anyone ever tell me that?* I thought.

I still remember the moment I realized I had come here to do something. In that moment, I knew with every cell in my being that I had a purpose. *Could it be true? Me?* I was hanging my daughter's clothes in her closet, and when I realized I had come here to do something, I just wanted to know what it was. In that moment, with all of my heart, I asked to know what that purpose was.

In hindsight, that was right before absolute chaos broke out in my life. Along with a seemingly steady diet of small setbacks and frustrations: My grandmother made her transition. My other grandmother had a stroke. I lost my driver's license for a year due to a fender-bender and short lapse in insurance. Lost my house in a foreclosure. And then my father-in law, who was coming for a long-awaited and much-anticipated visit, died of a sudden heart attack the day before he was to arrive. All of this happened in a very short period, and even though I had come to know a world of unconditional Love, I couldn't help feeling that I had been cursed in some way.

More upsetting than anything was that the feeling of total connection, joy, and peace, which had come with the "awakening" the year before, was slipping away. In a strange way this slipping away didn't seem directly connected with the circumstances as much as it seemed coincidental to them. The enthusiasm and joy I felt upon waking began to wane, and an emptiness the size of the Grand Canyon took its place.

What in the world is going on? I thought to myself, as I observed the sudden turn of events.

At the same time, there had been a profound discovery of who I was. I had come to know myself as a spiritual being and had an absolute, unequivocal knowing that everything was Good—that everything happens for Good. Even with that knowledge, there was a hellish aspect to this stage on the path. I wanted to go back to my previous state of awareness, but it seemed to have disappeared as quickly and mysteriously as it had come. I honestly don't know how I got through that time.

I do remember one evening while getting up to go to the restroom, my body suddenly went into a kind of shock. It began to shake, and as I observed this happening, the thought came to me that this was what it was like to have a nervous breakdown. It was as if there were two roads in that moment. One was to follow that energy and see where it led (most likely to a facility where I could get some help), the other was to stay there with my daughter. I chose the road that led to her. My body stopped shaking and I went back to sleep.

From what I remember, I just continued to put one foot in front of the other, stayed open to the adventure, continued to trust Life no matter what it brought, and laughed—a lot. At times, I lost track of whether I was laughing or crying. I would often observe myself in these states, and after awhile it didn't seem to matter that much whether I cried tears of joy or tears of pain. It really didn't matter that much anymore. It was the experience of being awake and alive that was beautiful.

Unloading the Baggage

In times of initiation, we may feel so out of sorts we resort to behaviors we have previously left behind. We beg God, or someone or something, to tell us what is going on. If enough of our attention is engaged in the questions, the answers *will* show up. Whether or not we are receptive to them is another story.

During this phase in my life, a message that kept coming to me through various avenues was *"The first time I'll do it for you, but then you will need to do it for yourself."* Looking back, I don't recall the different forms that message came in, but after awhile I began to understand. There was even a dream I had about a year after the whole experience that seemed to make some kind of sense of it all.

In the dream, I was in a large circular room, very high in the sky, sort of like the Space Needle in Seattle, but it seemed to reach into the heavens. The windows were made of crystal, and the light coming through was astounding. There was a feeling and a sense of beauty and elegance everywhere I looked, along with a feeling of timelessness.

Excitement filled the air as many people talked with one another. The only problem was that I didn't know anyone there. I was thinking about talking to someone, then decided instead to go to the elevator. I saw that I had a bag with me and picked it up and made my way over to the elevator. I had started to become conscious in my dreams at that time, and realized as I was dreaming that the bag I was carrying represented my "baggage."

There was an elevator attendant, and we nodded and smiled at each other as the elevator doors began to close. As soon as the doors shut, the entire elevator slammed to the right and I was thrown up against the wall. Then it swung just as harshly to the left. I had been thrown to the floor, and I looked up at the attendant in panic.

He looked straight into my eyes. "Don't worry," he said. "This is what's supposed to happen. Hang on!"

I was just barely able to get my hands around one of side rails before we began to drop. It felt as if the bottom had dropped out, and soon we were falling faster and faster.

The pressure was unbearable. At some point I began to think my head might actually explode. I tried to scream but couldn't. This seemed to last for years. Just when I thought I couldn't take another second, the elevator came to a very gentle, graceful stop.

I gathered my senses and stood up. I picked up my bag, and when the doors opened, I walked out into what seemed to be the core of the earth. It was dark and damp and had an earthy feel about it. There was something very comforting as well and I felt like I had been there before. I was on familiar ground.

As I began to explore the surroundings, I heard the attendant calling, "Excuse me, ma'am. You forgot something."

I turned around and looked inside the elevator at a red Radio Flyer wagon full of shopping bags. There were an amazing amount of bags in the wagon, piled so high not one more would fit.

I smiled graciously at the attendant and told him, "Oh, I'm sorry, but those aren't mine."

His face was suddenly very close, his eyes bright and clear. "Yes," he told me, in no uncertain terms, "they are."

After the elevator experience, I was in no mood to argue the point, and it is truly not in my nature to argue the point, so I went back inside the elevator and pulled the wagon out, grumbling all the way.

It was not long after that dream that I was guided to a Spiritual Psychology Master's program, which holds the theory that you cannot help others heal until you heal yourself. This makes perfect sense, since it is not just tools that heal, but consciousness—that is, awareness of Love, of What Is. Most of the work done in that program is experiential, and the students become their own case studies. It is a brilliant premise and a brilliant program. After attending that program and continuing my studies with various teachers, I became aware of emotional blocks that I had never worked through and that were still running my life in many ways. I also became aware that much of my desire to heal others was coming from an unconscious desire to heal myself.

Dreams have a way of conveying messages that we may be unable to hear in our ordinary waking hours. Keeping a dream journal and recording anything that comes through in the dreamtime can be extremely telling and healing. I am sometimes astounded when I read some of the dreams I had in years past and their prophetic messages which, at the time, seemed nonsensical.

There are many different kinds of dreams. Some foretell future events, some are warnings in our present lives. I once was dating someone who, in a dream, began to suck the side of my hip until I was screaming in pain. It was a clear message I needed to leave the relationship, which I did. I hadn't realized just how draining the relationship was until after I left. Some dreams are actual connections with loved ones who have crossed over to the other side, and upon waking I am convinced I have shared time with them. In some, I am so busy that I wake up feeling like I've been living an entirely different life while asleep in this one. Others are very vague and make no sense at all until I begin to write about them, and in the writing of them, the meaning begins to materialize before my eyes. There are times when I mention a dream to a friend and they see an angle I hadn't even thought of, and it resonates or, oddly, has great meaning and relevance for them. I once had a friend share a dream that had no meaning for her whatsoever, and as she told it my mouth dropped open. She dreamed, in great detail, a situation I was going through which she wasn't aware of, along with a wonderful solution.

Dreams can be such a rich source of information and pleasure, and for those who pay attention to them, they tend to become even more so. You may even begin asking yourself, "Did I dream that, or did that really happen?" And then after a time you may begin phrasing the question, "Which dimension did that happen in?"

You're Being Purified

Before ever making it to the school in spiritual psychology, there was still the challenge of trudging through a major purification stage. I worked at a bookstore at the time and relished the experience. Being an avid reader from an early age, I loved everything about it. I loved the smell of books upon entering the store first thing in the morning. I loved recommending books to customers and the ensuing conversations. I loved building elaborate book displays in the front windows, reminiscent of early Lego masterpieces. I loved finding books for customers who had only the faintest hints as to what the book was: "Well, I know it had a blue cover...*um*...and I think the author's last name is Smith. Yes, that's it, do you have that one?"

I also adored the people I worked with. They were such a creative, fun bunch, full of novel ideas to keep things interesting. One day we tried to speak using only book titles.

Do You Know Where the Red Fern Grows? Go Ask Alice, I'm in the Zone.

Sometimes we special-ordered books on specific bizarre subjects, such as the Illuminati Seven, and read further into the conspiracy when none of the books came in.

One of my fellow workers, named Reese, was a theology major in school, but he was one who possessed more than a mere intellectual understanding of theology. Along with being a practical joker extraordinaire, sometimes when we worked together he would pose philosophical/theological questions and we would ponder them, sharing our insights as we went through the day.

When my life began to fall apart, I would come in and he would console me: "Sorry to hear about your grandmother." Then, "Sorry to hear about your license." And "Sorry to hear about your house," etc., until one day he just stood there and didn't say anything for a while. "I don't even know what to say anymore," he finally said.

I didn't either. We both stood there looking out over the stacks of books, contemplating the mystery of it all. We were opening the store together that morning, and we proceeded to shelve the carts of books before the store opened to the public. Some time later, I heard a yell from one of the aisles.

Reese came hurrying out. "Hey, I know what's happening!" A look of inspiration on his face, enthusiasm filling his voice: "You're being purified!"

It was said with the joy and innocence of a child discovering the dynamics of gravity or the recognition of a word for the first time. He waited for the inspiration and enthusiasm to make its way over to me.

It never did. We stood there for what seemed like a long time.

"Oh, that's great," I said. "Thanks. I mean...oh, wow. Hmm ..."

Some things are just about impossible to respond to with any kind of grace, and "You're being purified" is probably one of the more impossible.

When around friends and acquaintances who are going through

purification at different levels and magnitudes, I have forgotten the mushy brain state and the inability to remember any metaphysical principle ever learned, which seems to come hand in hand with the experience and have said something to the same effect: "You're being initiated, purified, chosen!" The enthusiasm is never matched, but it can be comforting to have another person see something other than total annihilation and devastation in your life when that's all that's currently being presented to you. It's also a fine thing to remember the openings that follow these times of initiation. Everything that's not in alignment with that next level of awareness you have been living in is falling away, be they physical possessions or mental and emotional attachments. The "problems" in your life have become too big for you to turn to anything other than God. You can't do it by your own will. In this stage, no one else can do it for you.

Sometimes it takes a lot for the Universe, for God, for your Self, to get your attention. But don't worry, eventually It will. You *will* get your attention. And when you do, when you really start to listen and do what your Soul is begging you to do, you will look back and bless whatever it was that put you back on track.

Still, before you get to the point where you are looking back and blessing, and if you are not quite in a place in which you are able to bless it as it is happening, it can seem quite a harrowing experience. As well as the destruction that may appear on the outside of your life, the destruction of the inner self can be even more challenging. People like to have good reasons for finding themselves in the fetal position in the corner of the room, rocking like Elvis in his prime, humming such inspirational tunes as "We all live in a yellow submarine …"

It's all well enough when your exterior life is falling apart. You can have the luxury of experiencing life from the mental state of an overripe banana and feel pretty justified about it. But when everything is going really well on the surface, and that feeling starts coming, it's another story.

There are ways of being, ways of thinking, ways of seeing the world, which are not in alignment with the vision of the Soul. These ways have to be leveled so we can realize what is Real; so that we won't just continue to learn different ways to survive in a world that we are experiencing through limited ways of thinking and being; so that we won't be tempted to think we need to change others, or the world, rather than change ourselves and our perception; so that we have the opportunity to practice what we have learned and come to realize that God, Love, and Life are our salvation. Nothing else. The understanding and realization of what those things really are, and the understanding that our spiritual practice is the way to our salvation. That it *is* our salvation. Not a drug. Not a person. Not a new idea. *Only* being Awake.

We're conditioned to see ourselves and our lives in general as something to fix, as opposed to an unfolding process of discovery and insight. This way of seeing things could mean the difference between getting a drug to "fix" the problem, instead of finding the answer to what the "problem" actually is. The problem could very well be that our True Self is getting really tired of playing out a life that has no real meaning for it. The Universe is screaming cold, and instead of moving out of the cold to find a warmer area, we are told to take an anti-depressant, or we begin to self-medicate through various addictions in order to take away the sting of the cold. No matter. In the end, we are still living in the cold and not moving. And to the part that is the most real in us, we become not much more than death warmed over.

Prescription for Purposeful Living

I lovingly refer to 1997 as my year from hell, knowing full well there is no such thing in Reality. Still, it seems appropriate to refer to it as such. It was the time when everything fell apart.

It was the next year when everything was going seemingly well. The emptiness lingered and I still had some things to work on, but for the most part, everything was fine. An inheritance had come through from my mom's parents, and I had started back to college full-time. With ten added years of experience, school was a piece of cake, and I actually liked a few of the classes. Money was no longer an issue. I had some friends I enjoyed. It was good. Life was good. But the empty feeling, which had been gnawing away in the background, started to come to the forefront of my awareness.

I dropped my daughter off at school one morning and came back home to get ready for school myself. As I was walking across the floor, the most overwhelming feeling came over me. I literally could not take another step. I kicked off my shoes, went back into my bedroom, got under the covers, and cried for hours. I went and picked my daughter up after school as if nothing was wrong, and continued the same process the next day. I was already halfway through a semester with a full load of classes, A's in all of them, and when I shared this strange occurrence with a friend, he said maybe it was because I was afraid of success. I pondered this. I did have a history of not completing things, but for some reason that just didn't seem to be it. I couldn't put my finger on it, but something was severely off.

I ended up keeping my freshman composition and life drawing classes, both of which I absolutely loved, and dropped the others. That feeling was still overwhelming, and I begged the Universe, my Higher Self, my Soul, to tell me what to do.

"Just tell me, what am I supposed to do?" I asked.

I was feeling so out of sorts, I thought I was going to lose it. If I wasn't so desperate and so willing to do whatever it took, I might have missed the message or chosen to ignore it.

It began with my stepmom, also known as my angel-mom, out in Palm Springs. I mentioned that Ariel's teacher had told me she was asking too many questions, that she was getting up out of her seat to help others too much, that she was beginning to be a problem in the classroom.

"Why don't you homeschool her?" she said.

Hmm...I had started to look into that before she went into kindergarten, but that was right around the time I had left my marriage, and I needed to go back to work full-time. It was a different story now; I was back in school. Well, part-time, but I had other things to do now. Homeschool?

A few days later, my neighbor (and Ariel's best friend's mom) was walking by and stopped to chat. "I've decided to take the kids out of school and homeschool them," she said.

Homeschool, huh? How about that? What a coincidence.

Then the clincher. While talking on the phone with my friend Christopher, laughing at the fact that Ariel "asked too many questions" in school, he suddenly said, "Hey, I know—you should homeschool her."

The *Twilight Zone* theme song began playing in my mind.

"Hey, are you still there? Hey, I was just kidding. I don't even know where that came from. Is that even something you can do?"

That was it. I had no idea how to do the homeschooling thing but then I remembered I didn't need to know how. That is the coolest thing about the whole deal (or the worst, depending on the level of your need for control). You really don't need to know how to do the thing, you just have to follow the next step as it comes.

I ended up finding an organization online, attending a weekend conference, and hooking up with local groups. That was several years ago, and I have yet to understand exactly how we're doing it, or even what we're doing at times. My daughter has come home to learn, but most of the time I get the feeling she's only there to continue to provide me with lessons.

One summer we went to Paris together. At first I thought it was a little extravagant, but in a perfect world…and then I remembered it *is* a perfect world. Hey, if you're going to study art …

Once during meditation, I had a big, dramatic, on-the-floor, fists-clenched argument with "God" when one particularly disturbing picture came into my mind.

"You don't understand, I just can't do that," I said. "I'm too shy, too socially retarded. I think you've made a big mistake. Thanks for the offer, but this is just a little too much, you know? I'm sorry, but I really, really, really can't do that!"

Good, a voice came back, *no one asked you to do anything!*

"Excuse me?"

You don't seem to understand. The part that is scared is not the part that is going to be doing the work.

I climbed up from the floor, slightly embarrassed, slightly relieved, and a memory of Gilda Radner from the old *Saturday Night Live* TV show came into my mind.

I looked up to the heavens from where the voice seemed to originate. "Oh," I mumbled in a small voice. "Never mind."

So much for the drama.

It's easy to forget that the part in us that is scared and resistant isn't the one being asked to do the job; it's being asked to step aside—to get the heck out of the way, if you will. If we can remember that it's not a limited and fixed idea of ourselves that is being asked to live the vision, but is only being asked to surrender to the vision, to our Soul's intention and our Soul's life, we will understand that there's really nothing for us to do. Nothing. In fact, the less we do personally, the better. In doing the inner work, we simply become more our Selves. In living from our Soul's will for us, we come into alignment with the nature of our true Selves, of Life Itself for that matter. We end up becoming the thing we originally experienced ourselves surrendering *to*.

There is an Intelligence within that knows far more than the conditioned mind could ever hope to. If we are willing to ask this Intelligence for guidance, surrendering what we think we want and who we think we are; and if we develop the patience and courage to follow the signs and the answers this intelligence reveals to us, our path becomes effortless.

Well, effortless to the Soul. Hell, perhaps, for the ego.

By taking action on this inner voice, this intuitive self, and by continually living in a space of surrender and trust, we eventually start to identify less with the limited ideas and more with the eternal and infinite presence.

In our past, we have usually had to surrender to other people's will for us. It was sometimes necessary for our survival and socialization at the time. We tend to take that idea of surrender and think that's what surrendering to our Higher Selves will be like. There is a big difference, though. When we surrender to our Higher Selves, we surrender to the part that is purest about us, the part that knows our potential and what we have come here to do. We are surrendering to our bliss, to our true beauty, to the genius within. During childhood, we may have had to surrender to ideas about us that weren't even true. We may have had to surrender to a way of life that was lived in fear and survival. We may fear that we will have that same experience when we surrender to what we think of as God. We are afraid of surrendering because we equate it with giving up parts of our self and becoming less, which might have been the case in the past.

Once we understand that surrendering to God is not surrendering to some outside force that will take over our lives and make us do things we have no passion for, but is the same as surrendering to our Self—that part that knows exactly what is best for us because *It Is Us*, the surrender becomes easier.

Hmmm…Maybe "easier" isn't the word.

Less traumatic. Well, maybe not.

More welcome.

Yes.

My house is on fire

and though my limbs burn
and my mind races around
trying to grab the 'important' things,

a little voice says,
This is not a fire of destruction

Burning away the old thoughts and beliefs
too small and short sighted,
too limited for this expanded vision,
too sane for a Heart's dream

Though I can feel my heart burning
with sadness,
confusion,
longing,
regret,
fear,

things
that haven't frequented my home
for
so
damn
long
now

Amid all of this
I hear a whisper,
This is not a fire of destruction

My mind
now barren of the answers
that once so easily found their way there

*I wonder how
it could not
be a fire of destruction*

So I stop

and allow the burning

*and in the stillness
the old,
outdated overgrowth
burns away*

*clearing a space
for the new ideas
fresh growth
to be nourished
in the full light of the sun*

*It was
in fact
a
fire
of
the
Heart*

Belief
The Foundation of Experience

I can't believe
this happened again!
When will they stop?
When will it end?

Then ever so gently
I hear a tsk, tsk, tsk, tsk,
And I think to myself
"Something's amiss."

Have you forgotten
again, my dear child?
How much you forget
In such a short while

But don't you worry
I'll tell you again
And then you'll forget—
Then again, we'll begin.

Do not just believe
what you can see
But come and play
a new game with me

Only those who have learned
to master this game
Will come to know peace
Will not live in blame
So if you would like
To truly be free:
It's as *you believe*
Then so shall you see!

If you don't get a handle on what you really believe and understand what a profound impact those beliefs have on your life—that they *are* your life, in effect, your manifest life, the life you experience on a daily basis—you will forever remain a victim of circumstance.

"Hey," you might say, "I thought the book was called *beyond belief*."

All in good time. Before we can go beyond something, first we have to master it to a certain degree. Without a firm foundation, which comes from becoming aware of limiting beliefs, exchanging those beliefs for ones more in alignment with who we really are, and experiencing the effects of that work in the physical world, we will not have a strong enough conscious anchor to move to the next level.

What do you really believe? To find out, you just need to fill in the blanks:

The world is _____. Women are _____. Men are _____. Work is _____. Money is _____.

Now think of your current experience with these things, and about the truth of the matter.

Well, I just did, you might say.

No, you just told me your beliefs.

No, I just told you what is true.

Okay, okay. Now, why do you believe the world is a scary place?

Because it is. Just look at the troubles right now! Look at the people starving, war, terrorism, global warming. Why, my neighbor just got robbed. Not to mention all of the things that I've gone through. The world is a scary place. Any idiot can see that.

Well, that's true. But, moving along, not everyone sees it that way. Not everyone believes the world is a scary place.

Well, they must be crazy then.

After questioning, and releasing, many limiting personal beliefs and watching situations change 'miraculously', I often think:

If this is crazy, bring on the straightjacket!

What's really crazy is to be an all-powerful, divinely creative being and believe yourself to be a victim of circumstances.

There aren't certain people who are randomly lucky and who get to live what one would consider to be a wonderful life. On some level, they have agreed that life is wonderful, that there is more than enough to go around, that they are in relationships to nurture and grow into greater expressions of themselves, and that Life is Good.

Charmed and harmonious lives and prosperous and loving relationships aren't random events, even when it looks like they are. If, in our inner world, we believe that life is a struggle, we will live in that world. We will consistently experience it as such. In fact, there is no way we cannot experience struggle consistently in our life experience if that belief does not rest within our minds. We don't even have to be conscious of beliefs for them to affect us. In fact, when we are continually experiencing life in a negative fashion, we can pretty much bet we are not aware of the limiting beliefs which we formed throughout the years, and which hold us in that limited pattern of experience.

The person next door to us might be experiencing the same exact "negative" circumstances, but have a totally different internal reaction and response. Our responses absolutely have an effect on our experience farther down the road. The person who believes there is opportunity in every seeming crisis will find it and use that evidence to further their development, strengthen their faith, and bring Good to the present circumstance, which will undoubtedly, eventually manifest as grace, or "luck," down the road, since this is the place they are living in now.

What Can We Change?

There is a distinction in what our beliefs seem to have the ability to manipulate. In the beginning of this chapter, the things asked about don't actually exist in spiritual reality—things like money, men, women, etc. If you think about it, there is no such thing as "men." There is George over there, and Fred, and William, but there is no such thing as "men." Who is "men"? What energy is "men"? There is the collective of all men now living on the planet, or who have ever lived on the planet, but that is much too broad and dispersed for us to be able to tap into, and if we think about it, it is not what we are tapping into when we personally think of men. There is the divine masculine, which pertains to certain qualities and ways of being that may be used in either a constructive or destructive way; but this is not what we are talking about when we speak of "men" either.

What we personally tap into when we think of men is what we have been told, what we have heard about and read about—basically, what we have been conditioned to think about in regards to men. We might also turn to personal experience to prove our point, failing to realize that our beliefs keep re-creating our experience.

The same is true of time and money, no matter how many brilliant rationalizations we can come up with. We can either go through life unconsciously proving limiting and negative beliefs to be true, or we can experiment in this area and begin to demonstrate what kind of life we can experience as we begin to consciously choose our beliefs. There is a difference between things such as time and money and those things that do actually exist in Spiritual Reality. Things existing in Spiritual Reality are conscious. They are eternal. They have their own intention. They contain their own energy. These things cannot be as easily altered or manipulated with our beliefs in the long run, since they carry their own unique blueprint of infinite possibility.

With anything containing a unique, individualized conscious energy, we would do well to ask to see only the Truth of what is there. To see what is inherently Divine and Real and to support that Truth. In the movie *City of Angels*, Nicolas Cage's character makes the statement "Some things are true whether we believe in them or not." There are many things we might want to believe, but we find in the long run these beliefs run against what is inherently true about the thing itself. While we may know that every person is a divine being, we may not know every Soul's main intention and mission for this lifetime. We may wish that someone were something other than what he or she is expressing, based on our limited understanding of Reality.

We may even wish our own Soul's intention to be different—until, that is, we begin trusting it and find that it leads us to joys beyond our wildest imaginings.

The Malleability of Experience

I'll never forget the first time I really understood that we are creative beings. Not that we have the ability to paint a picture or design a building, but that we are much more powerful than we ever thought possible, that our thoughts alone actually effect our reality—or more accurately, our experience of reality. And, the second understanding, perhaps even greater than the first, is that we have the power to change what we believe, which in turn changes our experience! That we are, in Truth, at cause and not effect.

I was about nineteen years old when I stumbled upon the book *The Power of Positive Thinking* by Norman Vincent Peale, which is about the effects of our beliefs on our life experience. At first it didn't make any sense. I had never heard of such a thing. It blew my mind. I thought it was nuts. Insane. Crazy.

My dad once told me that I almost drove him crazy with my *why* and *what if* questions when I was very young, and it is this insatiable curiosity that has helped me move past skeptical thoughts, which otherwise would have stopped me from exploring anything new.

There is nothing wrong with being skeptical. No one wants to be "taken." Until you start being "taken" to new levels of living. I mean, really, how do you know something doesn't work unless you actually try it out yourself?

This one was a biggie though, and some part of me knew it. The implications were fantastic. That we, *everyone,* every conscious human being on the face of the earth, had the power to create our experience merely through our thoughts! And not just that we had the power to, we *already were*, but probably weren't aware of it.

Whoa! Wait a minute. That's nuts! Ridiculous.

But, what if it were true?

What if?

And then the zinger of all questions: How can I prove it? I mean, if this stuff were true, it would change everything. Everything.

This guy seems to think he's found something here. I'd almost have to be an idiot *not* to try it.

I decided to try it out with an area in my life that needed a boost: money. Cold, hard cash. I wrote out a bunch of personal beliefs I saw operating in my life related to money. One was that I had to work hard for it. I was going to take out the "hard" part, but then I thought, *Hey, why would I want to work for money? If I'm choosing the rules of the game here, why would I want to believe that I needed to work for money at all?*

In that moment, I got it. A big "Aha!" If this stuff were true, the condition existed only because, in my mind, there was a connection between work and money. All I had to do was to disconnect the two. It was so wacky, so wild, it just might work.

It takes a lot to suspend your entire reality—your entire identity at times—to try these things out. If you weren't questioning your sanity before, you'll sure as heck start now. It all gets really, really weird at times.

I started working with the idea that I needed to do nothing to get money, and that I was worthy of lots and lots of money just because I existed. Why not?

When working with financial issues, we have to wade through all of the "root of all evil" crap, too. History not only shows the corruption that greed inspires, but the tremendous good accomplished by the philanthropists of the world. Think of all the good that could come from ghastly amounts of money in the hands of people who are here for the health and well being of every person on the planet.

It took a while, but as it turned out, the experiment was successful. A part of my mind still sometimes thinks the whole idea is ridiculous, even though I haven't worked for money in years. Go figure. That doesn't mean that I haven't had a job in that time—I just haven't worked for money. This is a big distinction, and only you know where your energy and focus are.

One day when I was working at the bookstore, a number of us were hanging out in the back room. The conversation turned to large sums of money and what we would do for it. This was before any knowledge of my future inheritance, and I could not think of one single thing I would do for money. There were many things I would do, but not for money. I didn't realize it until that conversation, but I had absolutely no interest in making money at that point. I loved working at the bookstore, so much I would have worked for free, and I usually did much more than was expected of me because of that love.

Of course, one could argue that I certainly had to be interested in making money to at least pay the bills, but to be honest, I really wasn't. There was no longer any thought of money or of getting a job. They held no interest for me. From that point on, the only interest has been in doing what that still small voice—my Heart, my Life tells me to do. In that intention and action, the money and any resources I've needed have always been there. The only time I fall under the illusion that they aren't, is when I start holding a limited idea in my mind and start looking *outside* for something to force an idea into existence. Whenever I'm in service to the Soul—getting my own limited agenda out of the way—more shows up than I could have ever possibly asked for.

If you think about it, money is only another form of energy, but it does not have any inherent worth or value. If you are working for love, truth, excellence, beauty, wonder and discovery, you will find yourself truly onto something. This does not mean you need to quit your current job; you only need to make a very subtle yet profound shift in awareness to choose to work for your Soul instead of for money.

If you allow the awe-inspiring Spirit within to motivate you, rather than money, your entire life will change. The seemingly insignificant daily decisions you make will change, since the bottom line is no longer the dollar, but the Soul. You will find that the intent and energy you act with is just as important as the action itself. You will also find that it doesn't matter what job you have or who your boss is. You can choose to work for your Self, for Good, for your Soul, no matter what you happen to be doing.

When you can truly "take no thought" as to how you will be fed or clothed, no matter how many hundreds of people tell you "you can't do that," and when you seek only to give, the blessings will become "too big to receive" because you have come into alignment with Who you really are and how things really work. This is why tithing, giving ten percent of your earnings to the place(s) or people that spiritually feed you, seems to work so miraculously.

A few years back, I heard a speaker talk about tithing, and I knew it was my next step. I had been giving a lot already, but this was definitely a jump. Ten percent off the top?! Nevertheless, I decided to do it, and some months into the process, I was informed that there was even more money to be distributed from the same inheritance. In fact, it wasn't a small final distribution like I had been told it probably would be, but an amount larger than both initial distributions. I mentioned this to the broker and he said they hadn't expected that at all, and in fact, in all their years had never seen the likes of it.

This whole concept of giving without thought of what you're getting in return can be very hard to come to terms with, since you have probably been taught your entire life that it is important to be immediately compensated for what you give. We go to school to learn how to make a living, to figure out how we will make this money stuff so we can do and have the things we want. In this paradigm, the underlying, unconscious intention of one's life is focused on acquiring and/or saving money.

This underlying intention on money automatically puts us out of alignment with the full energy and intention of the Soul, since we are consciously or unconsciously focused on something that does not exist in Spiritual Reality. The two cannot exist side by side because they exist in different dimensions, and we will find ourselves feeling torn. Believing we are working for a Higher Cause. Actually working for money in the world. (Which, in the end, will only accomplish worldly things.)

When you align with your Soul's intention for your life, you align with your true nature. Your true nature is infinite abundance. Infinite. This abundance does more than source worldly concerns because it does not come from the world. It may look like wealth, but it is actually something far beyond.

In this prosperity paradigm, the only thing one needs to work on is locating and removing the limiting beliefs that are keeping one from experiencing abundance that is the natural state of one's true Being. When you do this, you will start to become more aware of every time you say, or even think, "I can't afford that." Your word is your law. Every tiny electrical impulse of worry or doubt keeps you in a lower-level life experience and restricts your manifested life experience. In allowing that thought to pass through unchecked, a future situation of not being able to afford something is created—as *soon as it passes through your mind* and especially after it passes your lips.

As you begin to understand the power of your words and thoughts, working for money will become an outdated paradigm. You learn that by changing your thoughts and feelings about money, you are able to experience a life of material abundance. As you become more comfortable with having money, and more cognizant of the thoughts blocking its presence in your life, you will build a solid foundation. After the blocks are removed, you realize that no one "out there" was ever blocking anything from you. After you train your mind to think differently and begin to release the limiting thoughts, you then go to the next level, taking absolutely no thought about it, and experience it only as a reflection of the Love you are expressing, the Love You are. The only thought about it then would be where you would like to invest it. The ego likes to invest in the illusion of safety, in the illusion of the future—it likes to invest to make money—but the Soul looks only to invest in what is generative to Life.

Wealth is the natural effect of a mental state of Abundance. It's not just something that you have acquired by means of your own device. If it holds you hostage by taking your attention and peace of mind, you are not living in and from Abundance; you just have money in the world.

Another definition of abundance is having a conscious awareness that everything you need for the highest expression of your soul is here, right now. This may include money, or not. Abundance is knowing "I Am Prosperous."

Knowing You Are.

Period.

From this state of consciousness everything else is added. If someone is attached to the physical expression of money, then they're not really free. They're living in bondage to it. To something that doesn't even really exist! How silly!

Another example of true abundance is to have an absolutely ridiculous amount of money, have it all taken away, and in that transaction remain in perfect equanimity. That is true abundance. That is true power. That is true joy. True faith.

True knowing which has nothing to do with the things of this world, only to do with the kingdom Jesus talked about. The Kingdom is awareness of Heaven.

Awareness that, in this moment, everything is working together for Good, regardless of how it may currently be presenting itself. Looking at it this way, we can see that abundance doesn't really have as much to do with money as it does with our attitude toward money—and everything else in our lives.

To the extent we are trying to figure out how we will do something, like "make money," to that exact proportion, we are blocking the natural flow of true abundance in our lives. The more we realize our Natural Self, the more we will simply come to know our natural state, which is abundant. Our outer state will then begin to reflect an inner realization of our true nature. The realization won't come from our work in the world but from our love of the world. It can take the *form* of work in the world, and it might even *look* like working for money, but it won't be. When you find true abundance, you will no longer work to attain something in trade. You will instead view it as a sacred opportunity to use your inherent gifts, talents, and *being* in service to Love, to Freedom, and to Heaven on Earth.

We may also need to challenge the deeply held beliefs and ideas we hold about "work." When we choose to grow, to take classes and read books that further our conscious awareness; when we realize spiritual qualities on deeper and more profound levels through daily practice; and when we take action on our hearts' behalf, using every moment to align more fully with who We really are, can be a hundred times more challenging than going into a building for eight hours a day and "working". The clincher is, it's also a hundred times more rewarding.

As long as we are living in a world where "I scratch your back, you scratch mine," or, "I'll give you this little bit and make darn sure I getting back what I deserve in return," we are not open to our divine inheritance. This type of mentality keeps us living in a very limited universe when, in fact, we live in a reciprocal universe. If you aren't giving beyond belief, you can bet your bottom dollar you won't be living beyond belief either. This type of giving isn't restricted to the material plane, but relates to how generous you are with thoughts about others, your intention to follow the voice of your Soul, and how committed you are to truly going beyond what you currently believe to be your limit.

Even after being conscious of this information and experimenting with it for over twenty years, there are always new limiting beliefs to be transcended. That part just floors me. Living beyond belief isn't a one-day workshop, but a lifetime of challenging one's limiting beliefs. The great thing is that you get to live in larger, more expansive, more creative, more beautiful, more loving, and more adventurous worlds as a reward for your "work."

Upgrading the Program

The assumption we make as humans is that there is a world "out there" we need to maneuver ourselves through and interpret. We have assumed that there is not much we can really do about this world "out there," and use much of our energy adapting ourselves to this fixed and objective physical reality. We make this assumption because the world out there seems so real. It would only be logical to believe in that reality and experience ourselves at the effect of that world, because in the physical realm that's the way it feels. What the mystics of the world have found is that this is the great illusion.

If we have someone to remind us of the illusion and if we have the curiosity, desire, courage, and commitment to test out another way of going through life, we can find ourselves living in entirely new worlds.

If we think of a computer, we can see that our beliefs are like the software we load onto our hard drives, but they are not the hard drive. We might have the finest computer systems available, but if we are running old and outdated software (the beliefs we were brought up with, the ones that came with the system, so to speak), through these wonderful systems we will continue to run that limited program over and over. It's not that our current beliefs are "bad." We made it to where we are today with them and they have provided a means to experience life as we have been, up until this moment. But sitting where we are in this moment, we might realize that our life experience is somewhat limited by some of the beliefs we are continuing to run. Our ability to be of service, to love, and to make a difference on this planet may be restricted. We may be inspired to step into new areas but find that a limited sense of possibility is getting in the way of taking the next steps.

We can choose a new program.

We can choose to upgrade to the finest software and use our "system" to its greatest possibility and capacity. In the process, we might find we have to add some memory to accommodate these new programs. We may have to begin to seriously remember who we really are to even dare to upgrade our beliefs.

We can begin these upgrades by making statements that at first sound absolutely ridiculous to the logical mind, because we know they do not represent our current experience. Saying and feeling "I am wealthy and prosperous" between calls from bill collectors and visits from the Repo Man might say you're ready for a stay at the local sanitarium, but others who have done this work and have seen the results know that if you have the discipline, the heart, and the persistence to continue, your financial situation will transform slowly, but surely—or even miraculously overnight.

If you really do the work, there is no way it cannot happen. *If* you don't go back to the usual distractions. *If* you don't get tired and run off to find another belief system that puts the power and responsibility once again outside of you. And *if* you don't go on to something else without completing the experiment. Rest assured, it will happen.

How will you know when the experiment is complete? When you've succeeded.

By having faith that thought is indeed creative and that we can effect our experience in a positive manner through the conscious application of it, we can attempt one of the most worthwhile experiments of our life. Even though I say "thought," which implies only the mind, there is an aspect of the emotional body involved as well. You have to believe it with all of your heart. A monotonous mumbling of certain words won't do much more than "prove" that this is ridiculous.

You have to really *Believe*.

Literally with *all your heart*.

You have to get to *Yes!* You have to get to *Knowing it is done!*

And if you really, really want to see results, you have to get on your knees, baby, and start thanking your lucky stars!

Some may see this as escapism or denial at its finest (among other things), convinced that you're just ignoring the facts and living in the land of airy-fairy.

It's not that you're denying there are problems in the material world. You just begin to understand what's really going on—what the masters, prophets, and sages of the world have understood—and you come to have new definitions for those problems. When you truly get a sense of what's going on here, that thought is indeed creative, you know that to focus your attention on a problem is to exacerbate it. If you are able to do a 180-degree turn in consciousness and give back love where there is anger, hope where there is despair, kindness where there is hate, faith where there is doubt, you are effecting that situation in such a positive way it is incomprehensible. If you truly become aware enough to have total control of your emotional reaction, everything in your world will change.

When Einstein was asked how he handled the critical remarks his peers made about his work, he responded that they didn't effect him because he didn't live in that world.

There are times when powerful points need to be made to awaken those in an unconscious slumber, but these points are made consciously, from an inspired place of vision. They are points that instigate positive and progressive change. A message given consciously with strength and power, with the fire of the heart, is a catalyst for transformation. The same energy can be destructive when it is coming from a place of fear and unconscious personal reaction.

When everyone else around you will only be able to react to the situation, thereby strengthening it's negative effect, you will facilitate change for the better by refusing to buy into what you see with your physical eyes. The truth is that people who talk about this as an escapism route have not yet found the spiritual strength to hold a position of equanimity. They do not understand that they are adding fuel to the fire by believing in, and being upset over, something that exists in part because they continue to feed it with their attention! They are living in the same state of mind in which the problem was created. In that state of mind, creative solutions don't exist and one becomes caught in a merry-go-round of recycled problems. That consciousness lives in a world of problems because that is all it has been taught to see. It lives in a world of problems to be solved, instead of a land of infinite possibilities, creative solutions, and adventures to be lived.

We have been taught that we are at the effect of the physical world. This is not true. The world we are living in, our conscious awareness, is actually the one that really matters. It is the one that really matters because it is "at cause." It is creative.

Our conscious awareness was never meant to be a problem-solving machine or a mere victim of circumstances. This is not to say that we should just pretend things are fine when we're going through a purification period and are stuck in the illusion. By being able to release strong emotions through a creative outlet or some other healthy avenue with the intention to truly heal (as opposed to releasing emotions to bond with others, bond with ourselves, or feel justified), we can neutralize and transcend the negative emotion and use that energy to propel ourselves into a new awareness. If we allow ourselves to embrace our feelings fully and mourn something we may never have given ourselves permission to mourn, the result can be tremendously freeing. We can come to see that the beliefs we took on surrounding an incident in the past have no influence on our current situation, save the influence we continue to give it by holding it in our consciousness.

When your intention is to heal and see the Truth, as opposed to merely vent, emotional releases tend to have very different outcomes, including liberation and new understanding and insight as opposed to 'more of the same next week.' When your intention is to change and heal at the emotional level, you create a field of energy that will draw various resources to you., be they teachers, healers, books, or other opportunities that will enable you to release blocked energy and limiting beliefs (i.e. move to a higher level of vibration where those energies and that world doesn't exist.)

Who Do You Think You Are?

We would not consciously choose to be a victim, but by remaining unconscious of our inherent divine nature, that's what we do everyday. Every time we say that someone else made us feel a certain way, or—God forbid—act a certain way, we are handing our power and our lives over to others. We might as well be little puppets on a string as we let people and events in the material world, in conjunction with our limited beliefs, yank us around and cause us to respond unconsciously. Sometimes it just takes a little reframing to bring us back to our center, where we can cut the strings to limiting beliefs altogether and truly be present and at choice in the matter.

Let's begin with a simple (yet dramatic) example, if you happen to live in a heavily populated area.

You're driving along the freeway, enjoying the day and listening to some great music. Without warning, a car cuts you off.

First scenario: You slam on the brake, curse under your breath in surprise, then curse out loud at the driver. You think how drivers on these freeways are idiots, and think about all of the times in the last week alone someone has been thoughtless while driving. How do these people even get their driver's licenses, you wonder. Everyone in this city is so self-centered and egotistical that it makes you want to move out (or back out) to the country. Of course, there are other problems there, and you proceed to think about all of those. You tell others about the jerk that almost killed you on the freeway. You find lots of sympathy, and soon many people are agreeing and relating their self-centered, egotistical, incompetent bad-driver horror stories.

You feel justified and have a sense of belonging. You feel better for the moment.

Second scenario: You slam on the brake, curse under your breath in surprise, thank your angels, realize that the other driver must be either really upset, have other things on his/her mind, or really need a vacation. Whatever the reason, you see the driver could use a little prayer. The need for forgiveness never even enters the picture, since you didn't take the action personally. You send them your love and you go on your way and probably never even think about the incident again.

It might not be possible to stay this conscious every moment of every day—but then again, why not? If you are aware that you are a Divine and sacred Soul, pure consciousness manifesting on the physical plane, the incident wouldn't even bother you because you wouldn't take it personally. In truth, we are all God in expression. That is just a simple fact of who We are. I know that's who You are. The real question is who do *you* think you are? Who do you think yourself to be?

I was listening to a radio talk show one day when my daughter was a few years old. The host told a story about a master who was able to remain calm, like the eye of the hurricane, in spite of absolute chaos around him. Something clicked in that moment and I actually saw that this state of mind was something I was capable of obtaining.

If he was on the planet, he must have been human, I reasoned. Why couldn't I do what he did? Why couldn't *I* have that peace of mind?

It could have been due to lack of sleep and a long day with an exuberant toddler, but I couldn't think of a reason. It was a big shift. Before that time, I had always seen greatness as something outside of myself. The great authors, speakers, scientists, artists, etc., were in the special-lucky-genius category. It was really the first time that I made the connection that I was capable of being a master. That it was actually in the realm of possibility and that someone wasn't necessarily born into these things. That these were things one actually worked toward and became. That all the masters of the world were born just like we were, and they all came into the world the same way we did.

It seems the greatest disservice to all of mankind to create a story that someone came from anything other than the womb. It makes it impossible for us to live at that level simply—*and only*—because we believe it to be impossible.

Myths, metaphors, the archetypal realm of gods all provide inspiration and energies we can tap into to benefit our experience on earth. If we take mythical and metaphorical stories literally, place miracles and revelations in other time periods, and put ourselves in the "lowly human" category, we have done a service to no one. Rather than follow the teachings and examples of the spiritual masters who came before us, we are taught instead to put them in a separate category and worship them, which doesn't do much for our spiritual development, but does a lot for our ego and its paradigm of separation.

After returning from a meditation retreat, an insight came that the spiritual masters of the world were just ordinary guys and gals with extremely disciplined minds and a ton of beliefs that supported them. Period.

That might be a big stretch for some, but you might remember one of those masters saying something like, "All these things and more shall you do."

Ah, but why should we listen to him? What did he know?

I think he mentioned something about us being gods too. Hmmm...I wonder how that one slipped through the editing process.

There's one belief beyond all others that does more disservice to the human race than any other: that we are born in sin.

Believing ourselves to be born in sin gives us an excuse to, in fact, be a sinner, whatever that might mean to us. There's actually no other way we could be, if we truly believe that's what we are at core. Incredibly, there's not even anything we had to do to earn this coveted title besides come into the world.

The notion that there is a god outside of us that we need to be in good favor with in order to get the things we believe we need to be happy, all while believing we are sinners (which would undoubtedly not put us in good favor with that god), puts us in a Catch-22 more debilitating and ridiculous than anything ever created since the beginning of time. We put the great teachers and prophets of the world on pedestals and label them as special, but in reality, we are all prophets because we are all self-fulfilling prophecies. What we say about ourselves shapes our actions and behaviors, and, with the understanding that everything is connected, our world as well.

To "sin" was originally used to imply that we were moving away from our divine nature, not as a statement of who we are at the core of our being. Our thoughts and actions may be out of alignment with our true nature, but at core, in a dimension we may not be currently aware of, We are still Love.

We're not just the things we tell ourselves we are in our inner conversations. We are infinite, and we hold the qualities of the Spirit in infinite measure within us; they only need to be realized. We find we can then be more than we've ever allowed ourselves to believe and to be.

Right now, you can picture a situation in your life that you would like to be different. If this situation changed, you would be better off. Others would be better off. Become aware of something you see as limiting about yourself. Something that keeps you from experiencing what you know in your heart of hearts you were born to experience. Or think of something that seems to stop you from taking the next step you know you are being guided to take. Once you have a picture, ask the question:

In order for this limiting situation to be true, what belief would have to exist?

"For that situation to exist, I would have to believe _____ _____."

Aha, there it is. A seemingly innocent little belief. Think of this as mental dissection. It was painless, wasn't it? Except for the fact that you had to experience the limiting condition for a moment while you thought of it. So, there it is, a little critter running amok in your head, creating havoc in your life and in your sense of wellbeing.

Doing this little exercise once will do nothing. Doing it several times a day, or as soon as a limiting thought pops in your head, will.

For those of you saying, "Oh, I know that already," the question is, how diligently are you practicing it? What area of your life are you currently growing in, and what would you need to believe to go to the next level with it?

Think again of your current situation. What would the ideal outcome be in this situation? What would the absolute ideal be? What would you need to believe in order for this ideal situation or circumstance to exist?

"For this circumstance or situation to exist, I would need to believe_____."

"Well, duh," you might say. "But I don't believe that."

I know.

"Well."

Well.

"Well, it's not true."

Only because you don't believe it's true.

"But it's not."

Until you are willing to own and accept the power of your words and thoughts and move beyond the idea that you are a victim of life, such conversations in this area can become copious versions of that old baseball classic, "Who's on first?" We can argue till the end of time about the order of materialization (which came first, the chicken or the egg?), but when you get past all of the arguing, all of the clever reasoning, all of the logical deductions, what is left? If you aren't living a life of love, joy, and enthusiasm, adventure, prosperity, and health, you may have cleverly won the argument, but at the cost of an outstanding life.

Taking the Witness Stand

Imagine that on some level we are all participating in a metaphysical court of law. As "victims" in this world, we have all been taught to argue for our own limitations, for our own innocence and another's guilt. Oh, and we have circumstantial evidence. Boy, do we have it! We can have very impressive cases with loads of evidence, but we are forgetting one factor. On some level, either from an unconscious Soul level or from our beliefs, we have created the very circumstances we are blaming others for; and we recreate it every time we think or speak of it.

We might even have been taught to believe that god is a judge who hands out punishments and rewards. I hate to break it to you, but there is no one else in the courtroom. You are the judge. You are the jury. You are the witness, the victim, the audience. You are even the one taking down what everyone says on that funny little machine.

In fact, the court reporter is a very powerful position, and it serves us to cultivate this position in our awareness. Removing ourselves emotionally from all the different internal aspects and influences, while looking at things objectively, is imperative to recognizing limiting patterns and beliefs so that we can transcend them.

I was once in a psychology class where we were asked to describe a person after he had briefly entered the room and left. Everyone remembered something different about the person's appearance, and when he was brought back into the room it was found not one person had offered a perfect description. Some weren't even remotely close. There's a good chance we have a very biased perception in what we would regard as a painful past experience. Even when we think we are right, when no one, nothing, can have us believe any different, being right is absolutely worthless to us if we are not using the information for our growth and development. We can argue the best cases, but we have to ask ourselves when we are argue, who are we serving? Are we serving the victim in us? The part that believes itself to be weak and wrongfully injured? The part that believes in the illusion of separation? Or are we serving the qualities of the Spirit within?

We must learn to make empowering interpretations of our circumstances. Somewhere along the line, we need to be given the correct interpretation of the law, the Universal Law, so that we can use it to our benefit.

An impersonal law that states: *As you believe, so shall you see. What you focus on, you get more of. Thought is creative.*

It does not state: believe only things you can see; then live in reaction to what you see.

We can live the life of our choice. We *are*, in fact, living the life of our choice. But, as you may have noticed, we can only consciously choose if we are aware that we *have* a choice. When we understand that thought is creative and we make choices that lead us to be more conscious of them, we can become a victor of circumstances, as opposed to being a victim of them.

It is our choice. We can bring our Higher Selves to the witness stand and see everything from a different light, and in that new interpretation, everything can change.

Take the story of your life (*Reader's Digest* version, for our purposes). First, put the victim on the witness stand and write down what comes forth. Next put your Soul, your Higher Self, on the stand

and see if you can come up with any other interpretations than the victim in you just did. Same life, two interpretations.

Victim: "As a child, I felt alone and unwanted. I didn't get the love I wanted and didn't have the support I needed to express myself. I had a lot of talents I never developed and felt mostly misunderstood and ignored. I was very troubled as a teenager, even to the point of being suicidal. I got in with the wrong crowd and took drugs. I almost died because of some bad drugs. I got married to someone who was mentally, emotionally, and physically abusive. He manipulated me and used me and I wasted years of my life going nowhere."

Higher Self: "Growing up in what I experienced as an unstable and unhappy household, I felt very alone, which led me to a deeply introspective and richly imaginative life. The lack of connection I felt growing up led me to search for deeper meaning. I became fascinated with why people do the things they do, which has led to an understanding of myself and others that I would never have had without these circumstances to motivate me. I was a troubled teenager and took drugs, leading to a near-death experience that helped relinquish my fear of death and expanded my conscious awareness of the nature of Reality. I was in an abusive relationship for eleven years where I often felt like a prisoner. I believe I now experience a level of freedom that many people without that experience cannot imagine. This experience has taught me that true freedom has nothing to do with circumstances, but is a state of mind. This realization, in turn, led me to understand that true happiness doesn't come from the right circumstances, but is only a state of mind. It has all been a wonderful adventure, and I look forward to discovering more aspects of myself while mining the gold that has been buried for so long. I have the advantage of being a late-bloomer, beginning anew with years of life experience and wisdom under my belt."

It's amazing the difference we feel when we see our lives from the victim's perspective as opposed to the Soul's perspective. We can take a current problem (i.e., opportunity) in our lives and let the victim have its say, then the Higher Self, and discover that we really do have access to the answers for all of our apparent problems. It does take practice, dedication, and discipline to develop a greater awareness so that we are able to hear the voice of our Soul. We also need to continue to expose ourselves to spiritual, philosophical, and psychological teachings and alternate explanations of reality to keep our minds fresh and develop our ability to access that wisdom.

Praying without Ceasing

A chapter on beliefs wouldn't be complete without mentioning the incredible power of prayer. Years ago, I would have wanted nothing to do with it. I didn't believe in it. I was a skeptic of the first order, and, as an atheist, if I did have a prayer it would have been to keep those nutballs who thought they had found God far away from me. But alas, things change.

We might have been taught that prayer is something we engage in when things aren't going so well, when something is off or we are in crisis and want things to be different. "Okay, God. This is it, show me what you got," we might say. Or on the other end of the separation spectrum, "Let's see if I'm worthy and deserving enough for you to give me what I'm asking for. Please just this once. I'll never ask again. I promise. Puh-lease! I'll do anything." Sometimes we get the results we want. Sometimes we don't. We forget that we are not five years old and that "God" is not a man in the sky with a little red suit and a bowl full of jelly.

The problem, for one, is that we're praying to something we understand to be outside of ourselves. It's a big misunderstanding, given that we are co-creators with the Universe. Unconsciously creating circumstances and then praying for them to be different is not the most intelligent way to do life. Another problem with the way we have been conditioned to see prayer is that it is something that we sit down and do once a day, once a week, or in extreme crisis, as if our thoughts are only creative in that moment. As if we are not creating *every* moment of experience.

We've got to understand that we are continuously creating our experience through the thoughts and energy we choose to focus and act on. Praying—real prayer, which is "believing ye already have"—is simply doing this in an intentional, conscious manner. While we start by "sending" our thoughts, after a time, we realize what we are really doing is consciously communing with *What Is*, and through that communion, *seeing* what Is.

We see it *first* in our mind, then in the physical world.

First in our *mind*, then in the physical world.

First in our mind, *then* in the physical world.

Prayer is brilliant, wonderful, powerful. It *is* the answer. But prayer is not a once-a-day endeavor. It needs to be a passionate, all-consuming intentional focus until it creates a pattern so deep in our consciousness, we no longer even have to think about it. We have to remember that in essence prayer is not something that only happens in front of an altar, inside a temple or church, or when we decide to.

The thought we believe. The thought we engage. Put our energy into. Hold on to. Embrace. Agree with.

That is our prayer.

That thought you just had about your mother-in-law? That was your prayer for her. That thought about your lack of financial resources? That was your prayer for your financial resources.

Thought is creative. What you thought about that person whose cell phone just went off during meditation? That was your prayer for them.

And have no illusions. You are never really praying for someone else. You're the only one in the courtroom, remember?

Thought doesn't suddenly become creative the moment we begin to pray. That is ridiculous. It's been said that worrying is like praying for something you don't want to happen. If we're at a point in our lives where we are worrying about things, it's a good thing that every "prayer" we have doesn't come to pass, since every worry would come to pass as well, given the law. The irony is that the more we begin to realize the fullness and glory of our true nature, of our Self, the less we worry. The less we worry, the less we have to worry about.

We have to stop worrying before we *think* we can. Before we think we have that luxury. We have to train our minds to think, "I have nothing to worry about." We can hold that thought in our minds, in our hearts, and bring it into our meditations, conversations, and into the very circumstances that would challenge that statement.

The truth is, the less we worry, the more our attention is engaged in Reality. The more our attention is engaged in Reality, the more aware we are of the Good that surrounds us every moment. The more aware we are of the Good that surrounds us in every moment, the more that Good miraculously shows up in our experience. The less attached we are to results, the more results we get since attachment is just another form of fear. Attachment says, *I need this*. Life says, *I need nothing; everything is here already*.

It seems we get to a point where we could care less whether the circumstances are in our favor, but care deeply about where we are in consciousness regarding the circumstances, choosing only to believe the Good, see the Good, be the Good. Not good based on current cultural beliefs. Not necessarily good according to manmade laws or the good of agreed-upon rules, but *the* Good.

In the awareness of that Good, of Love, we begin to positively effect our circumstances more than when we saw ourselves outside of them. Even more than when we were trying to personally manipulate them by praying for something to change. Our attachment begins to fall away and we begin to personally care less, but spiritually become more. We become more of our True Nature, which is Love. Love without agenda or preference. We are able to love in places we previously couldn't even imagine loving.

And, it is in *that* becoming that we change the course of our realities and, on some level, the course of the evolution of the whole.

Inside our hearts
lies the essence of beauty itself
pure creation
pure intelligence
pure peace
joy's true home
bliss' resting place

and in our waking moments
the violence against our hearts
accumulates

with every unkind gesture we offer
every unripe word we speak
every unexamined thought we think
even the thought

even the thought

towards others
towards ourselves
towards our lives

creating a prison
with walls so thick we might believe them to be impenetrable
so subtle we may deny their existence
or so familiar we may believe them necessary

And still our hearts sit and wait
for the violence against them to stop
for the day when they are trusted, honored, chosen

the day when the key to freedom is found

And while we wait patiently
(or desperately)
for the key to open our prison doors
we forget
We hold it with our every thought and action

and every unexamined
thought
word and deed
becomes just another brick
separating us even further
from our longed-for freedom.

Projection
Polishing the Mirror

Mirror, mirror on the wall
You mean it's my issue after all?
I race and race
to change the scene
While my inner state
is reflecting.
Is that really me that I see
in the face of my enemy?
Reflecting the parts
of myself
that I've denied,
put on a shelf—

Only when
I can really see me
and forgive myself
will I truly be free

When we begin to accept total responsibility for our lives we come to realize that not only are we creating what we experience of it, but on the other side of the spiritual coin, our experience is a reflection of our own consciousness. It is the greatest freedom to use the information being reflected back to us to clear our field of unconscious limiting behaviors, beliefs, and judgments. This way of understanding and interacting in the world shatters the illusion of separation and the stance of victimhood altogether, since we see that no one is doing anything to us; we are simply watching our inner state of consciousness being projected onto the big screen of life.

To the degree this work has to be incredibly liberating—a beeline to Freedom, if you will—it also has the potential to make us feel incredibly degraded and humiliated. It is actually only degrading to the false, manufactured self, the part that feels it needs to defend itself and make a case for its innocence. The part that actually believes it is less than perfection. The part that in Reality doesn't even exist.

If we can identify less with the part that takes offense and step back to observe what comes into our experience with a detached curiosity, working with projections can become some of the most transformational work we will ever do. And it can actually become quite hilarious after a time. Well, sometimes after a very long time.

We can choose to shrug off this whole idea as radical self-absorption, but in that shrug we also shrug off the much-needed clues from the Universe, from our Self, from Life for our healing and ultimate freedom.

It is quite easy for us to see someone else's wrongdoing. It is ridiculously impossible to see the same behavior (or the judgments we carry) in ourselves. This is because the part that is upset about the situation in the outside world is, in fact, the very part that is "guilty" in some fashion of the same behavior.

Before you shut the book altogether, I need to say that when we are dealing with projections, much of the time we are dealing with metaphor. Working with projections can become an art in itself. Keep in mind that this is not an exercise in debating moral and ethical issues. We will always find someone who agrees with us when we have been wronged by another, but finding someone to agree with us does nothing to alleviate the cause of our upset state. This is because the reason we are upset has nothing to do with a person or situation outside of us. In truth, there is no one, or no thing, that has the power to take us out of our peace. We can argue that point as well, but when we begin to see the limiting transformative value of arguing points, and when we would sincerely like to try a new approach in dealing with negative emotions, we may find taking full responsibility for our emotional upset to be a great opportunity. If a person or event triggers you emotionally and takes you out of your peace, you can be absolutely, positively, one-hundred-percent sure that there is some form of projection going on.

A subject like this can be a breeding ground for misunderstanding, and in no way do I condone behavior which is out of alignment with someone's True Nature or Goodness, but if you understand the physical world to be illusion and the spiritual realm to be real, you have quite a different perspective of things. If you have the understanding that Life is Good; that there are no mistakes; that We are, in essence, Spirit, which can never be hurt or injured; and that on a Soul level nothing happens without our permission, then we are much freer to explore alternate explanations of cause than if we live purely from a material awareness.

People who truly understand the illusion of death do not take it as a license to kill, but become quite incapable of violence since they have glimpsed the true nature of Reality and its unifying truth of Love.

We are all here in support of each other's growth and awareness, even when it doesn't look that way from our limited, physical-world perspective. We are all here to experience the true nature of Life and our Selves, which is Unconditional Love. We are here to embody a peace beyond what we might acquire from temporarily favorable conditions in our lives. Working with projections is a way to weed out anything in our inner realms that keeps us from knowing our Selves as Unconditional Love.

Reflecting on Projection

If someone made a disapproving comment about the blue dress you are wearing, when you are actually wearing jeans and a t-shirt, you might make certain assumptions about that person's state of mind, but the statement wouldn't offend you. It couldn't offend you, because you knew you weren't wearing a blue dress and that it had no factual basis in reality.

At the same time, if someone told you that you were stupid, and if that comment took you out of your peace, you would have two choices. You could have an emotional reaction and blame the other person for "making" you upset, judge them as rude, insensitive, and quite possibly stupid themselves; or you could stay conscious, choose not to react, and go to a new level of freedom. In this sense, true freedom is not given, but earned.

If we choose the first option, we remain victims of circumstance and are doomed to live at the whim and impulse of a universe we consider random and unstable. We cannot say that we don't live from victim consciousness, yet continue to respond to others with knee-jerk reactions and finger-pointing behavior. It is not only a hypocritical stance, but involves a lack of awareness that is not sufficient to our evolution at this time. We must understand it is not what someone else did or said to us that upset us, but the judgment we held about ourselves that it triggered. The enemy is indeed, within.

No statement or situation has the ability to upset us unless something inside us agrees with it, corresponds to it, and carries a similar vibration. Our mission, if we choose to accept it, is to locate those patterns of energy within ourselves, the beliefs and judgments, that the person or event rubbed up against and set off in our own psyche. This same dynamic is in effect when you take a drug. It's not just the drug going into your system and having an effect on you. It's the properties of the drug stimulating, or inhibiting, what is already within you.

Polishing

The key to growth is actually doing the work. What a concept. We can have an enormous amount of information and tools, but unless we use them, they are worthless. We can all relate to a time in our lives when we had known about a tool or a certain action that we wanted to take, and when we finally did it, a whole new dimension of life opened to us. Theoretically understanding something is a good thing; taking action on it is a whole new ballgame. The first can be illuminating, the other absolutely life-changing.

A few years ago I stumbled upon an exercise that has given me incredible insight into areas of my psyche that needed healing and clearing. As we start clearing the sludge of negativity from our consciousness, we begin to realize, at greater levels, the Spirit, the Power, the Love, that dwells within. More energy becomes available to us every time we let go of what is not Real about Us, about the Other, or about Life. We find ourselves in creative, inspired, peaceful, and loving states more frequently. Our vibration continues to increase. Unhealed energy, negative patterns, and limiting beliefs will not be able to exist in this atmosphere, in this "higher vibe," and will need to surface in consciousness in order to be released. That lesser vibration within us, that pattern of negative energy, will continue to attract a person or event that will stimulate that particular form of unhealed energy until it is healed and released. This is why we find ourselves repeatedly attracting the same type of people or situations into our lives. This is why we feel the same anxiety, anger, alienation, etc., over and over and over again.

These feelings are not "normal." Negative feelings are normal to the ego and normal to the human experience. They are not normal to the Self, the Soul. In fact, they don't even exist in that dimension. When we find negative emotions surfacing as the result of another person's behavior, we are on the brink of an incredible opportunity if we remain conscious and avoid merely going into a reactionary response. The offending person or event really did nothing to you except provide you with an opportunity to see your next immediate area of growth and where there is work to be done.

Most likely, this was not the way we were taught to see the world around us as we were growing up. We have been conditioned to see life as a struggle and ourselves as having very little power in that struggle, save the power we receive by using our personal force or might to change circumstances in the physical world. For those daring enough to experiment, this is a path to freedom from that struggle and from the need to ever force anything again.

The following exercise can be extremely helpful in realizing and releasing those patterns of stuck energy within us that keep us in unconscious and reactive behavior patterns. I have found it to be like having a side-view mirror, reflecting our current blind spots as we cruise down the highway of life. As with many life-changing exercises and practices, at first I thought it was complete hogwash.

A few years ago, I had a friend I really wanted to help. Although he hadn't asked for any advice, I could see that his Soul was crying out.

(Mayday, mayday. This is your captain speaking. You have just encountered one of the first signs of projection.)

He was so smart, so darned intelligent—if he would only put it to better use, he could influence the world in such a positive way. And he was so angry! There was so much anger in him, he really needed someone to help him find his way and to heal that.

I pondered his greatness, reflected on his predicament, and found a book that would help him. (He had never actually asked for any help, mind you, but I was determined to help the poor soul nonetheless.) The book was *Dreams Do Come True* by Pamela Oslie, and it contained very basic, well-explained ideas of beliefs and how they are causative in nature. It included some fun exercises, and I began to do some of them before I gave the book to my friend. I came across an exercise in which you were asked to write down something about someone who is upsetting you. *Well, that was easy*, I thought. Then in the next part of the exercise, you write what your advice would be to them, advice that, if truly heard, would change their life.

My advice went something like "Oh sweetie, you are such a beautiful, wise soul. If only you would believe in yourself more! You have so much talent, but you're letting your fear hold you back. The world is a safe place, if only you would believe it. You need to let people love you; let them in and let go of the anger. There's so much anger in you, sweetie; you need to heal that. It's holding you back from experiencing the life of your dreams."

There were a few more parts to the exercise, and when I got to the end there were directions to go back over the material, reading it with a different perspective. I read the advice over as if my Higher Self were speaking directly to me, as the instructions directed. If you take this advice, your life will change, the book said.

Obviously, that was a waste of time, I thought. I guess it only works sometimes or in some situations. Hmmm…well, at least the book will help my friend.

I shrugged off the exercise, but it haunted me a little. How could it be so off, I wondered? I was one of the least angry people you'd ever meet, while my friend was beating people up when they really pissed him off. And that stuff about talent? What talent? How silly that exercise was! And I surely didn't have fear. I had an awakening experience that changed my life, darn it! I didn't live in fear anymore.

I forgot about the exercise and gave the book to my friend. I don't think he ever actually read it, and when we went our separate ways, he gave it back to me. I was shocked to pick it up about six months later and remember what I had initially written for that exercise. In that span of time, I had started going to small group meetings based on the book *Women Who Run with the Wolves* by Clarissa Pinkola Estes, Ph.D., and had begun to journal every morning while working through another book, *The Artist's Way* by Julia Cameron. An incredible amount of anger had surfaced in that time, as well as a greater appreciation and realization of budding talents.

I was absolutely blown away by the fact that the advice to myself couldn't have been more right-on than if I had directly channeled my Higher Self. Then I realized that was exactly what had happened.

Oh my God, I thought, the world really is just a reflection.

After I had acknowledged and dealt with my own anger, I noticed that angry people didn't upset me anymore like they had in the past. As I started healing my own emotional upsets and developing my talents, I wasn't as compelled to cheer others on while ignoring my next steps in the process. Also, as I began to really dig in deep and do my own healing work, I stopped seeing others as unhealed and stopped needing to compulsively "help" the people around me.

These aren't random events. From the perspective of your Soul, the part of you that is Pure Spirit, they are only neutral events coming to you in service to your healing, growth, and awakening. If I didn't continue to do the work (take responsibility for being upset) I would have probably formed beliefs about certain groups of people being angry, and the cycle of cause and effect would have continued in a very unhealthy, self-defeating manner. As it was, even though I thought the exercise was silly (wildly ridiculous even), on some level I was still open to it and continued to hold the intention to grow.

After this revelation, I started working with every single situation that caused an upset within me. I became almost obsessed with the whole deal, but after awhile I noticed a few things. I noticed that every time, every single, solitary time, there was resistance to the "advice." Every time, there was a part that could not see the correlation. Could not see how the advice related to myself. The other thing I noticed was that when I was able to step back and get my ego out of the way, when I would go with a "What if it were true?" attitude, a door would open—sometimes just a crack—and I would be able to see a place in myself where the advice just might be useful. Just might have some value.

Oh, there was a third thing I noticed. I was beginning to feel so peaceful and content, so aware of who I was and what Life was, so full of joy again that nothing in the physical world had the power to take me out of that state.

I must say I was not so gung-ho about projections when I first started to experiment with the theory. As I have said, it has been positively life-altering, but in the beginning I thought it was ridiculous. Maybe it worked once in a while—about one in ten, maybe. But then I wondered how it could be true only some of the time. If it was one of those universal law thingies, it wouldn't only be true some of the time. If it was a law in effect, it had to be operating indiscriminately.

I found that I was the one discriminating—literally and figuratively.

One of the interesting aspects of working with projections is the level of degree. Like the paradoxical nature of life on planet earth (i.e. the illusion that looks and feels so real and the Truth that is invisible to the physical senses), it is at once brilliantly simple, and from another perspective, exceedingly complex.

In an abstract sense, there is no big or small. There just Is. Anger is anger and there is no level of degree. There is no big anger or small anger. There is no distinction between a murderous rage and a mild feeling of irritation. From that state, there is only the emotional response of anger—period.

On the other hand, in our perception of and experience with the world around us, we definitely account for different levels of one concept or form. For example, in the abstract world, money is only an idea of money. In that thought, there is no specific amount, only an idea of what we have come to know as money, which is really only another form of energy, which in Reality isn't needed and doesn't exist. Yet in the material world, we definitely have awareness of varying levels or degrees—or in the case of money, amounts. One dollar is not the same as one billion dollars in our material world frame of reference.

It is very helpful to keep this in mind as we work with projections. If we see someone in a rage being verbally abusive, and if that rage upsets us, it does not mean we are acting in that manner toward others. It does not have to mean that we are a volcano ready to go off any minute. If we have an emotional upset and/or feelings of condemnation and judgment toward this person, it does mean the episode has triggered something within us which we can choose to look at, get information from, and heal.

One key to remember is that you are still the only one in the courtroom, to use the earlier analogy. On some level, there really is no other relationship you have other than the one with your Self, or, with God. On that level, the whole thing really has nothing to do with the other person. It only has to do with your reaction and the specific advice you would give to the other person.

Another part of the equation is that something has triggered a negative emotional reaction within you. It really gets your goat, so to speak. Something you simply find a flaw with or wish were different is not necessarily a projection. The exercise only works with something you have energy with. (Although you will find the energy becoming more and more subtle as you continue to heal.)

You are appalled, offended, and annoyed that the other person could be so _____ (fill in the blank). It is judgment of the highest order. The greater the offense, the more intensely you feel the emotion, the more significant the opportunity for healing and accessing a storehouse of blocked energy.

Someone in a class I once attended made a great distinction between discernment and judgment. Discernment is an observation made in the moment, while judgment is something you carry with you after the event has passed.

This exercise works best if you are aware of your feelings and can be (sometimes painfully) honest with yourself. From the beginning, we are usually taught to hush up. To be quiet. Stop crying. Be nice. We learn to repress our feelings to the point where we are no longer even aware of them. If that is the case, for the healing process to work, you might need to let go of some of your favorite distractions or addictions in order to allow the energy to surface in order to transcend it.

In introducing this work to others, I have encountered people who have argued that anger can be healthy, that sometimes we need to be angry. I would ask the question, which part is it that needs to be angry?

There are different levels here, and on one there may be a repression of anything that seems bad in order to be spiritual or good. Denying our feelings and pretending everything is fine when we don't feel fine is not the answer. But we also have to realize that only the ego would need to be angry, prove something, hate something, or condemn something. Only the ego needs to be right. Many times, people are addicted to their emotional outbursts to the point where those outbursts become a way of life. We can be pissed off about something and the more intelligent we are, the more able we will be to justify those reactions. But we might want to further explore the concept of healthy anger. While it isn't healthy to stuff feelings inside, it's just as unhealthy to be caught in a cycle of negative energy that plays itself out continually. Anger is actually a surface-level feeling. Underneath anger we always find hurt and sadness. This work is not about trying to be perfect; it's about realizing the inherent perfection within—which is completely different. Completely.

To see the way this exercise actually works, let's use a specific example. Even though this example might not apply to you personally, you can follow it to get a feel for the complexity and simplicity of projection at work.

Suppose there is a homeless woman who is wheeling her bags of stuff in a shopping cart across the street while you sit in your car and wait for the light to change. She looks as if she hasn't taken a shower in weeks and is having a very hard time with the cart.

There are unlimited combinations of thoughts and emotions that might run through someone's mind while this scene unfolds in front of them. That, in itself, proves that what happens in one's individual psyche has absolutely nothing to do with the event. You might think it is the event itself that is responsible for your reaction, but if that were true, everyone would have exactly the same response.

A few thoughts in response to this scene may be: "My God, we live in a modern society and we can't even take care of the people who need it most." Or, "How could anyone let themselves go to that point? That's disgusting." Or, "There goes another one of those panhandlers who just want to get a free ride while I have to work for a living." Or, "Why doesn't someone help her? She obviously just needs help in getting back on her feet—that's just horrible!"

Notice that while you may agree with any one of these statements as being the correct answer, we are not dealing in the realm of right or wrong. For the time being, we are not dealing with "this world." In each situation, the person's conditioned mind is making assumptions about the will or plight of the woman described and is basing their reaction only on what it can see from a very limited, material-world perspective.

In reality these strangers know nothing of the homeless woman's real situation. They can't see the whole picture, only what the conditioned mind has dictated to them based on their beliefs and experience. They don't have access to information regarding that woman's Soul intention, and what this Soul is accomplishing by experiencing life in this fashion. They cannot see the dimension of her that is not even being touched by this experience. They are caught in the illusion. From this perspective, the current situation in itself is neutral.

Until, that is, we have a reaction to it. The more emotional energy those earlier statements contained, the more opportunity there is for healing.

For us to be open to the healing available, we first have to get it out of our heads that negative reactions are bad, and that we are wrong for being upset. If we are in judgment about the emotional reactions that surface within us, we can go into denial and pretend that everything is hunky-dory, while at the same time building an inferno of repressed emotions and a resistance to the healing that is possible for us and those around us.

We have been taught to place so much judgment on emotions—which ones are good, which ones are bad or undesirable. In reality, they are nothing more than signals that there is something to work with here, something to look at, to explore, and to embrace. We may have become afraid of our emotions, since, when we repress them, they reach a threshold which can cause us to blow up inappropriately. Choosing to own our personal upset and work with energy that surfaces, diffuses such unconscious emotional outbursts.

We might have come to over-identify with our emotions and believe they are the most accurate source of information about the world around us. It is true our emotions give us information, but the information is about false perceptions within our consciousness, rather than about others "out there," when we are holding them in judgment. We may get a "bad vibe" about someone or something, but again, these internal warnings are neutral information coming from a strong belief that we are protected, not from unhealed energy, and the information is not emotionally charged or accompanied by a judgment. Even when we get "bad vibes" we are still operating in the limited realm of duality, in a sense of separation. In an expanded state, there is only Love. There is nothing to fear, nothing to drain us, nothing to be protected from.

In our first example, the person sitting at the light made the statement that we live in a modern society and was upset that we couldn't even get it together to help our own. If this person decided to take on the challenge of being responsible for his personal reaction and realized it as such, he could choose to try something different.

If he so chose to experiment with the exercise, he could get himself into a state of compassion for the government, for example, and his advice might go something like, "You people really need to shape up here. There are people in need and you keep putting your money into things like wars. Why don't you take care of your own people! Why do you have to take on everyone else's problems and make them your own? When did you forget that you are here to take care of your own? Remember 'of the people, by the people, for the people'? If you concentrated more on taking care of your own people, which is your foundation, you would be a country of strength!"

As you might be able to see, such a rant has nothing to do with the woman or the government, but only that person's consciousness. This person has choices. He can let that negative part stay in control so he can feel self-righteous, and continue to see his target as wrong and his own view as right. He can find people to agree with his opinion. Or, he can make a radical decision to see that there is something else going on and that his emotional upset is a reflection of something happening inside of *himself*. If he read over his own words from the position of his Higher Self giving him sound advice, he would gain valuable insight into an area of his life that could be transformed—*if* he chose to take the advice.

This person might own his own company and suddenly realize that he has been putting a large amount of money into areas which don't empower or enhance his employees' quality of life and by changing this his entire business could go to a whole new level. He might work for someone else and realize he has been spending an inordinate amount of time at the office while neglecting his family and kids and his Soul is telling him he needs to spend more time with them. He might live alone and find that the whole message from his Higher Self, his Soul, pertains to his relationship to his Self. Maybe he is focusing a lot of energy on helping others but is neglecting his own growth and could even be using threats of violence in his internal dialogue. He could even be using threats of violence or bullying behavior with others and not even recognize it as such.

As you can see, there are no cut and dry interpretations. When you are doing this exercise for yourself, you first have to be able to put yourself into a state where you "forget" that the advice you're giving the other person will be coming to you next, and then totally focus on the task at hand without editing anything. As you read back what you wrote, which you now understand to be coming directly from your Higher Self, it will be helpful to read the advice metaphorically at times rather than literally. There are countless ways to interpret this advice, but there are usually certain words or phrases that stand out which make it important to really get into the exercise and not to analyze anything as you're writing.

The person in the car didn't know he was doing an exercise. You will. When you are upset with another you have to forget what you think you should say, and just let it come from your Soul to their Soul.

This exercise doesn't excuse us from being human and living in the physical realm. It doesn't mean we become indifferent to the plight of others by using this kind of exercise to rationalize situations away and failing to be a space of love, kindness, generosity and service for others. It's not that we become uncaring or unfeeling; what we become is far seeing, a light, a positive force, and truly helpful rather than emotionally triggered and drained. It is incredibly easy to be swept up in the illusion when a strong emotion is accompanying the message. We can feel very good about being "right." But there is so much more available to us than simply being right and feeling justified. When we're right, we have to be left too. We have to be in a state of separation. In an illusionary world existing outside of Love.

Using the former example of the "bag lady" crossing the street, we can choose to "help" by seeing the woman for who she really is, by knowing with an energy of peace and gratitude that, on a Soul level, all is well for this woman's life. If we are so moved, we can take physical action and help out by buying her a meal or finding some other way to be of assistance. We may simply want to offer a warm and generous smile. Because we are no longer motivated by emotional upset doesn't mean we won't feel called to be of service in the physical world—far from it—but to truly be of service to the homeless woman we have to see through the illusion and see who she really is. We have to see her as a dimension of Love and allow our action to originate from that space. That is probably the greatest service we could offer anyone we are helping, to see him or her as the light that they are. It is most definitely the greatest thing we can do for ourselves.

It is a wonderful thing to feed the homeless in the physical world, it is only that while we "feed" others, we want to make sure that we aren't feeding the illusion as well.

If we try to help others while silently cursing those who don't help, or if we are so disturbed by the illusion in front of us we are simply trying to fix something that doesn't even really exist in a higher dimension or vibration, our efforts will ultimately be in vain. We're not here to fix something that appears to us to be broken; we're here to transcend our limiting perception and see the world as Love sees it. As Itself.

Recently there was a woman who had taken my seat at a conference. I went to another area where I was told there was a seat saved for me, and at the last minute, that one had been taken as well. This usually wouldn't be something that would get to me, but I began to feel a little peeved. I instantly brushed it off and held that little peeved feeling at bay, pretending it wasn't there. As luck would have it—or grace, you might say—a meditation followed, and since it was so present, I decided to work with it. In my mind, I did the exercise. What would I say to those people?

"Dang it, you guys keep taking my space!" was all I could come up with. During the conference, I was becoming very aware of an identity of shyness, which I realized had nothing to do with the greater dimension of my being, with who I really was, with what I really was. That was it. Those dang false identities kept on taking up the space that was there for the Higher Self, for Love, for the Masters, for Life to express through. This may sound silly to the rational mind, but it's not the rational mind that needs to be engaged in this process. It is more a process of intuition or gut feeling.

You'll also notice that the "advice" from your Higher Self gets very specific at times. Even if one hundred people were upset over the same thing, they would all choose different words to voice their protest much as the man in the car did.

We also tend to project emotions of extreme happiness or excitement onto certain people or events as well. We put people on pedestals and believe they are special while failing to see the same levels of brilliance in ourselves and everyone else. The same principle applies, though. You can only see in someone else that which you possess in yourself. If you find yourself enraptured by another's presence, know that you carry the same potential within you. Maybe not identical type of expression or gift . But maybe. Begin expressing the qualities you see so clearly in that person right now in your life, and while you will still appreciate and admire that person, you won't be looking to him or her to supply you with a feeling. In Truth, no one can make you happy. No one can even make you *feel* happy. There are those who can make our egos happy, but no one can make *Us* happy because We are perfect Peace and Joy.

How could you make Joy happy?

Most romantic relationships begin by way of projection: by seeing qualities that another person possesses as distinct from who we are and idealizing them for this reason. There's nothing wrong with appreciating—heck, even worshipping—another for the brilliance of being and the greatness of Spirit which moves through them, but we have to be realizing and releasing that energy within ourselves as well. Otherwise, we come to depend upon another for a feeling we naturally carry within us. Until the time we realize who and what we really are, we are just projecting onto others what we haven't yet come to see and experience in ourselves. Haven't discovered the unique way Love moves through us, connects us with the Divine, which puts us in extraordinary states of ecstasy and bliss that does not involve any other person, or thing, on the planet.

Being the Change We Wish to See

If we are using any part of our lives to hurt, condemn, disempower, or belittle others, we are not part of the solution; we are part of the problem. We might discern situations, people, and areas where there is room for growth. We might be called to speak out in service to waking people out of a slumber that is destroying their peace of mind, their true potential, and maybe even the planet; but in doing this we won't feel self-righteous or have a judgmental attitude if we are in the awareness of what *Is*. At bottom, we will harbor a deep compassion and love for those who have wandered so far away from their hearts. As long as we are living in a world where it is "us against them," we are perpetuating the very ideas we are seeking to eliminate. We could walk a million miles for peace, but as long as we continue to hold hateful judgments against people who perpetuate wars, peace is only a concept for us.

At best, it's a nice fluffy idea. At worst, it's an outlet for us to unleash our own unhealed anger and fear instead of working to release old patterns, and acknowledging that we are temporarily caught in the illusion.

"We need to be the change we wish to see in the world," the peacemaker Gandhi said. If we are not working diligently to be that change, to realize who we are and who everyone else is, our ideas of peace are impractical, hypocritical, and very airy-fairy.

The manifest world is merely a macrocosm of our own current inner reality. Period. How can we expect our world leaders to hold their bombs when we can't hold our tongues in our communications with or about others stemming from our own unhealed experiences? And our ego, which can only experience separation, will fight to the death to justify its positions of righteousness. But these positions are ultimately self-defeating. They cannot bring good, they cannot bring peace, they cannot bring joy, because they are of a different nature and can only create more of the same.

The day will come when we finally see the folly of fighting for our idea of peace and gain the awareness and spiritual power to actually *be* peaceful. When we can live in the vibration of peace, it will manifest in our lives. We will begin to see evidence of the world becoming more peaceful around us because we naturally attract similar vibrations. Relationships, situations, and living quarters will begin to reflect this newfound peace within us. We will even see it out in the world, where we formerly hadn't been able to. Newspaper articles, conversations, television programs. Peace Is. In Reality, it's Everywhere.

We will be able to live the change we wish to see in the world, and, in effect, give life to that world by living in it today.

It's not to say that we won't be able to see a world of unrest anymore; but when we see unrest with our physical eye, we will know there is an unseen Reality beyond it. One which can be coaxed into manifestation by keeping our attention on it. After we come to know ourselves as peace, it's not that we may never again go through times of upheaval and angst, but it will no longer be a constant state, only periods of purification, rebirth and healing.

Peace does not ask us to ignore the current manifestations of unrest on the planet, to pretend that they don't exist, or to serve a personal agenda at the expense of the whole. Sometimes Peace asks us to stand up for our Self for Life, for our fellow human beings on the other side of the planet, and for the planet itself. We can be an empowering presence for Peace without getting caught in the fight if we let our Soul speak rather than our personal resentments.

If we allow the Vision to speak for us, it comes from an energy of Peace, since Peace is the Vision. It is done from a place of absolute wholeness and awareness of what really Is. If we allow the unhealed projections to speak for us, the energy is polluted by hate, anger, pain, and judgment.

It is ironic that the same words may come out of our mouths. The only difference will be in relation to the level of consciousness on an energetic level.

I have to say that the part of me who used to be addicted to excitement and drama used to think that peace was boring, that love was boring (unless it was a five-star drama being played out). Used to think that joy was hokey.

But that was before I realized I was only experiencing my ideas of these qualities, not the qualities themselves. I had no comprehension of what true Joy really was. Or of Peace. I was caught in an addictive cycle to keep myself unaware of the deep emotional upset within, which made it impossible to release it, in order to realize what true states of wellbeing actually felt like.

The conditioned mind pooh-poohs things like Joy and Peace because it can't experience them—it is simply not capable of it. It can only experience its idea of things. A concept of things, but not the things themselves. The idea has to be transcended, or relinquished, in order to experience the actual quality.

It has been said that peace is not the absence of war.

It is not just being semi-comfortable or temporarily free of conflict, it is an absolutely amazing, brilliant and dynamic sense that everything is right with the world. It is a silence that screams in ecstasy.

In these purer states of consciousness, Life is absolutely enthralling, even when "nothing" is going on. You realize the beauty in everything, everywhere, and freedom takes on such a different meaning it needs to become an entirely new word for it to be properly comprehended. It is no longer about being free to do what you wish, when you wish, but about being free from the limiting beliefs you hold about reality, and about saying yes, yes, yes, Yes to Life!

Before I realized this other state of reality, life was a flat, one-dimensional, subjective drama of cause and effect. It was ridiculously easy for me to become lost in the drama, caught up in the game, cast out from "god's" good favor for making a mistake. After waking up in this other realm, though, and seeing that everything in the material world was relative, that I was "at cause" of my experience, and in Reality I was "at Cause" period, that there was no god "out there" to hand out goodies, the mirrors began to tell stories.

Stories I didn't want to hear at first.

But, when I have the courage and humility to look into those images and, well, reflect, to ultimately know that none of the lower vibrational manifestations are Real, to continue to align with what is Real, and at the same time discern where in consciousness I am living my daily life, I'm then able to release the lesser energetic patterns and allow for the greater, more Divine aspects of my Self to come through. These Divine aspects seem to be covered by the old conditioned beliefs of the mind, and it is sometimes through the awareness and understanding of these old beliefs—by bringing them to light and finding forgiveness—that we are able to dissolve them.

There is actually no greater gift than the current mirrors in our lives.

If we use them correctly.

If we use these mirrors to see what we need to work on in our consciousness, they are a tremendous gift and can serve as supreme allies to the Soul. Tools for true healing and transformation. If we use them to deny our areas of growth and to simply judge others, they become our world of illusion, our world of smoke and mirrors, our world of justification and rationalization at the expense of our peace of mind, and, on a larger scale, at the expense of peace on the planet.

And because the images we refuse to see will only continue to get closer and closer until we can't deny them any longer, when we don't take responsibility for our emotional terrain and do the work on ourselves, they can eventually become our own personal hell.

My heart
held a dream
the world seemed intent on destroying with its wicked laugh
cruel insults
and harsh ignorance of truth

Although …

one day
I found
when I stopped laughing at my own dream
no longer insulted my own wisdom
and began to recognize my own ignorance of truth

The world stopped to pause

and opened
in a new way
And I realized it only to be a reflection of myself

Intention
The Rudder of Your Ship

Just beneath,
your desire
your longed-for love
your heart of fire

lies the spirit of that dream
the part that drives
the part
unseen

the part that makes it come to life
the part that fuels
the part that lights,
The part that directs
and charts the course
the part that is
the power, the force

As you aspire
to a great ascension
you must align
with your Soul's Intention

What is the intention you have for your life?
The question is one of astounding significance. Your strongest underlying intention is charting your course as we speak. If you don't have an answer to the question, then an unconscious intention is steering your ship without your knowledge.

You may currently be operating from many intentions you are not aware of. They may have formed early on in life while you were trying to figure out how to operate and survive within your family structure, how to understand and honor a religion you didn't fully understand or believe in, and how to be a productive member of an economically based society.

If we look inside ourselves, most of us have the underlying intention to "be good," since in childhood when we were good, we were usually rewarded. In a sense, this is true in a universal way as well, because of the law of karma—cause and effect—and what we put out into the world, we tend to get back.

But, a lot of the time, being good meant going along with the program even when it didn't feel right to us on a deep level.

And always there was that carrot dangling on the end of the stick: the carrot of love if you are good. The carrot of a good life if you go to the right school. The carrot of fulfillment if you get the right job and buy the right things and marry the right person. The carrot of the picket fence. The carrot of heaven.

The problem is, the carrot is always dangling in the future, and even when you do manage to get the carrot, you could end up even more frustrated than when you began, as you realize it was just a damn carrot.

Carrots may satisfy the personality for a time, but there is a place that will never feel content until you begin fulfilling the intentions of the Soul. When you begin to fulfill those, the carrot of heaven will no longer motivate you, since you will have found that heaven isn't a place you get to in the future. It's a state of consciousness you live in while you are on Earth, when the intentions of your mind begin aligning with the intentions of the Soul, and when you are engaged in action on Its behalf.

There are many different levels of intention. The intention of the Soul is always to grow and expand, to evolve or, looking at it from another perspective, to be realized at greater levels. The individualized soul, as opposed to the collective Soul, may develop talents and capabilities while in human form, create works of beauty and inspiration, complete and satisfy agreements made in other times and other realms, learn particular lessons, pay off karmic debts, and most simply, experience and demonstrate eternal qualities and be Itself while on the earth plane in physical form.

The personality, or conditioned mind, may have another agenda altogether, such as staying safe and comfortable and keeping us diverted and distracted from anything it experiences as painful or uncomfortable.

When one consciously embarks on a spiritual journey, it may create a great conflict of opposing intentions within one's being. The initial purpose of embarking on a spiritual path is to align the intentions of the Soul with those of the personality or mind, which in effect creates a being who is fully present and fully in tune with the desires of the Soul, ultimately transcending the limitations of the fixed personality self.

Instead of the personality using the Soul, or God, to get what it wants, the Soul begins to use the personality and its unique gifts, talents, and ways of being for Its cause, Its mission, Its intention.

This is what is meant by having a pure intention.

To desire to be used by the Great Spirit of Life to fulfill It's intention on Earth. To have no other wish or desire, no hidden agenda, but to be used by this presence from the depth of our being. To be willing to sacrifice everything, everything, *Everything*, for it. To trust Life beyond anything else; to know that the Life within us would not have us do anything not in the best interest of our Selves or others. To believe in Life with a conviction that surpasses all else. And at those times when we don't feel it anymore, when we have lost hope, when we cannot believe—then to *know*. To know that we know that we know that we are here for a greater purpose, to live only, only, only, for a life that is of a greater wisdom, greater meaning, and greater awareness. To be a willing servant of Love, Life, Joy, and Beauty. To be the greatest lover that has ever walked the Earth. To want that Life to live through us so passionately, so deeply, and so profoundly in order that our lives will not be lived in vain.

This is one example we might have for our life's intention.

Another example is to try and make it through without too much suffering.

How inspiring.

The real irony is that when we go through life trying not to suffer, we end up creating suffering because that is what we are unconsciously holding on to in our awareness. The irony is so wild that if it weren't so tragic it would almost be funny.

It is also ironic that an entire religion was built around believing that someone else, someone who is not even physically alive, is going to save us from ourselves. That we can just "go to" heaven simply because we believe something about someone else.

And, on top of that, others *won't*, because they *don't*.

Maybe it's not irony at all; maybe it's just a shame.

The truth is, if you don't know you're in heaven now, you won't know you're there when you die.

Believing in Jesus will not "save" you.

Practicing his teachings will.

If you merely believe in Jesus, (or any other being as a point of inspiration and guidance) while continuing to gossip about other people, continuing to believe yourself a victim while blaming others for your upset, failing to quiet your mind in order to hear the inner wisdom and guidance, and failing to act on that guidance; you will merely cross over to the other side and, more than likely, be a little disappointed in yourself.

You don't get a brand-new consciousness just because you die, because you believe in someone else, or because you followed someone else's rules while you lived. You get one by coming to know who you really are, and by working to become a more enlightened person while you are here on Earth. And by realizing that Heaven is Earth and Earth is Heaven.

You get a "new consciousness" by having the sincere intention to become more loving and giving, more grateful and disciplined, more trusting of Life, and more aware of what's really important. And what's really going on. You get one by becoming more Real. More true to the Soul. To your Self. To Life.

If the intention you hold for your life is not to become more conscious, more aware, more loving, more service-oriented, but only to suffer less, or to simply acquire knowledge in order to personally gain something, then there is only so far you can go. There is a limited amount of awareness to be found in that intention. There is a limited amount of heaven to be found on Earth in that intention as well as a limited amount of what you can bring to the world.

When we go to school, our main focus is to develop our minds. Our intellects. To learn things so that we can survive on Earth and take care of the physical body. Get a good job, go on some nice vacations, and enjoy a nice retirement.

How different would it have been if we were taught that each of us is an integral part of the Plan on planet Earth? Part of a plan to bring forth more Beauty, more Joy, more creative solutions and brilliant ideas so that we may celebrate Life and serve the Magnificence of Life and of Our Selves? That we were here to share our individual genius. Contribute greatly to the whole. That we were *necessary* to the planet—otherwise, we wouldn't be here.

Having an intention to merely develop our minds intellectually limits us to that way of being in the world. We are multidimensional beings. We are not just our minds, although many would have us believe just that.

We are taught opinions and rational worldviews, by people with letters behind their names, as if the letters signified anything much more than many years spent memorizing information and other people's theories. When I changed from a BA degree to a BS degree, I laughed out loud as I thought I heard a voice announce, "I thought you would like that one." There are times you really do just have to laugh at the irony of it all. When are we going to really figure this stuff out and get on with it already!

There lies a great chasm between intelligence and wisdom. Intelligence is to the mind as Wisdom is to the Heart. Intelligence without wisdom is a formula for disaster. Without the understanding of the interrelatedness of all of Life and the innate intelligence of It, our personal intelligence can indeed become a dangerous weapon. It steals softly the very soul of our collective existence as we sell out to the great illusion of separation, including the great mandate of competition. As we are competitively nurtured and ushered into this competitive way of being, we are told that this is a "healthy" way to operate in the world.

If we are aware of a competitive tendency and make light of it, we can play with it and have some fun. But usually we are not aware of it or what it does to us, such as compromise our values and unconsciously put us into a paradigm of separation and scarcity. If we look at our neighbors, our co-workers, our clients, our friends, or our lovers, as people to outdo or manipulate instead of as an aspect of our Selves to support, appreciate, and love, we are fanning the flames of our ultimate destruction rather than building a sustainable future together on the planet.

There are stages of individuation in every person's growth that need to be honored, but "us against them" is so ingrained in our collective consciousness, we just assume it is part of the human condition. We assume it is the best, or only, way for us to become motivated. The truth is, competition can only exist in a lesser vibration, in an environment of scarcity. When we have peeked into the Eternal Abundance and diversity of the Universe, competition is a profoundly silly concept.

We have been taught to believe that there is only so much to go around, based on evidence in the physical world. After this paradigm of scarcity is created, we are then manipulated by those with an agenda to do and be certain things. Actually, it is probably the only way to get things done that your Soul has no interest in doing. If you were doing what you absolutely loved to do, and this "work" was in alignment with a purpose greater than yourself—one which contributed to the lives of others and brought you absolute joy—you wouldn't need artificially created motivations. If you feel great about who you are, you are motivated to do what needs doing without someone breathing down your neck. You would take care of yourself and relish the opportunity to take care of others.

When you're in Heaven, you are inspired to do what you are doing. Not only would competition not appeal to you, it would be seen for what it is, a tool for separation. In the realization of a universe of infinite abundance, there is enough to go around for everyone. Our particular genius doesn't take away from others genius, but complements it. When we're in Heaven—in that awareness of Heaven on Earth—in Love, we realize there is nothing to compete for, nothing to "win." We come to understand that the greatest wins are those of our greater realizations of Truth. Of fulfilling our unique callings. Of our realization of unity consciousness and our inherent Divine Nature.

As our awareness expands, even in games or athletic competitions, we become more interested in playing rather than winning. We become focused on playing our best game, getting into a state of flow, on discovering a new aspect of ourselves or the game—not in beating someone. In truth, you can only take with you what you give away. Winning against other people is temporal. Extending love, kindness, generosity, and compassion to someone who is not acting in a way which would warrant it, is a true win—a win of the Soul—at which the ego will balk.

The truth is, we do not need to carry a consciousness of competition to move forward in our growth. In fact, if you carry the identity of a "winner," you will constantly have to create people in your life to win against in order to keep that identity. You're setting yourself up for a life of constant conflict rather than cooperation and harmony. If you forget that what you are doing to others you are really only doing to yourself, you may have many wins on the physical plane, but on the spiritual plane, if you win at someone else's expense, you "lose."

It has been argued that competition is the only way to build character and to motivate people. As my Oma used to say often when I was growing up, "Oh, owl-hockey!"

An intention of winning over someone or something else carries far less clout, far less Soul-motivating energy, than an intention of inspired and enthused focus. When a team focuses on beating another team, it is far less effective on an energetic level than if they were inspired to ask, "What is the highest potential of this team's ability to work together?" Or, "How can we contribute to a positive experience for the other team?" Those kinds of questions invoke a higher level of energy with which to engage; energies of wholeness, inspiration, and generosity of the Spirit. The Soul, aware of the unifying oneness of Life, knows that it can't "win" against itself, but it can aspire to demonstrate new levels of cooperation and mastery in the physical world. In this endeavor, the team is engaging its collective Self, just as we engage our Self when we are inspired, rather than engaging our egos in competition or winning.

There may be other intentions we might not be aware of, which are holding us back from living the life our Soul intended. Our upbringing might have steered our intentions toward playing very small. If we grew up having our decisions made for us, we might have felt powerless to do anything to make a difference in our lives, much less in the world. We might have bought into the doom-and-gloom theories that were unconsciously handed down to us. We may have been taught to ask ourselves "Who in the hell do you think you are?" instead of "What brilliance and joy are you here to experience and demonstrate?" We may have been taught to focus on our weaknesses and frailties. Our sins. Our mistakes.

We might have held ourselves back with an imaginary vision of doom, playing so conservatively that we ended up altogether bored by the game. Or we may have held back by becoming vigilant, constantly on guard, measuring and gauging others, and constantly calculating instead of remaining open and trusting in our Selves, in the Love of others, and in Life.

When we have the intention of playing God's game, as opposed to our own, we find ourselves playing a game grander than we could have ever dreamed possible. We begin to trust our Selves again. We trust Life again. We find we know where to go, who we feel comfortable with, who our teachers are, what our next project is, and what we need to practice in order to stay in the flow of life. We find we actually do have our own answers. Who knew?

All this will happen effortlessly if we consistently remember and connect with the intention we have for our life. What is it really? What do we really, *really* want?

Soul Desires vs. Personality Desires

A personality desire is quite different from a Soul desire. A personality might desire a little red Corvette. A soul might desire world peace.

There is nothing wrong with a little red Corvette. Little red Corvettes are fun. Soulful living is fun living. I imagine that our souls love riding around in little red Corvettes. What would a Soul have to do to get a little red Corvette, though? It could use the knowledge that thought is creative, and use affirmations and visualizations in order for it to materialize.

If the little red Corvette comes by these means, we find that ultimately the car becomes less important than the "miracle" surrounding its appearance. The Soul will be more fulfilled by the demonstration itself, rather than what it has specifically demonstrated. It will be fulfilled by discovering the law of cause and effect and its own co-creative abilities in the world, along with the implications for what it could mean in other areas of its life. The car becomes somewhat irrelevant in that picture, and the likelihood of creating an unhealthy attachment to it would be small.

If we get a job, work hard to make the money, and buy the car, there is no magic, no demonstration, and we could easily end up with an unhealthy attachment to the car itself. It will be seen as having great value, rather than our ability to co-create with the unseen forces of Life, since we had to personally work so hard to get it. We probably had to sell out our Soul's intention by spending hours working for money. Most likely doing something our heart wasn't fully engaged in. Then all that we sacrificed, all that energy, goes into the physical expression of the car. We can come to put a very high value on something that holds no real value to the Soul and really has nothing to do with what It is doing here. A deep-seated love/hate relationship can manifest in regard to those material things we have sold our soul in order to get and keep in our lives.

What would a soul have to do to "get" world peace? Where in the world would you even begin on that one?

First, just by consciously having that intention, you move out of living only from your "personality self." In fact, everything that is not peaceful within you would begin to surface and be healed, since the intention for peace would bring to the surface all that is not of that vision of peace. Yikes!

Living the life your Soul intended is not a cake walk. It's not a skip in the park to a personality that wants to remain the same and keep things comfortable and convenient.

So, why even do this stuff? Why not just stay in a job just to pay the bills? Why not live for the weekend or for a yearly vacation? Why not live for a future retirement, or a future heaven?

Because in truth that life is hell. It's a silent misery that most of us are content with for so long, only because we don't really, honestly believe that an alternative exists. At least not for us. This kind of life without vision and Soul purpose is rationalized by claims that "life is hard, and then you die" and other such nonsensical sayings from cynical minds that never discovered their inherent Goodness and the inherent Goodness of Real Life.

This cynical view of life is continually handed to us on a very deep, subconscious level, usually with great subtlety and finesse. On television, in between the daily collective manifestation of fears and limiting beliefs being pawned off as "news," we are told there is something we can buy that gives us peace, love, beauty, confidence, that gives us a sense of wholeness, of deep satisfaction and happiness.

It's a boldfaced lie.

Nothing you will ever buy can give you these things. They can fool your personality into thinking you have these things for a time, but the Soul will eventually see through the whole charade. This recognition usually happens through excessive pain and insight, finding that once you've finally got it all, everything your ego convinced you that you needed, you realize on a deeper level, on a Soul level, you really don't have anything.

Another thing to remember is that Soul intentions are soulful intentions. They are not pious renditions of what we think others, or some god we have created in our mind, would like us to say. They are passionate longings of the heart. They are intensely beautiful visions of the Soul. If world peace doesn't do it for you right now, it doesn't do it for you. There's no point in monotonously recounting something someone else has said because you imagine it might be good for you. There is no demonstration to be had in a monotonous, pious prayer. It must be a heartfelt, soulful, rich realization of the Soul—full of zest, zeal, and enthusiasm! Lofty aspirations and visions daring enough to be worthy of that which created you. Possibly daring enough to be called crazy. It must be seen, heard, felt, and tasted with every part of your being.

I mean, really, how excited can you get over a car, for goodness sakes? (Actually, given how we're trained by commercials to salivate over material things, we could, in fact, be quite excited. How sad.)

Now, how excited can you get about developing a talent to the point of genius? About a peaceful world where everyone is appreciated and honored? How excited can you get about being appreciated and honored for who you truly are in your own life? For absolutely knowing you are doing what you came to the planet to do? Or healing the most challenging relationship in your life to the point where it becomes one of your most loving and supportive? How would it feel to contribute greatly to the life of another? To your community? To the world? To wake up in dimensions you haven't even begun to imagine?

A part in us is probably so cynical that it not only believes these things are not possible for us, it may not even be able to see the incredibly awesome potential and value in them.

Imagine it, though. A deeply loving and supportive relationship with your mother. Your dad. Your children. Your boss. Someone with whom, in a perfect world, you would enjoy a deeply fulfilling relationship. Imagine that your life was full of relationships that were mutually nurturing and supportive. Ones that gave generously. That cared deeply. That honored, respected, and adored. Imagine a world where no one life was valued more than any other. A place where everyone was encouraged and supported in expressing their own unique Self, in their own unique way.

We have to ask the part of us that has become hard and cynical to move aside while we go for what in our heart of hearts we may not have dared to consider. Maybe not in years. Maybe decades. Maybe *ever*.

We have to get to the point where we see this as possible, or it never, ever will be, and our life will be lived from a very limited vision, or, more accurately, without vision. In the end, we may be able to say that we had some good times, maybe had some good friends and even what we considered a good life; but the seed of genius that had been planted into our soul was never allowed to grow.

Our divine inheritance went unspent.

The truth is, we might not reach "the goal," and things may turn out completely different than we had imagined, but by living an intention of the Soul, there is no way to live an insignificant and unfulfilling life. Even if you are never known by anyone other than the people in your immediate circle, you will have contributed greatly. In this alignment, there is no way not to feel a deep sense of fulfillment and belonging, as each step reveals another. You may find yourself not belonging so much to a certain group, but to the Soul of the World. To Life Itself.

The alternative is to live a life of resignation. Sold out to a little idea that only so much is possible. To the idea that material possessions are the "be all and end all."

To live in a constant state of trying to acquire more.

Intending to Surrender

After attending a profoundly inspiring weekend conference on global evolution, I found myself sitting in a broadcast room as a guest on a national radio show concerning spirituality. A friend had invited me to come see the show, since a client of his was the host, and when a guest had failed to show up, I was elected to go on the air in his place.

The conference I had attended ended that afternoon and I was still in what I could only describe as a heightened state of awareness. I knew it was no mistake that I ended up there that evening. As the show began, the peace and sense of awe and wonder I felt was replaced by sheer panic. At one point, the host told me I needed to remember to breathe, and one of the engineers gave me a little post-it note with the message "Smile," and a smiley face drawn on it. I was in trouble and I knew it. I soon realized that if it were up to me, it wouldn't be long before I passed out or started babbling like a madwoman. This was something I could not possibly do alone.

In that moment I had a strong intention to let that force, that power, whatever had put me into that chair that night, speak through me. I had the sense that the Universe had pulled some strings to put me in that seat, so the least I could do was get out of the way and let it speak. To say this took trust was an understatement.

As soon as the other guests started making their remarks, I began to think of certain quotes that would support my view of things and make my point. Then I remembered it wasn't me that was going to be speaking. I began a meditation, open-eyed so I wouldn't look like a complete lunatic, and felt myself going into to an altered state of consciousness once again. I began to see patterns in the lights and in the equipment around me that I understood to be part of a larger plan. There was a natural plan to it all, a synchronized universe that had an order that was so intricately planned down to the tiniest particle, and which expanded to the most far-reaching, infinite corners of the universe. It was absolutely perfect. There was nothing else other than this perfection. Nothing that man had ever created since the beginning of time, even came close to representing this steady and illumined stream of excellence and beauty.

I heard my name and realized I was being asked a question that related to the previous comments. As I began to lean forward, I had no idea what would come out of my mouth. There were some jumbled words flying around above my head, and it seemed to take minutes for me to lean the few inches to the mike, even though it must have only been a second. Miraculously, something coherent came out. As I leaned back into the chair after speaking, I even thought it was pretty good. Wow, that was cool, I thought.

The evening went on for a little while like that. Every time I was asked something, I thought about what I would say, then many times something else would come out of my mouth. Just as I began to relax, I was asked to comment on the "fundamentalist Christian" who had just made derogatory comments about homosexuals.

"Well," I said, "I don't agree with what he's saying, but I don't feel any judgment towards him."

The host looked like he had just been given first prize in a contest.

"Wait," he said, sitting up straight in his chair, leaning forward. "Let's stay with this for a minute. Are you telling me that you don't judge him at all? That he can say those things and you are okay with that?"

"Well," I said, "I certainly don't agree with what he said, but that's his opinion and everyone is entitled to their opinion. I don't judge him even though I don't agree with him."

"So then," he went on, circling in for the kill, "what does that mean? That anyone can do whatever they want and we don't judge them? What about Hitler, then? Are you saying we shouldn't judge Hitler?"

I immediately realized the trap I had been put in, and the question demanded a qualified response, as the question had moved into a different context and situation.

As I thought of all of the things I might say, such as, "It's not a question of whether you *should* judge someone; only a matter of whether you are or not, which in turn only tells you whether or not you are in a consciousness of separation and limited awareness." Or, "You certainly can judge him all you want—I don't care. But when you understand the laws that govern cause and effect, you wouldn't want to judge him. Not only would you be polluting your energy field with negativity, you would be releasing harmful chemicals into your body and polluting that as well, not to mention the environment around you." Or, "I don't see the benefit of allowing someone who is not even alive to put me into a negative state. Especially since there's not anything I can do at this moment to help. That wouldn't be too bright. I think he did enough damage while he was here."

As it turned out, those were the things *I* would have said, but I was not the one speaking. There were only two options open to me. Yes or no.

It was a very bizarre experience. I literally did not have access to any other words. I could almost see the two words floating above me and I became aware that, in some way I couldn't completely understand, this was one of the more important questions I had ever been asked. I also suddenly became aware that the room was filled with "guests" from another realm. I'm not sure if they were angelic, but whoever they were, they seemed to carry some clout. It was one of those moments where you can almost feel that God Itself is holding Its breath.

"Yes," I said.

I knew at that point there was no turning back, and I had no idea what was going to happen. I felt as if I had just jumped off a cliff, and immediately after the word left my mouth, I felt the most incredible peace and joy flood my entire being.

The host looked as if he was going to fly out of his chair in excitement. If it was first prize he had won before, this one would have been the Nobel. "Well, folks, she's obviously crazy, she's lost her mind! We'll be right back after this commercial break, don't go away."

A palpable hush fell over the room. No one would even make eye contact with me.

And it *just didn't matter.*

The freedom and bliss I was feeling was almost more than I could stand. Being thought of or called crazy had always been one of my biggest underlying fears since I was very young. I have questioned my sanity many times in searching for Reality, and there were many times I was convinced that I was, in fact, crazy. In that moment, everything became excruciating clear. I was suddenly able to see everyone's intentions. It was as if a veil had been lifted, even though, as I think back, there wasn't anything too shocking to be discovered.

The man sitting to my right, who was the "fundamentalist Christian," believed in what he was saying and thought he was helping people by showing them the way to salvation. He was also there to sell some books. He had a good heart, and we had a few nice exchanges during commercial breaks. The man to my left was bent on proving his theories and seemed to quite like the sound of his voice and the cleverness of his mind. He had a lot of excess energy and, during the show, he was rocking so forcefully I thought he might take off and fly into the sound booth. The host was after one thing: Ratings—to advance and promote himself professionally. We were not so much people to him as we were pawns in his game—new age nutball, hardcore fundamentalist, philosophic blowhard—all pitted against each other. Not truly intended for a deep and sincere exploration of spirituality in society, as the topic would imply, but to create friction and dramatic energy for listeners to feed off of. I felt no judgment in seeing this. There was nothing "wrong" with it, but after a while I had to hold back the laughter that wanted to bubble up. It suddenly all seemed so silly and irrelevant.

Child's play.

Interestingly, later on in the show, the host asked me a question leading with, "You're obviously an intelligent woman …" and the man to my left actually started to laugh. He was having problems holding it back and had to hold his hand over his mouth. The amazing thing was I felt no humiliation. It was as if I couldn't be humiliated, because the part that was capable of being humiliated wasn't even there. I actually thought it was funny too. Maybe not "ha-ha" funny, but definitely peculiar. In that moment, I don't think I would have described myself as "intelligent," at least not in the common sense of the word. In fact, I wouldn't have described myself as a "woman" at that point either.

After the show ended, the host gave me a hug and asked if I was all right, as if to say, "No hard feelings, okay?" I gave him a big hug and assured him I was fine. I was actually doing better than ever.

Walking out of the room, I found the others averting their eyes from me. It was as if everyone was thinking: "Maybe if we don't look at her she won't be able to see us." Or, "No sudden movements and everything will be fine."

Not only had I not been harmed or committed for speaking my truth—or rather letting the Universe, Life, Love, speak through me—but I was in ecstasy. The two-hour show seemed to have taken all of about ten minutes, and nothing could bring me down. On the way home, I asked my friend what he had thought about the whole thing. He seemed a little quieter than usual and admitted that the Hitler comment was a little much. That surprised me since I had thought we were on the same page, and I went through the explanation. Then he understood and said, "Well, when you explain it like that it makes sense." I began to think back on the show and to run certain parts over again in my mind. Holy moly, I did sound like a nutball! On national radio, too. I started to wonder if the comments hadn't made things worse for the new thought/new age movement (if anyone had even been listening).

As the hours went on, I grew more doubtful as to whether it actually had been a success. Without going into detailed explanations, it seemed that people who thought "new age people" (what I had unwillingly been labeled) were weird and nutty anyway would just be able to make their case even stronger. Before going to bed, I asked the question, How could that have possibly been a positive message?—not expecting to receive an answer. Surprisingly, one came.

Believe it or not, what you say is not as important as what you say it with. Underlying everything you do, there is an intention. The purer the intention, the higher the vibration. Even though you may look back over the evening and not think of it as a success, in another realm it was a complete success. You were able to move any personal agenda or fear aside. In that way, it was profoundly successful.

I also got that the incident was in fact a test. Not a pass/fail test, though. When you take judgment out of the equation—there is no sense of failing because there is no set standard, and therefore nothing to fail at—it becomes merely a litmus test of relativity. Rather than seeing it as a test now, I can see it was just an opportunity. An opportunity for me to stand in what I knew to be true, to trust that inner voice, to express from the deepest part of myself, and to simply be an outlet, a space, a place for Life to express. An opportunity to discover that I wouldn't be hurt even when what I said was blatantly crossing the bounds of what a "sane" person would say (if judged from a purely material-world perspective). It was an opportunity to trust with a capital "T" and from that perspective, it was a success.

Success is an interesting thing in itself. It is relative in terms of our frame of reference. Success in the material world and for the personality, or success of the Soul. There is such a fine line here, many fail to acknowledge its existence or to see the abyss which actually sits between the two. The distinction rests in your underlying intention. Only you know what that is. When you have the intention to work for God, Life, or Love, and you come to understand that that means you will always be Self-employed, no matter who you might experience as having to work for, everything changes. You start to become very aware of your personal will, the limited ideas of the mind, and the potential or the Success that comes from surrendering that personal will to serve a Higher Purpose. That serves All.

The personality freaks out time and time again because it experiences all of this as a loss. Loss of control. Loss of power. Loss of freedom. Loss of…everything. But the part that is fearing the loss is not you. It is only a manufactured, constructed, fixed idea of who you are.

I realized then that things I said were going to be misunderstood by some people, possibly even the people I was closest to, and I realized how that concern had caused me to hold back my entire life. I also realized that holding back was akin to being imprisoned, to not living.

If I am looking to gain anything personally, I am operating in a lower, limited vibration. Even though I may be able to pass along valuable information, I will ultimately not connect with people in the deepest way if my intention is not for All, for Life, for Us, if instead, at its core, it is really to serve my personal agenda. My professional agenda. Pay my bills. Take care of my own. This is not said to invoke an attitude of irresponsibility, but rather a profound understanding and trust in Reality and in Life to provide.

In the world of effects, it can be quite indistinguishable unless you take a little closer look.

Where is the focus?

Where is your focus?

If you have a list of goals derived from any intention other than to discover deeper dimensions of yourself on a more intimate basis, to mine the gold that is buried within you in order to support, to love, to benefit and to serve the whole, then those intentions are not worthy of your true greatness.

We can accumulate phenomenal amounts of goods and possessions when we understand the universal law of cause and effect, and begin to clear our consciousness of limitation, but we can also create imbalance if we are acquiring these goods at the expense of others. If our intention is to sell x amount of goods, without regard as to whether it is useful to another or in alignment with that Soul's purpose, then we are out of alignment. If, on top of this, we use our knowledge of psychology to create the appearance of scarcity, in order to manipulate and persuade others for our own personal gain, we are coming from a place of limitation, even though we may believe and can convincingly argue that what we are doing is "good" for people.

The foundational intention of selling resides in the principle of persuasion, whereby potential buyers may not know what is "good" for them and the seller has to help them see how much they need what is being sold. Sharing is different. If we are sharing ideas or products that we have found beneficial, we talk about them with an intention of service and if the other person would like to try that product or use that service, he or she will—not through persuasion and a clever strategy on behalf of the seller, but through the benefit of the product or service and its usefulness in the person's life.

It is very interesting to see people who are sharing being mistaken for people who are selling. We have been so turned off by the whole concept of selling that people who are enthusiastic about a discovery and who just want to share it with the world can be mistaken for people whose primary focus and interest is in making money. If we work toward accomplishing an agenda that we have created with our mind, with limited worldly concepts, as opposed to letting that power within us work to accomplish Its agenda through us, we are stuck operating from that limited world.

We cannot work for our Soul and our ego at the same time. This distinction can be quite impossible to discern in the material world because only we know our true intention. Therefore, it is not our responsibility to even try to figure out the intentions of others; only to become clear in our own. The clearer and purer our own intentions, the clearer the intentions of others will become to us. There are no villains here, only different levels of awareness of What Is. Are we asking: *What can I get?* Or, *What can I give?* Life becomes absolute bliss when we are only, only, *only* asking *What can I give?*

We are taught that if we don't actively work to get things, we will end up with nothing. This is a lie.

In fact, it is more than a lie—it's a prison! When we discover the Truth, the question *What's in it for me?* becomes an old shoe that just doesn't fit anymore.

You can't really "get" anything, anyway. Even if you do manage to acquire something, if you imagine it to be outside of yourself, you know that it can be gone in one sweep of fate. There is no security or peace or joy in acquired things, only in further realizations of the Truth. The Truth that We are that which we are seeking.

Just as it is not our job to figure out other people's intentions, it is not our job to convince others of our own. When you give unconditionally, love unconditionally, and live unconditionally, there may very well be people who misunderstand your intentions. But it really doesn't matter what other people think of you. It doesn't matter that they mistake the Soul's intentions. *It really doesn't matter!* The only thing that matters is that you are absolutely clear as to what your true intentions are and what is influencing them. In truth, it's between you and God. And in Truth, there is nothing between You and God.

Besides, in the end, everything comes out in the wash.

Pure Intentions Produce

As I've mentioned before, ever since I can remember, I was obsessed with finding out who I was and what I was doing here. As a child, I would say I was haunted by these questions. I don't think there is a coincidence between having an awakening experience of such magnitude, and asking those questions to the point of obsession my whole life. In fact, awakening to the Authentic Self has absolutely nothing to do with anyone personally; it is only a matter of where one puts focus and intention.

All I really ever wanted was to know who I was, how I got here, and what in the world I was doing here. That's it. That's all that really ever interested me. My only real intention in life was to find the answers to these questions. I don't know if I actually thought I would ever be able to answer them, but I just couldn't stop asking. When answers started to come, it blew my mind.

The Truth always blows your mind.

Upon reflection, I see these were not intentions of the ego. They were questions asked for the pure sake of knowing, not to personally gain anything. If your intentions are driven by an insatiable curiosity and a sense of discovery, adventure, wonder, beauty, and awe, then rest assured, awakening is at hand.

Of course, sometimes some little bugger—some limiting intention—may find it's way in, but as long as you stay in practice and continue your intention to grow, there's no way it can survive for long. With our intentions we create fields of energy, which bring to us exactly what we need to fulfill that intention. It can take an immense amount of patience, from the ego's perspective. It takes a tremendous trust in one's Self, and in Life, but it is always worth the "wait."

When I was around twelve, I stumbled upon Nietzsche's *Beyond*

Good and Evil. I felt as if an entirely new world had opened as I learned that there were other people on the planet questioning reality. It was as if I had been on the planet for years and had finally found someone who spoke my language. Soon after, I read portions of Emerson's essay "The Oversoul," which I remember pondering for months and years afterwards. I was transformed and transfixed as different books began to find their way to my hungry mind. I searched, yes, and some came quite by accident. It seems that sometimes books are just as much in search of you as you are of them. A year or two later, I found an old copy of *Man's Search for Meaning* by Victor Frankel in a pile of books in the corner of my journalism class. This was another book that had a profound effect on me.

I didn't attract a mentor of any significance, which, in hindsight, seemed a necessity for me to turn entirely away from the world and form a deep connection within. For a while, I envied others when I heard stories of them being taken in at an early age by people further along the path. My only mentors were those men and women whose words of wisdom jumped off the pages and into my heart and mind, and caused me to ask deeper questions about myself and my life. I had epiphany after epiphany, paradigm shifts, and intense and profound experiences with these writers, but I longed for someone I could actually talk to in person about these things. As the years went by, I became more and more introverted. At the same time, I loved the fact that I was "working" alone, since I could go at whatever speed I wanted and experiment with life without any restrictions or admonitions. Without a singular set of beliefs handed down and expected to be taken on as my own.

From where I sit now, it is so clear that we all have unique and perfect circumstances that have led us to this current moment in our lives. There has never been a "mistake," only infinite opportunities to see that what is in front of us is part of the plan we are choosing, part of the path, part of the call.

Love uses everything for Its Purpose.

It does not serve us to try and live up to a limited idea of perfection, to believe that we have committed an unforgivable act, to think we have made too many mistakes, or to berate and judge ourselves for our pasts. Being harsh with ourselves when we don't fit into our idea of right or perfection is a ludicrous way to do life. It is a life of constant stress, pain, and suffering; and it is one that most of us have been conditioned to live.

In Reality, there is no past. There is Only Now. You can start fresh right now. Right Now. In fact, you can start new every day and even in every moment!

It's so ironic that when we stop judging and start loving, when we stop trying and just start being, everything begins to fall into place with little or no effort. When others start seeing your inner work being reflected in the material world, and ask you what you are doing, and you tell them, they may have many reasons why such a way of doing things is not possible or won't work. They then go back to scurrying around and tell themselves and others that you were just lucky.

Luck is actually the language of the victim. It signifies that you believe you can be unlucky. Grace, however, is something altogether different.

It was Louis Pasteur who said "Chance favors the prepared mind." Indeed, we need to create the condition within ourselves that invites "luck" into our life. There are no special people who are randomly lucky or graced. On some level, they opened up to receive the abundance that Life is constantly giving, and simply Is. Receiving is really just another form of giving. It is actually giving in disguise. Receiving is all about giving Life the space to give of Itself. If you are not open to receive, you will have limited resources to give.

Also, when we say someone is lucky, we usually have an idea of what is good and we assume because that person has attained that specific thing, we assume that attainment makes that person lucky. We measure everything by what we value, and if we have been taught to value something highly, such as money, and have never truly questioned why we value it, when someone acquires a large amount we might assume that is in their best interest. From a physical reality of scarcity and fear, money is always seen as good because from that position, it holds power. The problem is that we see it holding the power We truly are, but are not fully owning and expressing.

Intending to Grow beyond our Beliefs

When the intention we hold for our life is to grow and evolve, to truly step out of the way of the thoughts we have *about* anything and be willing to be an open channel for Life to live Itself through us, then the revelations, love, joy, and sense of purpose and meaning in our lives far outweighs anything the material world could provide. The irony, once again, is that when we choose to turn away from what we have been told about ourselves and the world, and truly search for the answers within, the more we become ourselves, the higher our vibration, and the more of these "good" things we naturally and gracefully attract into our lives without necessarily working directly for them in the world.

When I was in my early twenties, I worked at a gas station near a gated community that contained homes worth several million dollars. Some people from that community would come in and complain about a man who had won the lottery and had purchased one of the homes there. It had been a while since he had purchased the home, and he still had sheets and blankets hanging in the windows and an old pickup truck in the driveway.

After a time, the story came in that the man had committed suicide. I often reflected on that story, along with another incident that just happened to have occurred within the same community.

I was in my teenage years when I went with a friend to pick up one of her other friends. I couldn't believe the house—or should I say mansion! I had never known anyone who had this kind of a house, and I was feeling very impressed and somewhat intimidated by the sheer size and magnitude. The three of us were sitting in the kitchen when the girl's mom walked in. I don't think I had ever seen a more miserable person on the face of the earth. It seemed as if there was a dark cloud around her. In my mind I began to equate lots of money with miserable and suicidal. Similar situations throughout my life "proved" to me that large amounts of money were something to be avoided at all costs.

When the inheritance came in, something had to give. It was either the money or the negative beliefs. Most people assume, as I did at one time, that if I just had enough money everything would be fine. I would be free. I would be happy. By that time in my life, I knew that wasn't the case, but I never realized what challenges the money would bring. Along with the money came guilt issues that I needed to work out.

Why me? I thought. Why can't everyone have more than they need?

I had to work through any judgments surrounding money and, more significantly, people with money. The main problem was, I took it personally. It became *my* money, rather than just money. When I think of it as *the* money, there is no problem. When it becomes *my* money, I somehow believe I am personally responsible for it and need to personally protect it.

This seems to be the key to anything that puts me out of whack with anything. I start to take it personally.

The truth is, money in itself is neutral. It is not good or bad. It just is. We create the beliefs we have about it. If we believe it will give us something we don't already have, we are setting ourselves up for a divine disappointment. If we believe anything outside of ourselves will give us anything we don't already have, we are in for a rude awakening. We can, if we like, choose to grow by making goals outside of our self. We can have a great idea we would like to pursue and take steps in that area. If that action in the world is a stretch for us, it will cause us to grow and reach a higher level of vibration because we are living more fully.

In time, we will find the goals unsatisfying on a deep level if they didn't originate as a vision of the Soul and if they weren't given to us as we followed clues that were reflecting the possibilities. If they merely came from watching someone else and wanting what they had, or from an imagined need of the personality, they were coming to us in a state of separation, rather than from a true vision of the Soul. We will have grown in order to pursue the goal, and in that growth, we may begin to hear some of our true Soul desires.

Another possibility is to have a deep, heartfelt, passionate, and inspired intention to realize our true Self, which we connect with on a daily basis. We can continually ask ourselves, completely letting go of what came the day before: *What am I really here to do? What is my next step? How can I serve? What is my unique genius?*

Then when steps are revealed to us, we take action. If the action is in alignment with a Soul Desire, with a Soul Purpose, it almost seems silly to say, "We take action," because it becomes so apparent that all we need to do is just show up and the action is done through us. All we need to do is keep showing up with intentions to be servants to Life.

We are then not motivated by a material goal, but a deep, devoted love and desire from our Heart and Soul to be instrument of Life. In service to Life. Not to our personal ideas of life. Not to what we think we should be, or what we have been told is right for us. Material goals will undoubtedly be part of the process, since we are participating in the physical realm, but they will be afterthoughts rather than the thought itself.

We can't force ourselves to have a vision or make a spirit guide appear and tell us step by step what to do, but by having a Soul intention we open our awareness and hold a space for these things to occur. Then, not necessarily in our time frame or with our ideas of how it should look, the life our Soul intended miraculously begins to unfold, and with each step the vision becomes clearer.

We have been taught time and time again that we must take action in the world and work hard to get anything. This is another paradigm so ingrained in our thinking it is usually not even questioned.

There is another way.

We don't have to work ourselves silly with mindless tasks to have everything our Heart desires. We don't have to have endless steps, rules, and goals that plague our consciousness in order to grow and move forward. We can move forward at an incredible speed by relaxing into and putting continual energy into our deep heartfelt intention.

And then trusting, really trusting, *knowing*, that the Universe will provide everything.

Everything for the realization of our Soul.

Everything for the life our Soul intended to live.

Everything to realize Heaven on Earth.

Everything necessary to bring forward a win/win world.

We come to trust and know that It will provide for these things because in Truth, it is *All already Here*.

A win/win world is the one we can choose to live in now, even though we can find plenty of physical evidence that this possibility doesn't actually exist. That a win/win world is indeed impossible. Choosing to believe in, participate in, and live the impossible life is not living in denial. It is the very life your Soul intends to live. It is living in Freedom. It is living in Abundance. It is living in Faith In Service.

The other option is to choose to live in the world that most of our culture chooses to live in. One of consistent suffering, of recycled problems, of upsetting and impossible circumstances. Of many, many rules and conditions on life, limiting the possibility of miracles and grace enormously.

It is our choice.

We can live out our days with the herd and be nice and comfortable in our suffering, since, for the most part, we think what everyone else is thinking and do what everyone else is doing.

Or…

Or we can begin to live the life our Soul intended when it took on this incarnation.

What kind of life did your Soul intend for you?

What lessons are you here to learn?

What qualities are you here to master?

What gifts have you come to bring the world?

Who did your Soul intend for you to be?

Are you living the life your Soul intended?

If not, when did you sell out? And much more importantly, what would it take to get It back?

To know
you are seed
with everything needed contained within,

To align
with the intention of that seed
To nourish
the ground that holds the seed
To discover
how Beauty will manifest as You

The sun smiles and shines brightly on all
but only that which has
chosen Life
opens to the light within
and allows
its own unique flowering

shocking and delighting itself with
its pure essence
its pure magnificence
its pure radiance

And in the full bloom of its own divine nature
it does what it came here to do:
it rests in Beauty

Patience
My Will or My Willingness

Look over here,
sign up today,
in only one week
you can have it your way

You can have it all
if you just pay the price,
and if you sign up today,
we'll throw in some knives

No matter that all
who made their own mark
had to do their own work,
make their way through the dark

It is only the ones
who stayed with their questions
and didn't give up
at another's suggestion
found a way to the dream,
and found their true life
beyond all the obstacles
and through all the strife

Their time in the desert
was not done in vain
Such knowledge and
strength and wisdom to gain

'Tis not instruction
to just be complacent
But to realize the times
that require your patience

I can remember hearing from the earliest time "Patience is a virtue."
When I was very young I'm sure I wondered what in the world a
virtue was. Maybe I thought it was something like a vulture. A cousin
of the vulture. Actually, when you think of vultures, one of the things

that might come to mind is patience. Other things come as well, and this isn't the prettiest metaphor by any means, but you've gotta hand it to those vultures.

Once they find a victim, they hang out. Circling.

Waiting . Waiting. Waiting.

If we could only have the faith of a vulture as he waits for his next meal. He doesn't go flying off somewhere else to go look in the next desert. He waits.

He knows that, eventually, he will eat. Eventually.

When we hold the intention to realize our true Self, to have a real relationship with, understanding of, and communion with God, and do the necessary work, we are on a path that is not for the faint of heart. Not for the ordinary. Certainly not for the personality self. We are on a mission from our very Soul to realize and carry out Its mission on this planet. It is much the same as if we are circling the small-minded and conditioned parts of ourselves that, in truth, are only an illusion, and going in for the kill so that we may become greater, more authentic expressions of who we really are. This analogy may seem a bit ruthless, but we cannot afford to be naive about how cunning and sly that mind can be in keeping us confused and stuck.

One of the things that makes it extremely hard to venture onto the spiritual path is this society's overwhelming obsession with the quick fix. Trying to fit a natural, cyclical pattern of growth into a consumer-driven society, we run into such absurdities as "Spiritual Enlightenment in Ten Minutes or Less." We might chuckle when we hear something like that, but a place in our consciousness may still buy into the idea of such a thing. If we spend any time at all watching TV, we are constantly exposed to short clips of life. We may unconsciously arrive at certain conclusions from viewing life in this manner.

Maybe all this Soul intention stuff just isn't worth it. It's too much trouble. Too much work. If it doesn't come in a week (or ten minutes or less), it must not be working.

Unconsciously, we might expect something right now, might believe it is possible to have that Thanksgiving dinner appear right before our eyes without doing the necessary preparation. We want that thing in our life, whatever it is, without having to wait for it to bake. Without chopping the vegetables and mixing the ingredients.

Heck, we might not even have the necessary ingredients (i.e. spiritual tools and practices) in our kitchen yet!

It is just plain self-sabotaging silliness to expect limiting patterns that have been running within us for years will be realized and healed overnight. That's not to say that incredible leaps of consciousness cannot be made in what one might call relatively short periods of time if one is committed and one's intention is in alignment with the Soul's. It's just that permanent growth of any depth takes time, requires patience, and has cycles and plateaus—just like any natural growing process—and a false expectation may actually block our progress.

Advertisers only have thirty seconds or so to get across an entire idea or concept. Sitcoms and hour-long dramas show the same condensed version of life in order to tell a story that would ordinarily take many more hours, sometimes days, and in cases such as full-length movies, sometimes years. Films can be inspiring. They can help us see our lives and ourselves with greater clarity, help us put things into perspective and see things in a different context. They can inspire us, wake us up, and enlighten us. There is nothing wrong with discovering different ideas and seeing the world around us from another's perspective. Through another's lens. It can become a problem when we rely so heavily on this medium that it ends up dictating how we view the world and conditions us to a thirty-second-flash consciousness.

When we see a movie about a person's life, we obviously can't watch the entire person's life to show the impact that person had in the world. There are only a few hours, so only the big events, the highlights and turning points in their life are shown. We don't watch the characters sit and pay their bills, meditate, cook an entire dinner, or have conversations that seem not to have any relevance or great insight. This is an example of how peak moments in the physical world are unconsciously valued as the most important or worthy part of life.

The truth is, the down time in these characters' lives was just as important. The daily choices they made, the endurance, the persistence, the choice to follow their heart when things might not have been going all that well is a key we might forget as we watch these glamorous lives on screen and wonder why we were not blessed with such a rich experience. Everyone has greatness within them, a well of love that is inexhaustible and that moves mountains; we just need to realize that well within us and learn how to tap it. It is a process that involves taking a radical inner directedness, a process our culture seems bent on destroying before we even get started.

We are conditioned from the beginning to live our lives outside in, instead of inside out. We are taught to mechanically react to a seemingly random world outside of ourselves and to make our decisions based on what the world is doing, what others are doing, and by what we have been told is "right."

Images flash from sources all around us, telling us we need this or that now, now, now! The quick-fix hook of some personal growth programs might be effective in bringing people into a new way of thinking and seeing life, but a spiritual path is not a sectioned-off aspect of life that you can fit in a few days out of the year. It's not something that happens at a seminar one day and then you're fixed, you're done. It's a way of life. It's a way of expanding your daily awareness so that you are continually growing and realizing that Spirit is infinite, that You are infinite, and that on some level not only will you never be "done," you wouldn't want to be.

Surrendering the Outcome

It is impossible to have any amount of patience without understanding what true surrender is. The ego, or conditioned mind, might think it knows exactly what is best and how things should go according to its limited view of life (based on what it has previously been exposed to), and it may not be aware that an organized universe which governs everything in existence might have a little better perspective of the whole thing.

An analogy that comes to mind is one of waiting for water to boil. When we start a new project, get a sign to go in a new direction, take a step out, sometimes we may be tempted to stand over that water and make it hurry up and boil. We may want to stick our finger in and make sure it's getting warm, make sure the whole process is working. It's only in those moments when we can walk out of the kitchen completely that things really begin to move. The boil is somehow always a surprise, since you weren't hovering over the pot trying to force anything to happen in the physical world. Instead you were doing the inner work to release the limiting beliefs and negative emotions in your consciousness. Working to realize who you really are. And, instead of putting all of your eggs in one basket, or in this case one pot, had come to have many other pots on the stove in various stages of progress, leading to a balanced, rich and fulfilling life.

We must understand that our growth and awakening cannot be forced or rushed according to our limited ideas, plans, and agendas, yet can be heavily influenced and accelerated by our conscious intention to relax and surrender into the process itself.

We used to have a garden in our backyard when my daughter was very young. We only planted carrots a few times and when we did, we invariably ended up with pale orange stubs instead of full-grown carrots. There's always that tendency to want to get in there and see if something is done, to start trying to do it yourself without giving the process the grace to proceed at its own speed—especially when it's initially developing.

Under the ground, where no one can see, is where the real growth happens, away from the eyes or awareness of others. On the surface it may look like very little is happening, but be assured there is a profound restructuring and reorganizing taking place. This restructuring happens in the dark. If we are afraid of the dark, we can put off real growth indefinitely and never do the necessary work. We can work with surface-level material, living a surface-level life, and never delve into the depths of our being and explore that territory. The same territory we may deem terrifying, where our existential fears lie, is where the real gold is to be found. This is the place from which our greatest treasures are excavated.

When you are feeling and experiencing fear—not *observing* yourself feeling fear and being at choice in the matter, but actually in the thick of it—you know you are in the thick of the illusion, the unconscious dream of separation and pain. Asleep. If we want to be afraid of something, we should be afraid of sleepwalking through life.

When the Student is Ready

We must be able to come up for air on these journeys into the recesses of the soul. We must not get stuck in the darkness—or when we do, we must know when to ask for help from someone who has been on the journey and can assist us in finding our way.

In these times, we don't need someone to help us explore what's wrong with us as much as we need help remembering who and what we really are. Finding someone to help can be an interesting thing in itself. There are counselors and teachers aplenty, but who is right for us? Since we were taught from an early age that we did not have our own answers and had to look to others to tell us what to do, many of us still rely too heavily on the advice of others. We might pay outlandish fees for help and follow advice that does not truly facilitate the evolution of our Soul or bring us to a deeper awareness of who we are—and in fact, may lock us into one more limiting system of thought.

It is not that some people will not be extremely helpful in reminding us of what we know and inspiring us to practice what we know. It's not that there aren't many people sharing insights that will help us to expand our awareness. It's not that we don't want to circulate our money (our energy) in the direction of a true teacher or healer, since the action of appreciative circulation will put us in alignment with our true nature of abundance. It is only that we should not feel forced. We should not feel obligated or coerced. We shouldn't feel duped or taken advantage of. Our own voice and current understanding should not be hushed, but encouraged and respected. We should not be told what to do, but shown ways to arrive at our own answers.

It's the quick-fix advertisements that appeal to the ego, that tend to go to the highest bidder, that tend toward short-term profit, and play into a scarcity consciousness that we need to be leery of. We're used to paying big money for the best product—right now! That's how it works, right? Wrong.

Not in this realm.

You Can't Buy Consciousness.

It may help tremendously to have a true teacher who has done his or her own work, continues to do the work, and has a pure intention, but sooner or later you've got to do the work yourself.

And the work ain't easy. Anyone who tells you it's easy is lying. Even though it's not easy, it is very simple. It can be done in a playful and fun manner, but it's still not easy. Surface work is easy. Holding hands and singing songs is easy. Being inspired to live our dreams and initially connecting our hearts in a circle of friends or a workshop is not so hard. It's what surfaces to be released as a result of being in these higher levels of awareness that can prove challenging. Soul-searching forgiveness, sabotage behavior-breaking, releasing physical world attachments, and belief-busting work is not for the faint of heart.

You needn't pay through the nose for spiritual instruction or do things that go against your sense of internal integrity and ethics, but you do need to pay with your "life." A life that is run by small-minded ideas, ego-based intentions, and unconscious fears will never produce the life your Soul intended.

When you start to see the true nature of money, you become more conscious of where you are investing it. You feel called, or moved, to give back to institutions and schools that have helped you to recover the knowledge of who you really are and what life really is. You are inspired to contribute to educating and positively influencing others. This is a more organic way to circulate money. To pay large amounts of money up front or to give your total and complete trust to someone only because of their spiritual or professional rank is unhealthy. Just because your mind is open doesn't mean your brain has to fall out.

Then there is the flipside of this that says spiritual teachers and healers should be expected to do their work for next to nothing or for free. This seems to be inspired by our unconscious belief in money being the root of all evil and that anything truly spiritual and heart-centered shouldn't have any association with money. We can see where our consciousness is by taking a look at where we are circulating our energy—our money.

In one workshop I attended, we were each asked to go through our checkbook for the previous month to see where our energy was being directed and what our values really were, versus what we thought they were. I've always thought the "root of all evil" remark was a very interesting one from a material world viewpoint. It would certainly seem to serve a very powerful and rich group, such as a church, if their followers were to fully embrace that idea—or should I say fear it? The spiritual movement on this planet will never be able to move forward effectively until issues surrounding money have been fully resolved.

It is true, though, that spirituality is such a mysterious arena for many of us, we may assume others know more than we do; and we can be easily duped into thinking we need to have blind faith in order to be healed. Faith is not blind. Faith is trusting what cannot be seen, but that is entirely different from being blind. Faith is trusting in your heart. Your heart will never lead you astray, but, at times, your beliefs will. Your longing for belonging will. And certainly your impatience will.

There is a saying: When the student is ready, the teacher appears. It does not say, Get on the Internet and find a teacher.

When we come across someone who we find particularly helpful in guiding us, there is often the sense of grace surrounding the meeting, rather than of effort on our part. There are often serendipitous circumstances around how we came to find ourselves in the presence of a great teacher, healer, mentor or friend. A great teacher may not be a master of flipcharts but is one who is able to lead you back to your Self. One who may show you a map but not tell you what route you need to take.

We must be able to discern if a particular teacher, guide, counselor, or therapist is operating from a personal agenda to gain something or truly serving Love. We also might want to discern whether they are seeing their "students" as whole beings capable of finding their own way, and, actually as teachers themselves.

We also need to discern whether these guides and teachers are confusing a projection of their own desire to heal with a true calling. Many of those who exhibit an authenticity and true talent in the spiritual field, initially resisted the whole idea. Instead of striving to become great in their field, they put more energy initially into surrendering to the call of their Soul. In other words, it usually wasn't their idea.

Great teachers know that each individual carries his or her own answers within because they are part of the One. Their work is not telling others what to think, it is teaching them how to think, or rather facilitating processes which help others to become aware of the thoughts that are not serving their greater potential. They help others become aware of and remember that thought is creative, and that simply, Life Is.

Material world advice-giving would be a rare occurrence indeed, as the role of a spiritual teacher is not to try and fix our problems on the material level, but to help us realize the true nature of the Self and of Reality, which in return transforms and "fixes" material world problems. These type of teachings are designed to help us to discover a world where there are no problems—at least not in the sense that we formerly thought—and to provide tools that help us connect with the teacher within ourselves.

When anyone passes along advice to us, no matter how highly regarded they are, we would be wise to see if the information they give resonates for us. We might also be interested in how they relate to others and if they are, in fact, walking the talk. In fact, the main indicator of a true teacher is not what they say, but how they live. It is by their example that we become aware of the greater possibilities for our own lives.

On one hand, if the information we receive from someone seems to have value to us we might not care any further. Someone else's life on one level is really none of our business. If we have any emotional reaction or righteous energy surrounding how another chooses to live, or their ability to reveal Unconditional Love, we know in that moment it has ceased to be about the other person and that we have work to do within our own consciousness.

We also know that one who is in alignment with what they are teaching—one who actually lives the teaching—is carrying a higher vibration, and it is this vibration that effects us even more than the information they share. At times, we can be lifted up and have insights and revelations in their presence because they are emitting a high frequency. Our energy will correspond to that frequency, and we will find our own answers coming to us spontaneously without much need for advice. It is not so much what someone says, it is what they are transmitting energetically that is just as, if not more, important.

The other reason we might not want a guide who does not practice what they preach is their tendency to project their weaknesses onto us. If a teacher or healer has not yet found the place of wholeness within themselves and does not consistently touch that "secret place of the most high," they will see clients and students as those "out there" needing help, as opposed as to seeing the dimension within them that is already healed. They will see problems in others they need to be looking at in themselves. From that state of awareness they will not be able to discern the difference and may give us advice that is not beneficial to our growth.

You don't need someone to save you, you need someone to *See* you. But even if you are truly seen by someone else, it won't matter in the long run if you can't see your Self.

As healers and teachers ourselves, if we see someone as whole and complete, we are doing a service beyond what we could ever imagine. If you think about it, how do you feel in the presence of someone who holds you in high regard? Do you tend to let more of your true self out? Tend to shine brighter in their presence? Now think of someone who you are pretty sure sees you as incompetent or needing help. How do you feel in their presence? Notice that someone's assessment of you is actually a reflection of how they see themselves, just as your assessments are of others.

In a sense, we absolutely have the ability to effect people by how we see them and what we think about them. If we are looking for others' weaknesses and fitting them into a diagnostic system we have created in order to prove our point or get our results, we are not doing much more for people than traditional medicine, since it operates in the same mind set: one of "fixing problems." If we exist in a conscious state of wholeness, we help others come to realize that state of wholeness in themselves.

In Truth there is nothing that needs to be healed or fixed. In Truth we are nothing but utter perfection. True healing is always a revelation of this fact. The revelation that on the spiritual plane there is really nothing to heal or fix, since nothing has ever been damaged or touched in any way. When you are conscious of the True state of your being—really, profoundly, completely and utterly aware of who You *really* are, of what You *really* are, and of What Life *really* Is, you are no longer bound by any former limitation.

A couple of years ago, I ended up in the emergency room as a result of taking a nutrition supplement that contained fish oil. I had developed an allergy to shellfish some years before and had learned the hard way that I needed to be very careful of anything containing that ingredient. While recently eating a protein bar, I noticed my fingers getting numb and my entire body beginning to flush.

Oh god, no! I thought.

I looked at the wrapper, and, sure enough, it contained fish oil.

As my entire body broke out in a sweat, and as my throat began to constrict, and my breathing got shallower, something happened.

I remembered.

I remembered who I was.

It was very strange to be heading toward a full-blown allergic reaction and suddenly remember that I am not allergic to anything. I don't have allergic reactions. The I Am presence does not have allergies!

I didn't hope that the allergic reaction would go away or start praying to a god outside of myself for my throat to open up. I remembered. I remembered who I was. Not only did the allergic symptoms disappear immediately, I experienced this expanded state for several hours following the incident.

This was not the result of a miracle, but of being engaged in practice and, I believe, from hearing hundreds of similar stories of healing. Through our intention, our practice of meditation and prayer, through constant study and extended focus, we will find ourselves identifying less and less with a fixed, identifiable self (or multiple selves) and more and more with an infinite Being. As opposed to re-inventing ourselves, we're realizing our true nature. It is clear to me that I am not doing anything special or magical other than continuing to sacrifice the old ideas of who I am and continuing to play a guinea pig in this experiment called life.

The more we become aware of our true nature, the more we exist in a consciousness that is only aware of wholeness and perfect health, only aware of the perfection of its being. This awareness will begin to be reflected through the various bodies.

But, this process of remembering is not instant. It requires patience. Healing takes patience. Insight takes patience. Revelation takes patience. Wisdom takes patience.

Patience is not waiting. It is an act. It is, in fact, a radical act in our society.

Re-Writing the Chapters of Personal Creation

One of the best examples of patience I have ever heard came unexpectedly, as the most powerful things always do. I was at a homeschooling conference and the keynote speaker was science fiction author Tad Williams. I remember finding him to be an incredibly engaging and interesting speaker. When it got to the time for questions, I found my hand going up. It was strange because I wasn't nervous at all. Usually I would feel at least a little nervous energy when speaking in front of hundreds of people. I took it as a sign to pay attention. I asked him what was the best and the worst part of being a writer. I thought it was a question I was asking because of my curiosity about the writing life, but his answer gave me much more than I had anticipated.

At first, he said the best part was the attention and the worst part was writer's block. He laughed and asked if that was what I wanted to know. Then the look on his face shifted into a reflective state. He had been asked a very simple question and had given a very simple answer, but there was more.

To paraphrase, he said, The worst part about writing is when it stops, when everything comes to a halt and nothing is working anymore. Even worse is when I keep on writing anyway, because invariably I end up having to write the whole thing over. At those times, I have to just stop writing for a few days. It's hard because this is how I make my living. I have my agent and my editor depending on me to write. But I have to just stop and do something else. And the best thing—*the best thing*—about writing is, sometimes days after not being able to see how any of it is going to work, suddenly it all makes sense. I'll be just driving down the street, thinking about nothing, and then I see it. I see how this character fits over there and why that character is coming in, how he relates to the story and how it all works together. Then I rush back and start writing again. That's the best part.

What a perfect metaphor for life that is! It's those times when things are not moving fast enough, not going the way we think it should, that we want to rush in with our little ideas. We want to fix things, put in our two cents, and start running the show. We want to control it. Later—sometimes years later—we find that all our efforts were in vain, and we end up having to rewrite that entire chapter of our lives. We might have learned many things, but, in the end, what we really learned was one more way to do life inefficiently. One more chapter on "How not to live a life of excellence and grace," or "How to burn out."

It can seem so much easier sometimes to create it all ourselves. To have a goal and take it and run. To read a book and figure out steps one, two, and three. But this is not living in Grace. This is not Life. Life is a co-creative venture with the unknown. It is the unknown becoming known. Becoming manifest. Being Lived.

It involves the patience to wait for guidance and the faith that there is such a thing. It involves the Faith that we do live in an intelligent universe. The discipline to continue with your practice, especially when you don't feel like it. It involves knowing that the conditioned mind, the ego, is not really manifesting anything. The ego can only bring into its experience what it has previously seen and experienced. It does not have access to the unknown or to different dimensions of being. It only has access to a limiting idea of life. To the data it has taken in through the senses.

We have to be continually reminded that the conditioned mind, the ego, does not have the lowdown on all of creation in its entirety; and that at times, it might not know what is actually best for you. That Life—true Life—is a living, breathing, organic process which is continually unfolding.

Just weeks after that homeschooling conference, I was watching a video on creativity in which the director John Huston was speaking to the very same theme. He was saying that sometimes during a shoot he would know that something was out of whack, something wasn't fitting, and he would wait for a clearer picture, another idea to come to him. He said that in those times it's important "not to spook" and to shoot the scene anyway. There's a lot of pressure because of the money being spent by the minute, and people waiting around for you to roll. There are many things that could easily cause someone to spook in that situation. Most of us end up making a living rather than Living when we get spooked by mounting bills. Or settling for a relationship that we know in our heart of hearts is not in alignment with our true Selves when we get spooked by loneliness. Or becoming one-tenth of the brilliant, beautiful, magnificent, creative geniuses we are in potential because we get spooked by what people might say or think of us living that fully.

If we saw the highest vision for our life, it would be quite different than what we believe is practical or possible. What we usually take into account first is how we will pay our bills, and end up creating a life that pays bills. Our Soul could care less about paying bills. That doesn't mean we need to live on the street or live without being able to take care of our basic needs, but it does mean we need to connect with that part inside us that is absolutely unconcerned with living in order to pay bills and become aware of what it is prompting us to do with our time. In this awareness, we do not deny our responsibilities, but instead embrace a greater responsibility to the Soul. It is here to do Its special work, to use the gifts It has come in with to complete Its mission.

The ego, or conditioned mind, likes to have things comfortable and safe. It likes to know exactly what's going down. It wants to see the road for miles ahead and know exactly what will happen next.

On one level, from the ego's view, living life from your Soul is like driving in a dense fog. You have no idea what's coming. One day to the next is an adventure and a new exploration. In living a soulful life, we engage in our daily practice, listen for and act on the still small voice, and pay attention to the Universe within us. This universe reflects back to us, seeing itself as one in the same. It leads us to new adventures, discoveries, and experiences; to new ways of seeing things; to growing, expanding, and connecting with people while expressing new levels of love in our hearts. We find that even things considered old by time's measure, like a job we have worked for twenty years, a fifteen-year marriage, a residence we have inhabited for thirty years, are all made new. Every day. Every moment. Now.

There is just no end to the possibilities and opportunities. Neither is there any real comfort. Not in the material world. The only real comfort to be found is in the realization that You Are, that who and what you *really* are is timeless and eternal, free and unrestricted by anyone, anywhere, and anything. When you realize that, anything can happen in the world. *Anything.*

And you will not be afraid. You will not be worried. You will not be intimidated. You will not be talked out of what you know. You will not need to defend what you know. You will be part of a deeply rich and soul-satisfying organic process where you feel led and guided by the hand of Life itself. Could there be anything more worth the "wait?"

What Would Life Need to Wait For?

On another level, in another state of awareness, there is no need for patience because patience in itself implies that we're waiting for something to happen. When you are in the eternal moment, there is nothing to wait for because you realize everything is already here Now. There is nowhere to go or be except where you are right in this moment, in this place, in this awareness.

The more we can hang out in this awareness, without following a thought into the past or future, or even into the constructed thought of the present moment, the more we will attract our true Soul desires, because we are hanging out in the awareness of the Soul—in the Now. In the awareness of the absolute perfection of Life. In this space, all of our needs are already met.

When we first hear the phrase "Thou shall not want," we may hear it as a command, but later come to realize it as a prophecy. In the realization of Life as Love Itself, we discover a place where there is nothing to wish for or attain. What would we even need patience for? In a place of total acceptance of what happens, in the knowledge that everything comes to you in order for you to reveal greater versions of your Self, in a complete surrender to the process, a complete Trust in Life, there is no stress, there is no worry, there is no fear.

Knowing that everything is perfection, that everything is working together for your Highest Good, that you are guided and directed, and are acting on that guidance, what would you possibly have to wait for? When you allow Life to live itself through you, you, in turn, *become Life.*

What in the world would Life need to wait for?

When we are in this awareness, to others our actions (or essentially our non-action) may look like patience, but it is no longer an active verb in our life. It is only a word to identify a signal given to us as to how we might proceed in a certain situation. There is no exertion of will in this awareness, no effort, no forceful energy behind the act, only the impulse to just be. To just sit with whatever is present. There is an entirely different level of acceptance of Life and its unfolding process in an expanded state of awareness, and there is no need to try to manipulate or "do" anything of our own will.

Interestingly, when we are aligned, we find we are much more productive due to the added energy available to us as well as the ability to transcend what we call time. Anyone who has a picture of an enlightened person sitting passively, doing absolutely nothing most of the time, definitely needs another frame of reference.

Practicing Stillness

Just as the path to realizing the life your Soul intended will lead you to experience and realize Peace and Joy beyond anything you have ever imagined, it will at times also lead you through a desert of existential loneliness and separation as old patterns and ways of being are vacating your consciousness.

There are times we might even feel so drained and empty that a simple walk across the room seems an insurmountable task. As we move out of mere intellectual understanding of spiritual principles and begin to practice them, we begin to experience these feelings of separation less frequently. It is our practice of the spiritual principles that will sustain us in the end. A practice in which we dialogue with the Eternal, with our Soul. A practice that helps us remember the truth of who We really are. A practice that delights us, thrills us, and awakens us to our Being.

I was in my early twenties when I first started hearing about meditation as a means of attaining greater levels of mental function and clarity. It seemed asinine to me at the time. I didn't have time to sit around and do nothing. How absurd! Look at all those people wasting their time. What space-cases!

As a current member of the space-case camp, I eventually discovered the incredible power of quieting the mind and tuning in to the higher frequencies of Life. At a previous time in my life, a four-day, silent meditation retreat would have been near the top of my Ways to Be Tortured on Planet Earth list, but now experience it as an incredible treat to the Soul. To see thoughts, emotions, and physical disturbances without experiencing them as "me" is a freedom and clarity unsurpassed. Many a time I find myself enraptured in bliss, and it becomes impossible to hold back the tears of gratitude and joy in simply being alive.

During meditation there have been incredible insights, poems and songs, or long-forgotten memories coming to surface in the awareness. Mostly, it is what I take with me after the meditation is done and I "return to life"—or better said, while I remain in meditation throughout the day. There is an underlying peace and knowing in my heart. There is a deeper appreciation for life and a tendency to have more intuitive "hits," greater clarity, and the ability to remain in a firmer sense of equanimity when events in the world appear chaotic. There is the experience of standing on solid ground in the Eternal, and not having to rely on the shaky ground of the physical world for a sense of peace. Even more than any benefit, there is the opportunity to commune with Life Itself, with the Beloved.

I admit this was not my initial experience of meditation. I didn't have any book or instruction that I recall. I just decided that I was going to do it one day. I went and sat, and for the entire ten minutes I could not get the thought "This is the most stupid thing I have ever done in my life" out of my mind. Occasionally, that thought would be briefly replaced with things I could be doing instead of sitting there like an idiot. Those ten minutes were enough to realize there was obviously nothing to the whole meditation thing. Some people might get something out of it, but I was not that kind of person. They must be a different breed, I thought.

It wasn't until years later that I started to experiment with meditation again. It seems what we initially resist the most ends up being positively life-changing.

At a Sunday service I attended many years ago, the monk who was speaking made the remark that it was impossible to realize any level of enlightenment without engaging in a regular practice of meditation. I questioned this then, because I had experienced a "big shebang" type of awakening without ever practicing meditation. I still question this, because there are many different ways to realize ourselves at greater levels. For some, chanting better serves their needs; for others the practice of mystical dancing, drumming, or yoga works better. While I hadn't done any formal meditation before reaching that expanded state, in my early teen years I swam competitively and would swim for an hour or two at a time every day. It was always a time of reflection and deep inner silence.

Even though we may have things that put us into a state of relaxed flow, there is something unique about meditation in its ability to cultivate the observer within us. When we can observe ourselves experiencing, we are truly at choice rather than in reaction. We can experience the emotion, see the thought, and feel the pain rather than just identify with them. They are no longer "my" emotions, thoughts, and pain, but "the" emotions, thoughts, and pain. This simple distinction can put us into a completely different awareness and, in turn, at an altogether new level of choice. The higher our level of awareness of our patterns and reactions—and awareness that we have nothing to do with those things—the greater level of freedom we can experience. We can choose to react with Love, or not to react at all, and in that simple act we will not be releasing our unhealed energy into the collective atmosphere.

Another benefit of being patient in circumstances that would seem to require it, according to our perception of how things should be, is that we find the "favor" being returned. If we can be patient in situations with others in ways that we would appreciate if the circumstances were reversed, we find the universe reciprocating. We find that we are not simply lucky in our dealings with others by attracting patient and kind people, we are actually having returned to us what we are giving most of the time. We might also notice the greatest benefit of all, which is to discover we have more patience with ourselves. We feel relieved of the pressure to perform or to be a certain way, and we can relax into the process of our growth, of our Life, of our Being.

It came again this morning
A knowing
A cool, clear knowing
so different than those restless thoughts of the mind
It breaks through the stillness
a space created
giving the thoughts of the divine
a resting place
a place to call home
Sometimes not able to penetrate that barricade of useless thoughts,
outdated desires,
not yet found their way to their graves.
But

this morning it came again,
this knowing
that
'planted seeds will grow'
If
I could only have the faith of the sun
and know as it knows
It will rise again
in its own time
by its own accord
I remembered how foolish it is to dig up
newly planted seeds
Remembered I am not here to take my cues from the outside world,
from impatient buyers
wanting to buy the fruits before they have ripened
I have come
to be ripened by the sun, by nature herself, by the force of the world
to be held in the palm of life
to let it push its way into me
and test me for my ripeness
To let it decipher the thickness of my skin
my texture
my color
To let it determine my readiness to be used
to feed and nourish the souls of others
And

when I find myself as seed next time
I will remember to fall in love
with the dark soil surrounding me
knowing of its nourishment, its richness, its necessity,
understanding its ability
to shield me from the light
which would destroy me
in the embryonic stage
I find myself in now

Integrity
Aligning with What Is

In all that there is
in this grand universe,
there is only one Life
stepping in verse

Clumsily we try

to march against the grain
and find in the end
our efforts in vain

We pray and we hope
to be set free
but to get right with Life
takes integrity

It is interesting that we usually think of language as our main form of communication, since so much of the time it is severely limited in its ability to communicate on any level of depth. All of us have specific memories and definitions of words, which lead to subtle differences and nuances of interpretation.

What probably comes to mind when we hear the word "integrity" is honesty. Having integrity implies that you are an honest person. Saying one is "out of integrity" is a politically correct, polite, fluffy way for someone to say they believe another is lying like a sack of… well, you get the picture.

A deeper, richer, and more substantial definition of integrity is operating from a sense of wholeness. The word itself implies a state of integration. A state of being absolutely in alignment with your Soul, your true Purpose, your unique gifts and talents, your genius, your heart.. To be "in integrity with" something implies becoming the very thing you are in integrity with.

When you come into alignment with your true Self, you come into integrity with Life Itself. Into alignment with spiritual qualities such as Love, Peace, Joy, Clarity, Wisdom, Beauty and Abundance. As you align with these qualities, you don't just experience them from the ego's perspective. You don't live in the illusion that they are coming *to you* from an experience, a product you've used, or an astrological shift in the heavens. You are no longer under the impression that someone else holds the key to your ability to experience them. You allow them to come over you, so to speak. You become them. They become you. And if you think about it, the only way you could become them, is if you were already, in some sense of the word, "them" to begin with.

We are usually given many roles, and some we may have consciously chosen to integrate into our experience. When we are shopping, maybe we become the bargain hunter. When working out, Hercules. When at work, an organizational queen, etc. We might choose to play these roles, but unless we are consciously aware we are playing them, we might just be playing out roles we have been conditioned to, without any thought as to whether they are serving our Soul's purpose.

Even though we may think of them as serving our Soul's purpose, if we are aware we are playing roles, then we know we are not really in alignment with our greatest potential but have actually created a limited self that goes about doing limited tasks, in a limited manner, in service to a limited idea. The rational mind may convince us that creating various characters or inventing personas will help us accomplish our goals. It may begin filling our psyche with an entire cast to help us with our "purpose," while the true genius—the unrepeatable, unimagined, unique greatness within—goes undiscovered and untouched.

In case you may have gotten a different impression somewhere along the line, God doesn't need any help.

In Reality the conditioned mind doesn't need to create anything, and anything it does create will only end up getting in the way of the complete and utter genius of your being. The point of spiritual growth is to take away the masks, not create new ones in their place. You are here to transcend the personal mind, not make up a new one.

You don't want to fake it till you make it. In fact, you don't need to fake it; you just need to integrate it. Faking it now leads to faking it later. Life never needs to fake it. It *Is*. It just needs to let It be. We have to understand that we never need to think about how to go about creating something, we only need to create the space to allow the true manifestation, the inspired idea, to come forth. We need the patience to let it unfold, without giving in to the temptation of creating with the limited conditioned mind and merely doing what has already been done before.

By playing out a self-created mental role based on the ego's needs, you may indeed become a great actor. If that is what you choose, that is fine. If that is the greatest possibility you can imagine for success in this life, who will argue with you? On a surface level, and especially to other egos, you will most likely look quite wonderful. But real transformation has nothing to do with looking good to others. It has nothing to do with fitting yourself into society's ideas of success. It is an alchemical process that burns away what is not real in order to transform consciousness and realize What Is.

There's self-will, and then there's knowing the Self-will.

Through your ability to sit in the silence of your Soul, through your honest and sincere intention to know yourself and your purpose for this life, through your surrender, the Self will take over. Eventually It will.

The small self, the conditioned self, has to fake it—pretend everything's great when it's not because it imagines it has something to lose. This self is very concerned with losing face, losing its reputation or losing the imagined power it needs to remain under the illusion of control. Out of fear and denial, this self may recite empty words as the proverbial pink elephant tramples upon everything in sight and may resort to projecting everything it can't see in itself onto others. Hiding behind an illusion of control isn't having integrity. Pretending you're somewhere when you're not isn't going to get you anywhere.

What you want to do is be able to recognize and speak to the different patterns and cycles of growth, to discern where you are in those cycles at any given time, and to know that you don't need to fake happiness. In the realm of true Love everything is Good, everything is used for Good, everything leads to Good. You can use whatever energy is present for you right in this moment to catapult your awareness to God Consciousness. Instead of resisting, you can tap into the energy, the pure energy encased within everything, allowing Good to manifest in the physical realm. You see what is Real and you call it out, using the energy present—another opportunity to call out Good. To call out God. To call out Love.

Only the limited perspective of the ego would call something "bad" and want to wish it away. Only the ego would think there was an experience or a power that existed outside of Love. Only the ego would think that it, or anything else, was not Love. Only the ego would need to act, to fake it, to deny it.

Actually, we do need to act. Not with a script in hand, though, feigning happiness we don't truly feel. Not reciting love poems through clenched teeth or by playing a spiritual martyr. But act in integrity with the process, the flow, and the artistic brilliance true growth and transformation really is. Act with authenticity. Act and be real.

One might begin to see a contradiction of sorts here. How can we keep our attention focused solely on Reality while at the same time "be real" and acknowledge negative feelings and energy patterns? In Life, there is no contradiction. It just Is and will always Be. We can understand that level of Reality exists whether we are currently aware of it or not. As we grow and transform from the physical plane, we can use the seeming contradiction, the seeming paradox, in service to waking up to a greater awareness of Life. We can trust that everything comes to us in service to this awakening as we begin to hold the intention to become more conscious of our true Self.

We also have to realize that the integration process itself is just that: a process. A natural, Self-regulating, organic process.

As we begin holding an intention to really know ourselves, to discover and live our purpose, and as we continually act on the guidance that Life lays before us, we will find new roles spontaneously emerging. In fact, instead of calling these "roles," we could see them as energies that have been previously blocked from our experience and awareness due to limited ideas and identities. And instead of calling them new, it is probably more accurate to see them as treasures of the Soul that have been previously buried and unrealized, even though they may feel new since they never had the opportunity or space to be expressed.

There may also be times when, as these new energies and awareness are integrating, they take on a greater role, and may temporarily require more of our time and awareness. We may go through phases where we find certain modes of being as more dominant, only to find their strong influence fading after awhile. They don't completely fade away, but integrate into our everyday way of being. As a new quality of awareness, or as we integrate a new habit on the physical plane into our present experience, it can be a little disconcerting and feel a little strange. We might suddenly become obsessed with certain behaviors, certain fields of interest, certain parts of the world, and certain languages or practices. Even though it may feel disconcerting at times, in the end it feels wonderful to have a part of yourself, in a sense, returned to you. It feels wonderful to experience a greater sense of Self. The energy that begins to express through you can feel like a familiar friend you haven't seen in a long, long time. Even though we might be tempted to personify these energies (*Hey, wild woman! It's been a long time. Where have you been girl?*), we want to realize the difference between making room within our awareness for more of Life to express freely and acquiring a mind full of fixed identities and separate roles.

We may have had the experience of many characters running amok in our psyches, which were created out of either a fear of not being enough as we were, or as a survival mechanism. If you are reading this, know that you have survived. You have creatively made it through those circumstances to get to where you are today. Also know that some of these former ways of being in the world, the ones that kept you alive, may now be blocking the Life that is trying to express through you.

We may play out scenes over and over again, referring to a tattered and earmarked script that was handed to us, sometimes not even aware we've been referring to it. A script given to us by our parents on how to play the role of a good child. A script from our boss on how to play the good employee. A script from our TV or newspaper on how to play a good citizen. From advertisers on how to be good consumers. We look to the outside examples and try to conform and acquiesce to the rules that have been set by a society or family system, which, upon reflection may not have been serving us or those around us at all.

We may argue that these roles have in fact served us well. If we look closer, though, we will probably see they have actually served us in playing a role in a dysfunctional and declining societal system lacking in true vision and community. These roles have not necessarily supported us in realizing our full potential in different areas of our life and cultivating the genius within.

Are we playing the casting director or are we allowing Life to? At a certain stage in the game we may want to cast our own show. Why not? That might be fun. It's one level of theater. If, though, you are ready for the show, the performance, the thrill of a lifetime, you want to let Spirit, Life, your Self, cast the show. Most people who are now living outstanding, tremendously fulfilling and remarkable lives initially resisted the casting call of the Universe. It usually didn't fit into any picture they previously had of themselves.

"Whoa, wait a minute! That's not me. You've got the wrong person here. I think you want so-and-so over there. They could play that part much better than I can."

When we trust and follow Life's wisdom, we may be astonished to find that, indeed, we were perfect for the part. Who would have known? (Well, except for the ultimate casting director, that is.)

Self-realization vs. Self-preservation

When we step away from the information that comes through the channels of a corporate-owned media, we may begin to question what agenda lies under the information and begin to wonder if many of the decisions being made by our leaders are truly in integrity with Life. Are they truly empowering and supporting people at large? Is the focus on creating systems that ecologically sustain and enhance the planet? It seems many times decisions are made in order to sustain a political position and the interests of those who have invested heavily in that leader's position. To sustain an economic system that we in the west have grown accustomed to (using most of the resources on that planet) and wouldn't quite know what to do without. This practice is not in integrity with the expression of Life, but rather integrity with self-preservation. Of course, this happens at the expense of the planet and of society at large. I guess it just can't be helped. Collateral damage.

This misuse of power leads to an unbalanced society and one that is very much out of alignment with Reality. Of course, this misuse of power is only a macrocosm of the way many of us relate to ourselves. Most often, *we* are not looking for ways to empower and support our Higher Selves, to create systems and practices which enhance and sustain a higher vision and align us with Life. We might not be in integrity with the full expression of Life but actually in integrity with our own self-preservation.

This puts us at a supreme disadvantage, because no matter how

Living Beyond Belief

much we may accumulate in the world, no matter how clever and intelligent we may be at self-preservation, at the core of our being there will linger an emptiness or anxiety or a feeling that something is off. Not quite right. We don't want to be caught in preserving our self, in preserving limited ideas and agendas, but instead reviving our Self.

We have been taught to completely overlook our true, inherent power and instead seek to obtain power in the world in order to feel secure. It is only by living in integrity with your Self that you feel a wholeness that can't be attributed to any outward circumstance or person. A true sense of wholeness doesn't depend on anything someone may or may not do. It doesn't come from manifesting great and wonderful things or from accomplishing the mightiest of goals. It comes from within.

A true sense of wholeness comes from being able to find your true voice and communicate from the deepest part of your being. It comes from being able to see yourself in another and have great compassion, love, and understanding for anyone. At any time.

It comes from seeing yourself as the beloved and knowing that you are supported, directed, and sourced by the Universe Itself—not because you're special or have done anything special, but because you have realized that You Are the very universe. And so is everyone else.

It comes from trusting and loving Life to the exclusion of all else and discovering that this does not put you at a distance from others around you and your current projects, but closer to them because you actually *see* them. Their true Essence. As God sees them.

You are not chasing after an idea of life, you are *living It*. You are *alive*. You are flowing with the grace of the Universe, because you are in integrity with your true Life and have no need to pretend you are something you are not, or try and hide the joy and brilliance that you are. And, you are no longer under any illusion that a conditioned mind has anything to do with any of it.

Identifying the Identities

Not too long ago, I had been feeling a little confused since I was getting information that seemed conflicting, yet valid. On one hand, it was said that in Reality there is no fear. Fear is only an illusion. The

194

inferior and weak parts of ourselves are conditioned aspects and only continue to exist because we believe them to be true.

Well, that sure resonated, I thought.

On the other hand, there was the understanding that one needed to accept every aspect of oneself and honor it fully and that by embracing one's shadow, one would find the hidden gold.

Well, dang if that didn't sound true also.

Yet in my experience, I had been having dialogues with my fear, courting my self-doubt, bargaining with my shyness and not seeming to get anywhere except more deeply entrenched and engaged in the illusion and story around it all.

Then one evening I saw the movie *A Beautiful Mind.* The main character realizes that some things are not real. They seem as real as real as anything else around him. But they're not. When he discovers they're not real (and it does take some pretty strong convincing!), his solution is not to give them any attention. I mean, if you knew something had no basis in reality, you'd be a little nuts to continue giving it your time and attention. By refusing to give those things his attention, they began to disappear. They began to no longer have a negative influence on his life. He was then able to get a handle on what was real. There were later times that the illusions appeared to him, but he became very aware that they were only illusions. He no longer engaged them and was able to keep centered on what was really real.

A light bulb went off inside my head: That's why I'm not getting anywhere with these fearful energies. They're not even real. In Reality they don't even exist, and I'm giving them my full attention and asking what I could do for them.

I realized I could spend lifetimes engaging in dialogue with my fear to the point that it became my main focus. My best friend. There is a big difference between consciously directing emotional energy that surfaces in the moment and chronically indulging a small-minded idea that has nothing to do with who We really are. The latter can actually enhance its grip on our psyche and keep us caught in the illusion of separation indefinitely.

Again, this is where the art of growth and transformation comes in. To ignore the pink elephant in the room out of fear and denial will only keep you stuck where you are. To engage the pink elephant and build a nest for it in your living room will leave you with a very crowded house and probably a lot to clean up after. You have to discern where you are in consciousness and whether you are in unconscious denial or consciously choosing to deny the illusion. It is the difference between denial and Denial. The first is what we have all done at times in our lives when something seems too overwhelming to deal with. We rationalize, file the information in our subconscious, and simply "check out." But Denial is very different. It is seeing a negative or fearful situation from what might be called the mountaintop consciousness. It doesn't deny the physical appearance, but consciously chooses to engage in Reality rather than the appearance. This form of Denial may also be called Prayer or Communion or Knowing, and it is fueled by the knowledge that what we focus on we get more of. Thought is creative, and Truly God is all there is.

A side note of this revelation was something that happened as it was unfolding in my consciousness. I had gone to see the movie very late and had left the theater at about one in the morning. There were only a few other people who had seen the movie, due to the late hour on a weekday and the fact that it had just been released. As I walked down the back alley to the parking garage, I realized that I wasn't alone. At the end of the alley, right next to the entrance of the garage there was a very large, very tall, African American man. From appearances, he looked homeless and quite intimidating. Even though I made a mental note of his location and appearance, there was no fear (or any other feeling or assessment) around his presence. My consciousness was trying to fully grasp the impending revelation from the movie and the usual precautions simply didn't register. Nothing else mattered in that moment except the insight that my mind hadn't fully grasped at that point. I walked straight toward the entrance of the garage and, in so doing, walked within a few feet of the man. Right as I was passing him he lunged out at me. He got about halfway and stopped, seemingly frozen in midair. Then he stepped back. My mind was still engaged with the revelation, but I did notice his actions and thought it odd that he would try and spook me.

What a joker, I thought.

I walked up several flights of stairs, still caught in the revelation, seeing all of the implications it would have in my life. It was as if something was being rewired, reworked, reprogrammed, and reconfigured in my brain.

When I got to my car and put my hand on the door, I became very aware of my immediate surroundings, and I suddenly realized, or knew, that the man in the alley hadn't been playing around with me at all. He had fully intended to mug me, or worse. I wondered what on earth had just happened. What had stopped him with such force? It was then that the Einstein quote came to me: "They don't bother me, because I don't live in that world."

There really is a world where none of that exists. A world with no doubt, no worry, no fear, no shame, no anger, no hate, no violence. When that world becomes available to our consciousness it then becomes manifest in the surrounding world.

We could also think of this in terms of energy and vibration. At one end of the scale things like Joy, Peace, Freedom, and Love vibrate at very high levels. The energy feels light. In Truth, We Are the Light of the world.

At the other end of the scale feelings of violence, hate, anger, greed, selfishness, and fear vibrate at a much lower speed. The energy is much denser; it feels heavy and thick. These energies can be used as springboards, as transformational agents, as inspirations to change, but not guides.

Everything in the physical realm exists at varying levels of vibration. When we're vibrating at the level of Love, Joy, Clarity, Peace—God—energy existing in the lower levels cannot touch us because we don't exist in that world. Perfect Love truly casts out all fear. I wonder what kind of world we would be living in if we all lived in that world today? *Can you imagine?* What would our minds be capable of if we consistently lived in a space of Perfect Love? What would our world look like? Who would we be then? What would we do if our time and energy wasn't going into fixing problems?

We have to realize that we will never be able to experience that level of Living if we allow ourselves to continually be fooled by the appearance of physical world reality. We have to realize that there are parts of us, dimensions of our experience, that simply are not real—no matter how real they appear to us and no matter how intense the experience. We have to realize that experience is not the indicator of Reality. We can have experience upon experience of something that has no basis in Reality, but comes from a limiting thought we hold in our awareness. Things that don't even exist in the most Real sense of the word, continue to play out over and over and over again due to our inability to turn our attention from the them in our consciousness.

From this larger perspective of Reality, we may come to see that there may be many ways in which we identify ourselves, all of which originated from a very small idea of reality. Maybe even from a single experience. And from our interpretation of a single experience, without realizing it, we have chosen our destiny. These limited identities, the ones that put us in the proverbial box, do not reflect our True identity. They do not reflect the pure potential of Life that We are.

On the flipside, there are aspects of our Selves, aspects of Life, which we have denied, restricted, or held back, and which would truly enhance our Life experience if we were to realize, embrace, and integrate them. These are qualities and ways of being that are natural to us. They are the authentic ways in which we express. They are not acquired talents, but gifts of the Soul. Even though they are natural to the Soul, they may be seen as aberrations in a highly mechanistic and controlled atmosphere. We may try and hide these so-called aberrations because we have been told at some point on our journey they were not acceptable. Maybe they didn't fit into our own agenda at the time, which may have been as paramount as surviving or as trivial as trying to impress someone. We might have discarded them due to their lack of value in regard to that particular agenda and circumstance.

We might find clues to these natural qualities of ours in something we may have heard repeatedly as we were growing up:

"You're too _____."

Completing that sentence could give us a clue as to where our hidden gifts lie. Genetic influences make the situation very interesting indeed. We might come into the world with characteristics similar to those of our parents and may display aspects that they have fought hard to keep a lid on themselves. This might play out insofar as a son having a very sensitive nature. If the father had a very sensitive nature as well and learned to overcompensate by becoming a macho "manly-man" in order to fit in, his son's sensitive nature can be akin to poking an open wound. This could also play out as an outspoken and intelligent little girl provoking her mother, who has been conditioned to be nice and quiet and "keep a lid on it," at the expense of her deep insight and inner knowing. It can be the free-spirited one with unlimited enthusiasm provoking his father who used to be that way as well, but who had a father who had to show him that such excitable outbursts are not gentlemanly ways of being. We learn very quickly that behaving a certain way is not okay and will not be tolerated. Sometimes these ways of being and behaving are talked out of us, sometimes beaten out of us. We later come to judge that part of ourselves just as harshly as it was judged in us. And the cycle continues.

There is no need to judge the people we may see as responsible for cutting us off from a part of ourselves(dividing us against ourselves), since there are no victims or perpetrators, only cycles of energy that continue to run generation after generation. This social conditioning is also heavily influenced by cultural paradigms and norms. On a Soul level, we have chosen it all. We might want to understand, though, that if we are constantly shamed or hurt for being a way that is natural to us, we will learn to take cues from an outside world as to how we should act, and shut down parts of ourselves that are actually ways of God, of Love, of Genius, expressing through us. Ways of being that are necessary for us to serve our purpose on the planet.

When my daughter was about a year old, I enrolled in a mommy-and-me parenting class through the local community college. The parents were the students and were assigned written papers on our relationship and parenting techniques with our children. It was a wonderful class, not only for the developmental information and feedback, but for the support and connection with other moms. There were two exercises that were particularly powerful.

In one, we had to write the five most important qualities we wanted our children to possess when they were fully grown. We also had to write what we were doing right now to ensure that they would posses those qualities. Another was a discussion and written assignment on labels we give our children and how any label is ultimately disabling. I still remember the phrase used a lot during that time: labels are disabling. Even if we call our kids good, it pigeonholes them into a role and is still a judgment—despite that it's a "good" one. If we call our kids good for things we like them to do and then bad for the things we don't like, instead of understanding the root of the behavior, initiating dialogue, and allowing natural consequences, we end up training and conditioning our kids the way we do a pet.

One of the major parts of the "labels" exercise was to see where we might find something difficult in our child's personality and learn to see it differently. In looking for the lemonade in one of my daughter's lemons—a strong will and stubborn nature—I began to see that her stubbornness was not a sin or a weakness, but had the potential to be a great strength. Time and time again she has astounded me with her ability to run the course in pursuit of her vision when anyone else might have given up. It seems if we don't come to understand ourselves and reflect on our strengths and weaknesses in a compassionate, detached fashion, we could very well become a victim of them. It is utterly ironic that the very things that are our greatest strengths, our genius, have the potential to run us into the ground if they go unchecked and/or misunderstood. We also might end up running others into the ground by condemning them for the very things we have come to harshly judge and misunderstand about ourselves.

"You're too sensitive!" is something I heard a lot growing up. I can see that I have a predisposition towards sensitivity, although I don't know about the "too sensitive" thing anymore. How can you be too much of anything? As if God could have made a mistake.

Probably too sensitive for someone's idea of what is normal or comfortable. And I will say I could have stood to learn how to deal with the intensity I felt. It was like the greatest curse in the world when I didn't know how to deal with feelings that overwhelmed me or when I could only see the negative consequences they engendered.

I could feel when things were off and would become very confused and anxious—disoriented even—when people said one thing but I felt something different. I would question my perception and think I was crazy. I would feel things so deeply and profoundly that what someone else might brush off as a simple remark, I would take as the height of insult, would feel as if I had been stabbed in the heart, intentionally betrayed, and be upset for weeks every time I thought about it. And I just thought that's the way it would always be. That's the way I was born. Cursed. There were times when I really didn't think I could take it any more. Everything was just too much, too raw, too intense. I had to shut down. Shut down the emotion, the feelings, just so I could cope. Just so I could fit in. Just so I could survive! (I also remember hearing something about being too dramatic. Hmmm …)

After a while, I began to see the sensitivity in a different light. Maybe this wasn't a curse. Maybe there was some gold in there too. When I went back to college at thirty-something, I heard from my art instructor: "Wow, you have an amazingly sensitive touch." Hmmm… Then a remark from my literature professor: "An incredibly sensitive analysis." Hmmm …

And one day, during a presentation in another class, I was so touched by something I cried. I got a hug from another participant: "You're so sensitive," he said. He said it as if it were a good thing. Wow! I'd never heard that before. I saw once again that I was just being shown a reflection of how various qualities and dimensions of the Self had been integrated, after coming to terms with, accepting, and even eventually liking the parts I had formerly despised.

To Tell the Truth

As we become more integrated with Life we soon realize that we have a very hard time bending the truth for our personal benefit or comfort. As we grow in the ability to see the Truth of who We are, we are less concerned with defending and protecting egos, and we relate in ways that are more beneficial to the growth, awareness, and freedom of others and ourselves. This integration makes us much more aware that an opinion we hold is only an opinion, only our perception of a matter that is playing out in physical reality, and we aren't attached to it being taken as ultimate truth. We begin to differentiate between the facts and the Truth.

It's not that we become completely incapable of what we would call lying. Sometimes the Soul has its own reasons which the mind (with access only to a limited system of thought) can't encompass. It's just that we begin to understand the Universal or karmic law and realize there is nothing we can ever really "get away with." It will matter less and less what other people think about us, but living with integrity in our Selves, in our Mission, in our Purpose, will be of extreme importance. We will have less and less concern for manmade laws and rules based on a limited understanding of life and of who we are as spiritual beings, but will begin to measure our actions on how true to our Soul we are. The moral obligations and values that have been placed on us by others will begin to dissolve as a higher understanding of integrity begins to reveal itself to us. This integrity allows us to truly Live, to be true to our own values, our own character, our own destiny, to Life Itself. We do this not out of a sense of obligation and fear, but out of a deep and devotional love. We don't have to worry about consequences. They will be there. There are consequences for living within the bounds of manmade laws, of living in conformity and comfort while ignoring the callings of the Soul.

There are also consequences for living from your Heart.

As you truly begin to listen to and make decisions from your Heart, rather than from a constructed belief system, that constructed system and persona will be in conflict. But to be in integrity with the Life within, and have that life reflected in your living, you have no other choice than to live from your Heart.

To live from your Heart, you have to come to know your Heart. At first we may mistake the Heart for being that which brings the emotional and physical bodies pleasure, but seeking pleasure is a limited intention and will bear limited fruit. To fully carry out your Mission, to fully be your Self, you have to go beyond pleasure and into bliss. In this endeavor, you don't seek bliss, you don't look around in the world trying to find things that will bring you into a state of bliss; you listen for the still small voice of your Heart, take action on it, and do what you are called to do. Actions taken on the Heart's behalf align you with who you really are. Who you really are is bliss.

Even though the bliss thing might sound pretty good, the thought of following your Heart can be terrifying. You may feel that you wouldn't be accepted if you came out of the proverbial closet, whether it be the spiritual closet, the homosexual closet, or the "I'm an artist, not a lawyer" closet, but remember that keeping things hidden and buried takes a lot of energy. It may suddenly dawn on you that living in a closet isn't much fun—not too much space in there. A little dark and confining. When we finally get the courage to take that step out of the closet, we may find that the world as we know it begins to fall apart, because whatever was not in alignment with Life, with that vibration of liberation, of freedom, of who We are, begins to fall away, creating space for those activities, opportunities, and people who truly support our newfound sense of Self.

"To thine own Self be true." Not true to the man. Not true to the woman. Not true to society. Not true to limited patterns and agendas. Not true to what we think should be. To thine own Self be true.

To thy own Soul.

When you know you are abundantly blessed, that everything in your world contains unlimited opportunity to be the rich expression of who You are, what reason would you have to try and get something from someone or to try and hide something? What on earth would you possibly need to get away with? The only thing you're "getting away" with when you lie for personal gain at the expense of someone else or pretend to be something other than what you are is a further sense of separation, a sense of unrest and inner conflict, a sense of disease and maybe even the manifestation of physical disease. This puts you out of alignment with who you are, and from that space, conflict will continue to be created and/or you will discover many people lying to you.

Another thing you definitely "get away with" is not having access to the awareness of who You really are, which would, interestingly enough, bring you everything you ever thought you needed to lie or cheat or steal to get—and then some. Not only do you no longer need to lie out of a sense of scarcity or to protect the ego, there also doesn't seem to be much of an option in trying to stay completely politically correct when asked a direct question …

My daughter was on a community softball team when she was about six, and the coach's daughter was a pitcher. There were a couple of other girls on the team who pitched, and the rule was, if you can make it to practice, you can pitch. Well, the coach's daughter had some scheduling conflicts and she was not always able to make full practices, but she still pitched a lot of the time. This caused a bit of an uproar among the parents. I wasn't one of the ones upset, but some parents were upset enough for the entire league.

One afternoon I got a call from the coach. He said the assistant coach had mentioned to him that some of the parents thought the pitching situation was unfair and asked what I thought. I told him honestly that his daughter seemed to be pitching a lot in relation to the amount of practice time. I also told him that he puts in more time and effort than anyone else on the team and that I didn't have a problem with the situation. He was clearly upset by my feedback and started to lay out the entire year's schedule in order to make his case. At a certain point, I had to tell him I needed to go. We might still be there on the phone right now if I hadn't! I told him honestly that I didn't have an investment in being right, but he was the one that asked for my perception of the situation, and I had given it.

During the next practice, the assistant coach thanked me for stating my opinion. It turns out I was the only parent on the team that had said that I saw any favoritism. The parents acted as if they couldn't believe I had said something. I couldn't believe they didn't! I was genuinely and completely surprised by the sudden lack of communication when the sidelines had been so rich with it. And then again, I know there have been many times before when outer intimidation had won out over honest communication in my life. It also seems that when you find yourself intending to be in greater integrity, you may discover situations seemingly arising for the sole occasion of your practice.

How supportive the Universe is!

You can tell when you are sharing from the Heart, in that when someone disagrees with you, it has no effect on you. If you have shared from the ego, you are very attached to the result of your sharing and how it is received. It's fine to share from the ego's perspective, it's just a little exhausting and stressful. Being attached to what other people think and not being open to hearing the other side, takes a lot of energy. In another sense, even though the conditioned mind may hold an intention not to lie, it is less about choosing not to lie and more about becoming aware of who You are. When you know who you are, there is no need to lie about anything, because there is nothing to defend or be right about or protect. No belief system to defend. No personality to shelter. No reputation to uphold. All of these things have the potential to put us into a rigid, fixed, and, ultimately, incongruent state, since our unconscious focus is centered on defending a manufactured identity.

To live Life in integrity, in a state of complete integration and wholeness, you have to be prepared to live a life of total congruency and radical honesty. I don't mean to get weird here, but what if you authentically shared your truth with others? Not just for the purpose of being radically honest, but in order to be radically real, to be radically authentic, radically loving? Just as an experiment. To rest in the most vulnerable part of yourself and just let it fly.

If we were able to get our personal agendas and fears out of the way, we could speak from the soul and say the things we need to say, and therefore have a real relationship with the people closest to us. A real one. Not one where you could only say a partial truth out of fear you'd lose something or where you make so many assumptions about how others would react that you never even give them the chance to do so.

What happens when, out of fear, we don't share what is in our hearts is that we shut down on some level. Then the other person shuts down on some level as well. We can sense when things are being left out of the conversation. Have you ever had something that was bothering you that you wished to share (or something favorable), and when you chose to just "put it out there," you and the other person both came to a deeper understanding. A deeper awareness of Love? Didn't it feel like you had a weight lifted off of you?

True honesty, coming from the Heart leads to transformation. Not more of the same. By being real, we give our relationships the opportunity to go to the next level. And we get to find out if another is willing to go to that next level with us.

We also have to understand that honesty is not the best policy in all situations. You learn to recognize when your words lead to positive change, to clarity, discernment, peace, compassion, and love, or if you are just "being honest" in order to prove something or maintain the illusion of control. Honesty is not about converting others to your rendition of reality or constantly giving unsolicited advice. There are subtleties at work regarding the radical honesty thing that can't necessarily be taught. It is a discernment that comes from awareness, practice, and trial and error. You find yourself just "knowing" more and more when to speak, and you discover your heartfelt, honest communication leading to deeper levels of healing, insight, and relating with others.

And, maybe not initially, but in the long run.

Ask yourself if you currently have a relationship where you feel safe enough to say anything on your mind. An even better question to ask yourself is if you imagine the relationship you need for this level of honesty to exist outside of yourself. All of our relationships are mirrors of how honest we are able to be with ourselves. Self-deception can be a real roadblock to growth.

When you decide to share your whole being with another, including total open communication, open heart, open mind without judgment or limitation, then you are free. It does not even matter if the other person is sharing themselves fully. Eventually, the relationship will not work if your intentions are not in alignment. You will inevitably attract people who are more aligned with your level of openness and ability to express from the Heart.

On some level, there is not even a real relationship unless there is an element of radical honesty and congruence. A real relationship is built on the solid foundation of truth. A radical level of honesty does not take away from the mystery of the relationship when you are living the Mystery. In that space, you are always discovering something new. There is nothing mysterious about hiding your feelings out of fear.

If it is your pattern to try to get people to love you while inwardly feeling that some past action is so horrible no one could ever love you, you might want to think about a new strategy. If you are identifying yourself as who you were in the past, you are limited by those identifications. If you have truly transcended the old patterns, the old identity, the old life, there would only be one reason for you to share your past and that is to give examples to inspire others to transcend theirs.

Self-love and self-forgiveness are absolute necessities before we are ready for a truly conscious relationship. We have to do the deep forgiveness work with ourselves, with all of our imagined mistakes, until we ultimately realize that though we might do things differently now, we did the best we could at the time; and that everything that transpired was and is an opportunity for a greater awareness and expression of Love. This kind of understanding makes it hard to label anything a mistake. We don't identify past actions as parts of ourselves, but as past experiences that have no influence on our current experience. In fact, in Reality the experience never even took place.

If a relationship is issue-driven, most of the relating will be done out of fear. Past disclosures might be used as leverage to win an argument or to prove a current case, and the trust will be broken. We can use our relationships to realize greater expressions of love in others and ourselves, but not when we are going to them in search of ourselves. We have to realize that if we haven't done a good amount of inner work to release old patterns and stuck energy, our relationships will continue to be issue-driven. After all, we are still, for the most part, issue-driven.

If we have discovered the Love within and have come to truly appreciate the many aspects of ourselves, we won't go into relationships seeking something other than a space to share and to give. The true purpose of a relationship is not to fill parts of ourselves that don't feel whole. In doing that, we end up in a state of fear because we are relying on the other to make us feel whole when it is not their job. We become fearful they will leave us because we imagine them to be giving us the security or confidence that no one can truly give anyone. We might begin to compromise or change our values to fit more with the other person's ideas or dreams. There is a huge risk in sacrificing the life of the Soul in order to sustain a relationship that we have no business being in to begin with.

In true Soul partnerships, there might be times of compromise in schedule, in opinions, in living quarters, but never, never, never in the Self. If you think about it, who on earth would want us to compromise our Self, our Love? (Except for a fearful, controlling ego.)

If our intimate relationships are not helping us to see the greater aspects of our being and inspiring us to greater levels of love, we need to seriously consider what we are doing in them. If we are doing our personal work and not taking a victim stance, we must ask why we have chosen a relationship that does not serve the Love within and what it is reflecting to us. If our home is not the haven it has the potential to be, it is not worthy of Us. Many people seem to expect relationships to do what they need to be doing for themselves. You don't leave and find another to become happy; you realize the happiness within yourself and are able to give from that space of joy. You realize the peace and comfort in knowing your own Soul. You realize the adventure of Life, and you gain confidence in yourself by going out into the world and playing—in finding ways to express yourself and discovering your unique gifts so that you can share them with others.

If you are looking for love in another person because you don't have it in your life, you are going to attract someone who is looking for love outside of themselves as well. In that dynamic when your partner does something beyond the range of what is acceptable or right to you, your ability to experience love is threatened because you were under the illusion that the love was coming from someplace outside of yourself. If, however, you are already in love with Life, with your Self, with your Being, and your beloved does something that you don't agree with, it's not that big of a deal. You know your ability to feel and express love does not depend on their actions and are therefore not dependent on them for your happiness. You don't need them to act or be a certain way for you to be comfortable. You can be deeply in love and also be able to discern whether that relationship is generative and if both of you share the same values and are committed to the same degree of growing and expanding.

There is a freedom in this kind of relationship that is not present when we are under the illusion that the other person is supplying us with love. Certain limiting beliefs may surface to be released. Old wounds may surface to be healed. Much healing and growth can come out of a relationship that is not entrenched in fear.

If every emotional release or mental disagreement becomes a threat to its existence—and not just the existence of the relationship but the existence of love in your life—you become a captive participant instead of an unbounded free Soul. In this scenario, you are not free to love, but actually burdened by it. To that romantic who wants to bleed for eternity for the only one in the world who will ever be able to make them feel so loved or who must bear unthinkable atrocities in order to be with the one they love, this may look like a cold and indifferent approach to relationships.

It is only when you've had enough of the rollercoaster of "love," (which is nothing more than a projection party—a projectionship, if you will) that you are ready for real love. One where you are not totally dependent, not totally independent, but somehow both and yet neither, as you become interdependent. You are a team in the highest sense. You get to explore and develop your own unique way of doing a relationship without any former conditioning or past experiences to tell you how it should be done. You get to create something that has never been created before. You get to move into greater expressions and create things that would be impossible if you were operating by yourself. In a larger sense, Life is being served by the relationship as the relationship relates with and reflects You. When it's in integrity, that is.

Soul Integrity

No matter how tempting it may be to concentrate on a world (including relationships) outside of ourselves, the most important relationship to us and everyone around us is the one we have within ourselves. We can be in integrity with the intentions of the Soul, and with those intentions find the blessings too big to receive. When we have Soul integrity with our actions, we align with Life, and that alignment allows the manifestation of things that nourish the Soul, as opposed to filling personality needs or ideas of what we think we need. The next step is to have Soul integrity with our thoughts.

Not only do we act with integrity, but we think with integrity as well. In fact, we might want to start here, at the source of our world—the thoughts we choose to focus on. We can take total responsibility for our emotional responses while not falling under the illusion that anyone can make us feel a certain way. When a person or situation causes upset, we work with that energy until there is no longer a charge for us. In doing this work, we not only free ourselves, but on some level we help the entire collective consciousness move forward. This work, this inner adventure, to heal whatever takes us out of our peace is the greatest work we can do on the planet, since we know that it is our consciousness that is creative. Each time we uncover and release what is not true about us and other people, we allow for the greater expression of what Is to come forward, and in that transaction, we have access to previously untapped energy. We can then allow more Soul to express, more Heaven to manifest, and more dreams to awaken for us and for the person we were involved in the struggle with as well, since we are not holding them captive with judgment (i.e., our inability to see the Truth of who they are).

After eleven years of marriage, I was finally a free woman. I started dating again, and I had found myself saying the dreaded line quite frequently: "This is just a friendship for me." For some reason, there was an incredible amount of guilt associated with the exchange.

I found romantic relationships to be my Achilles heel, and I decided to stop dating for awhile until I could sort things out. I wondered why I kept attracting the same type of relationships and why I felt so guilty ending them. I mean, if something is not for you, it's not for you. But the "let's just be friends" thing was always taken so personally. I started to wonder how I would handle such a statement if it was coming my way under the same sort of circumstances. Wouldn't you know, I finally got my chance to find out. Isn't life just grand?

I fell head over heels for a guy a few years back and then later found that he was in the process of ending the relationship he had been involved in before we had met. Eventually I found out that the relationship was not ending, only on hiatus while the couple worked on some things, but only after I had sent out a handwritten ten- or fifteen-page letter baring my soul to him. Hey, you only live once right?

Well…that's another subject.

Anyway, he called to tell me that our relationship was just a friendship for him. It was very strange when he said that. I felt sadness and relief at the same time. I also had to seriously consider whether this was a friendship I wanted. We shared many common goals and values, and I found that I really did love him—meaning his happiness was more important than what I wanted from him.

It was an incredible test to remain in integrity at varying levels— at least, in the beginning it was. I noticed how easy it was to drift off into fantasy about him. I noticed my reaction when he would talk about other women. I also noticed when I began to get a handle on my consciousness and could be at choice in the matter. To truly be a friend. Not a vulture masking as a friend.

When we have a sense of wholeness, of integrity, we are in alignment with what is natural within us and cannot blame others for anything. We realize that people who formerly drained us or triggered us energetically are unable to have that same effect when we are grounded in the awareness of who We really are. When we are in integrity with our Selves, we continue to use the tools we have to weed out unwanted and unconscious ways of experiencing life. We come to integrate the many aspects of ourselves in order to eventually transcend a sense of separateness altogether and realize our Self.

In the end there is only one true identity, which, paradoxically and ironically, is actually a lack of identity. Personal identity, that is. Which, paradoxically and ironically, becomes more unique and individualized in its *lack* of personal identity.

What seem to be different roles we play are not separate identities that live within us. If we think of them this way, these identities may all have their own agendas, intentions, and personalities that may leave our minds feeling very crowded and very confused.

We really only have one identity—One Life, One Love— expressing through us in a multitude of ways. When we are in integrity with Life, our life becomes a life lived in Grace.

Grace takes diligence. Grace takes courage. Grace is not something you can force. It is the hand of God in your life. Even though you can't force it, you will begin to experience it when you begin to choose Love over whatever might be more convenient to you in the moment.

Grace comes by taking action on Love's behalf, rather than taking action on an idea of what is right according to a particular mindset, a limited identity, in a particular circumstance. It comes from putting your dreams and your true loves ahead of what may be popular. It comes from knowing yourself so well that you begin to clear the conditioned debris of your mind and have greater access to the song of the world, which is being broadcast 24/7.

Not everyone can hear the song of Heaven. It is available to everyone but will only be heard by those who take the time and the effort to find the channel. Things seem to happen as if Life Itself is conspiring in our favor. It's in our corner in the ring of life, although we find we have no desire to fight or compete. The only fight is within ourselves to battle those false parts of ourselves that would have us believe we are "less than" or "better than" or that we are separate at all. After the battle, we come to see that there really is only One Power. We realize we spent all that time wrestling with nothing but empty air. It was all just our imagination.

As we allow what is not real about us to fall away, we become amazed at how clear and beautiful everything really is. We don't live in pride, but in gratitude for the awareness of our True nature. When we leave behind the parts of us that were blinding us to the Truth, we begin to experience the divinity in everything and everyone around us.

Why do I entertain
these guests
I have no passion for?
no common values?
no heartfelt love?

Why do I take them in as my own
And feed them my rapt attention
while they trample across my clean floor
and leave their grime
and grit
for me to clean later
And with their pontificating presence
they leave a shower of lies
trails of untruth
a sea of confusion in their wake

and again
I wonder
how it was,
these guests

these small unconsidered thoughts

powerless in themselves
came to find their way to my temple of awareness
and why
again
I did not have the strength
or courage
or conviction
to simply
not invite them in

Unconditional Love
Beyond Manipulation

It's suddenly all so wonderful
so brilliant and so real
it's all the things that you've been told
but never thought you'd feel

It's the beauty of a dream
that's been cherished by the heart
that suddenly comes to life
and brings a brand-new start

You've searched for this elusive love
and traveled oh, so far
but in the end you come to realize
it's who You really are

Every human being wants love, from the serial killer to the greatest philanthropist. As a species, we crave love and attention. It might be said that some of us have been more successful in finding love, while the more destructive and dysfunctional element in our society have not.

We have come to think of and experience love as something that someone gives us. We usually believe we are quite lucky to have found this love. We might then "love" someone for a time—until their behavior doesn't fit into our model of "good" anymore—and then find that we have feelings that are quite the opposite of love. We may then have the experience of falling out of love. Maybe now we'll find the one, we think. Maybe fate will be kind to us this time. Or maybe we'll be unlucky in love and be subjected to a life "without love."

Most of us actually have no idea of what real love is.

Real love is not an emotion stemming from a positive projection. It is not a feeling you get from someone when he or she looks the right way and says the right thing. It is not something you ration out when someone meets your criteria of deservingness.

These things are not love. They are terribly limited ideas of what true love really is. They are hostage-holding paradigms of love.

Most of our notions of love have come from greeting cards, not examples of real love. They come from ideas that love is contingent upon a stimulus outside of us. Our personal examples of love may be ones of inflated emotional states, not opportunities to act from our heart in spite of our desire to act in judgment. Our notions come from emotional addictions, infatuations, and romantic ideas rather than the understanding of what it takes to hold another in real love. We have been taught that love looks a certain way, feels a certain way, acts a certain way, when in truth the heart doesn't operate in the mind's land of hard and fast rules.

The mind is one for rules. The Heart is one for Love.

Some people might say that the heart is one for feeling, but when most people say "feeling," what they are referring to is emotion. Emotions come in response to stimuli. Even a positive emotion, when it comes from an outward stimulus, is not of the Heart but a reaction of the emotional body. This may sound like a dehumanization of the heart, but it is just a way to make clear a subtle distinction between the Heart and the emotional body emitting signals, whether negative (bad) or positive (good). We've been taught that the heart is impulsive and flighty, that it is irrational and can get one in much trouble when followed. On the contrary, one gets in trouble when one is not in touch with one's Heart. One gets in trouble when one doesn't know what love really is and is only in touch with an idealistic mental concept that they are constantly trying to make real.

The Heart has no such intentions. It doesn't seek anything. It just Is. It doesn't think anything; it just knows. It doesn't just feel love, it recognizes itself as such. It is not sourced by the affairs of the world, but by the realization of Itself, of Beauty, of Life. The information the Heart contains doesn't come from an understanding of the physical world, but from the knowledge of Heaven.

It is the Heart that knows the power of true Love. The person who knows the power of the Heart is a person to be reckoned with, since they aren't serving a personal idea of love, but Love Itself. The Heart does not lead one paddling in various directions on a whim, chasing pots of gold over the rainbow or pining for princes to arrive on white horses. The Heart leads one to their True Life. It leads them to the Truth of one's Being. To the Space between the spaces, in the ever-present moment.

In this understanding of the heart, we see that love is not the airy-fairy, delusional state we may have bought into or become cynical about. It is only irrational to the fixed and conditioned mind. It is not unreasonable, but has reasons the mind and our personal agenda and preferences cannot understand. We find we don't want to choose between our minds and our hearts, but that we need to allow our bodies and minds to be used for our Heart's purposes. We also come to realize that love is not the cause of our suffering, but our personal understanding and use of it is. When we are no longer serving a fantasy but serving real Love, we find a totally different experience of love.

In truth, no one can make us feel anything. When we find ourselves falling out of love with another person, something is surfacing in order for us to heal. It was not a mistake that we initially found ourselves so attracted to and enamored by this other being. Many times what we consider to be love is only a projection of what our Soul is trying to get us to realize and express in our own lives.

In the beginning, we experience this other person making us feel alive because we can see so clearly in them what we cannot yet see in ourselves. It would make much more sense to put our energy and focus into discovering our true Self. When we are operating from a sense of wholeness and vitality, happiness and bliss, we may then be open to a partnership with another. From a state of wholeness, we would have a better sense of what we really need from a partnership. This need wouldn't be for filling something that feels empty, but fulfilling a true need of the Soul.

This doesn't mean that you will no longer be growing in the adventure of love; it is just that you will no longer be waiting in any way, shape, or form for something outside of yourself to fulfill you. Usually, instead of doing the work to find our Selves, we work on finding someone else. Many times we use relationships not to serve or to grow, but to distract ourselves from what our Heart is telling us. In distracting ourselves from what we need to be paying attention to, we project that tendency onto the other person. We then end up with two boats without a sail, each telling the other what direction they should be going.

The truth is, we can't really share ourselves with another until we have realized a Self to share. We can share our personal opinions, our personal preferences, and our personal experiences, but we won't be able to truly share our Selves if we don't have a sense of who we are beyond our ideas of who we are.

As discussed earlier, all of our relationships are mirrors. Whatever sort of love relationship we find ourselves in currently, we can use it to our benefit in order to grow.

Seeking true love and not settling for anything else is a daunting endeavor indeed. We may begin by searching through the Personals, but in the end realize that if we haven't fallen in love with ourselves, no one else will either. Not really. They may fall in love with their idea about us in the beginning, but soon enough that will become evident.

Many people might be content with a superficial relationship and end up with partners who are only involved to satisfy their egos. Relationships that are ego-based can be very hard work. It's very hard to control another person's behavior. To make someone be the person you wish they would be. To satisfy a black hole.

In the past, partnerships were formed from the necessity of physical survival, a need that is becoming obsolete in western culture. As women gained the ability to thrive without a man as a partner, we came together in partnership for different reasons. We then had emotional and sexual needs that wanted to be satisfied. Stereotypically, the woman "needed" the former and the man "had to have" the latter. We also came to have spiritual agendas, and longed for our soul mates.

As we do our inner work, we identify more and more with our true Self.

We find that more of our needs are taken care of by the Spirit and by the awareness of our Selves, which makes us more independent of personal need and less dependent on others to fill the places within us that feel incomplete. We are more able to give without strings. We are able to give independent of need because we have realized our sole source. Our Soul source. The source of our Heart.

As Spiritual Beings, we really only have one true need: to know our Selves. When we don't know our Self, we feel incomplete and end up chasing our ego needs around like a dog chasing his tail. When you realize the True Nature of your being, you are "in love." Now. With or without a partner, since that is your True Nature. If you are already in love with Life, with your Self, what would the purpose of an intimate relationship be? If not based on filling personal needs, on finding how to get what you want from the other person, it would it be based on…what?

The needs of the Soul to give, to receive, to express?

On Love. Sharing. Service. Creativity.

One could say that the ego wants love, but it really doesn't want love at all. It only wants its idea of love. A love where it gets what it wants. Where its need for control and comfort are met. Where the physical, emotional, and mental bodies are kept satisfied based on a limited idea of what is possible.

The ego, from a sense of separation, asks the questions: "What do I need?" and "What can I get?"

A Soul-centered relationship is entirely different because it is not built on personal need but on True Love. The couple comes together out of love, not fear. The purpose is not to fill up the missing pieces in each other, but to complement one another, to form a partnership that enables them to create something in the world they could not do alone, and, ultimately, to "fill up" the world in a positive way.

As we personally evolve from survival-based to service-based beings, our relationships will reflect this inner transformation. When we come more into alignment with our true Self, the question shifts from: "What can I get?" to "What can I give?" which *changes absolutely everything.*

Many may be surprised by and critical of the high divorce rate, but how can we expect marriages to last when we go into them trying to fill a personal need? How can we be expected to love the way we need to love in order for our Soul to thrive, when our cultural paradigm of love is an immature ideal with ego expectations, agendas, and rules? At a time in our lives when we probably have no idea who we really are and what on earth we are here for? Should we really be expected to keep a commitment to another that was made from a previous understanding of Life? Made from a previous identity that no longer has anything to do with who we are? If you are growing, your understanding of who You are and what You're doing here grows as well, which would undoubtedly effect the focus, choices and decisions of your life. What our Soul wants in a partner and what our ego wants in a partner could be two very different things.

We compare current divorce rates with a bygone era and assume that we are regressing. We forget that it's very easy to keep a relationship going when one party is subservient. There's not much of a true relationship at all in that scenario. As the patriarchal paradigm continues to fall away women are increasingly independent and truly able to choose. Some of these choices may initially come from a sense of personal empowerment, but as women—and men—become more spiritually aware, they make choices that empower the Soul, as opposed to decisions that simply empower the personal sense of self.

The high divorce rate may also mirror people's relationships with the religion they were raised with. People realize there are other options and become empowered to seek alternatives to what they were raised to believe. They can enter into a real relationship or marriage with Spirit rather than one that is unquestioning and subservient to outside rules.

At first, this relationship may be sought to satisfy ego needs as well, but if the intention remains to grow, it will evolve into a deeper awareness of Love and desire to be of Service.

True spirituality empowers the Soul, but not the ego. To say that it empowers the Soul is not accurate. The Soul *is* Power. You can't empower Power, but you can become aware of it on increasing levels. The ego is concerned with rules and being right, with safety and acceptance, and with getting what it wants.

On the other hand, the life that is filled with miracles, filled with peace of mind, filled with love, filled with Life, is one lived without much regard for rules—especially its own rules. In fact, It has little regard for itself at all. The conditioned self, that is. It desires to be love more than it desires to *be* loved. In being Love, Love is what is reflected back. Period.

You have to give real Love though. Not your *idea* of love. Your idea of love is limited and therefore will produce the result of a limited idea of love being reflected back to you. There are no limitations in Love. There are no hard and set rules. There are no conditions. There is no way to even know what true Love is until you begin to know your true Self. When you come to know your Self, you will come to know Love—a Love beyond your ideas of love, reflecting a Self beyond your ideas of self.

This is not a personal love, but a love that transcends the personality. A love that makes the personality quite uncomfortable and makes it want to shout at times, "Hey, what are you doing?" It is Love that doesn't have any particular idea of how it may manifest itself in any given moment. And doesn't much care to have an idea about it, either. True Love outlives a simple idea of love. True Love never does it "for your own good." And then again, it just might. True Love goes beyond being nice and into being Real. True Love asks to be used but doesn't become a doormat. True love holds no conditions. True Love does not base its conclusions about another person on his or her actions, yet is able to see the person in a clear light. True Love knows everyone else as Love, since it knows it as Itself. True love knows anything is possible. Especially the so-called impossible things.

To live in true love you have to be gullible enough, naive enough, silly enough, daring enough, bold enough, in love enough to really, *really* believe the "all things" part.

All things are possible.

All things. *All* things. All *things*.

All things.

What would this not include? There are no clauses.

Well, except the prepositional phrase that precedes the "all things" part.

With God.

With Love. With the *awareness* of Love. With the awareness of *Truth*. Of Beauty. Of Peace. Of Compassion. Of Joy. Of Freedom. Of *Vision*.

Anything can be accomplished with the awareness of these things themselves, not with our ideas about them.

An idea of what love would do will never produce the same results as what real Love would do. An idea of love would only be able to produce results from a mental idea that a person carried about love. It would definitely be in a higher intention, and therefore in a higher vibration than a more limited ego intention, but it would still be producing from the mental arena.

When you enter the arena of the Heart, you find yourself in an entirely different playing field. Love is the most powerful force in the Universe. There is nothing wimpy about it. It is not a romantic ideal, but its presence does awaken the romantic within us as we are dazzled and delighted by the beauty and possibilities that surround us.

The Conditions of Unconditional Love

There was once a study conducted on the effect of prayer on plants. The experiment followed the growth of three plants. The first plant was the control plant and was given sunlight and water, but that was the extent of its care. The second plant was given the same conditions of sunlight and water, but in addition, prayers were given for its growth. It grew faster than the plant that was only given the sunlight and water. The third plant illustrates the power of unconditional love: it was given the same conditions as the second plant—sunlight, water, and prayer—but there were no specifics to the prayer. There was no wish or expectation for it to grow or to do anything. It was simply loved for what it was. In that atmosphere of unconditional love, the third plant shot above the others.

What we think of as love is pretty powerful.

A positive thought directed toward someone or something for a specific effect can produce results. Real Love, though—Love without any conditions or agenda whatsoever—is powerful beyond belief. It is free to operate independent of the limitation of our simple ideas of good. It blows what we think of as love out of the water.

It is the faith that says, "You go, God."

When we allow the space for whatever form of Love wants to emerge, without our personal self getting in the way and trying to direct the course, we allow Love to direct it. In the energy of unconditional love, Life is allowed to positively thrive, far beyond our ideas of thriving or our ideas of what is possible.

When we can surrender our ideas, even our positive ideas, of what life should be and just simply love it, our lives begin to truly astound us. It moves to a level we could not have previously imagined. It is in this energy of freedom, of trust, of real Love that we find our Self.

This is the kind of love that some of us can't even imagine, which is good.

It is not to be imagined.

It is to be practiced. It is to be lived. It is to be mastered. Finally, it is to be realized as our True Nature. Anything less is an excuse to be less than we are capable of being. Anything less is a ticket to a lesser, more contracted, more mundane version of our life.

When our personal agenda comes into alignment with our Soul's agenda to realize Love on deeper and more profound levels, we may begin to notice a very interesting dynamic. We can only love others to the extent that we love ourselves. Or, said another way, we can only be in love with others to the extent that we are in love ourselves. When we are in love with life and with our lives, we tend to treat others in a totally different manner than if we're berating and judging ourselves or complaining about things. If we can't love ourselves unconditionally, we will never be able to share that level of love with others. We can only give to others to the extent we have given to ourselves.

In the end we find that sharing love is not so much a cause-effect dynamic, a you-give-me-this and I'll-give-you-that scenario, but simply a realization—a revelation that Love is really all there is. And that everything else is an illusion.

From this perspective, we can see that if we really love someone, the greatest gift we could ever give them is to love ourselves more. This is not selfish behavior, but Selfish. It is a paradox we must understand in order to really love one another. When we are in alignment with who We are, through Selfish behavior, we can love and support others in a way that we are not able to when we are just trying to please them. Such "pleasing" behavior is usually rooted in fear.

To really love, appreciate, and take care of ourselves so that we are able to love, appreciate, and take care of others is truly the only way to love. If we love at the expense of ourselves, it is only a matter of time before we will burn out or take care of others with resentment and judgment instead of the love and care we think we are giving them. The only way we can give or love at the expense of ourselves is if we are giving and loving out of a limited idea based on separation and fear—fear that our life is passing us by, that we won't ever get what we think we need to be happy, or that we won't be loved in return.

We have believed the lies that we are not enough and that we need to have certain conditions and things present outside of ourselves in order for us to be happy. If we live our lives as martyrs, working for what we believe is right, or if we "give" while condemning and judging those who are not giving as we think they should be, we are ultimately spending our time in an energy of judgment and condemnation—not in Service or Love.

If, in turn, we tune in to the energy of love in our Heart, we may feel compelled to share a perspective that empowers and strengthens the awareness of Spirit, compelled to unearth and reveal that which is being done out of fear and which is out of alignment with Life. But once we come to know the invisible realm as the Real and the physical realm as the potential manifestation of the invisible, of the Real, we are much more compelled to speak the Truth as opposed to report the facts. The Truth is, what we focus on expands. The energy we do something in is just as important as the task itself.

We don't speak in order to be right or to condemn or point fingers. We speak to awaken. We speak to enlighten. We speak for all souls to be free—even the ones we may have deemed the wrong-doers. We know that whatever wrongdoing someone has done, nothing they have ever done could change who they are. If it goes for us, it goes for everyone. If we are ruthlessly judging ourselves, we will ruthlessly judge others.

Even though our conditioned mind tells us that we will be trampled on and taken advantage of if we don't punish and condemn, this is not the case. If we are truly in a state of unconditional regard, others are lifted to that state as well.

In order for the collective to progress into an even greater expression of what it means to be human, and ultimately to demonstrate what humanity may look like as it evolves into its next form, we will have to sincerely experiment in the area of unconditional love. Blaming, shaming, and punishing will never be a solution for peace because it does not help the wrong-doer see who they really are, it only adds to the subconscious belief they have about themselves (usually then projected onto others) that they are somehow bad. Flawed. Evil.

The only thing that will end the cycle of violence and retribution on our planet is for people to understand their True Nature. In this understanding, it makes no sense to fight an illusion. Any illusion. To fight an illness. To fight for a cause. To fight another or project our unhealed issues onto others. Instead of having an agenda to expose and condemn others as we catch them in the act, we need to see them as God does. Instead of a rush to judgment, we need a rush to healing. Punishment perpetuates, Love awakens and heals.

We must become motivated to understand what might motivate someone else to act as they do. We must understand that it is a sense of inner powerlessness which leads one to seek external power at the expense of others. We must see that it is a deep-seated fear and lack of spiritual connection which leads to gluttony and greed. When we acknowledge that we, too, have those same impulses within us (and remember times we may have acted upon them), we can have compassion for those we see as acting unconsciously from a sense of separation.

What if, instead of pointing fingers, we pointed loving thoughts in their direction? What would happen if we held them in the highest possible regard, despite our opinions, despite our mind's objections? What if we refused to buy into the illusion, the scene our physical eye beholds, and bought into the Truth instead? What if everything really was working together for Good? What if it were true that we *are* really One, and that what we do for another we do for ourselves? What if the least among us appeared, on the physical plane, to be the most powerful, but were actually the most spiritually deprived?

The Honeymoon

If we are absolutely in love with Life and only choose to participate in those things that honor the precious gift Life is, those that bring the awareness and experience of Beauty, Peace and Joy, we serve Life. If we have an idea of what is right because others have said it was so, then we sacrifice our happiness, joy, and wellbeing to do this right thing, we are not serving our Soul, our Self, our Life, and in the scheme of things, we are not really serving anyone else either. These ideas of what love, life, and spirituality are may not have anything to do with what they really are, but with what we have been told they are supposed to be. In this idea, we might believe we need to sacrifice very real parts of ourselves, our curiosity, our exuberance, our healthy skepticism, and our discerning minds in order to fit into that idea. We might end up handing over our life to a monotonous and lifeless service, to a system that someone else created in order to fit nicely into someone else's idea of what spirituality is.

A Soul that continually frees itself from limitation, continually realizes Itself, and continually falls in love with Life, needs nothing from anyone other than to participate in Love, to share with and create with. This Soul doesn't need to recruit or be right. It does need to *Be*. It needs to be Love, to be Compassion, to be Beauty, to be Clarity, Wisdom, Joy, and Peace. It can only display these qualities to the extent it has been able to realize them as Itself. No more, no less—at least not with any consistency and especially not long after the honeymoon.

The honeymoon period is not just limited to a romantic relationship. It occurs in any relationship where there is a great deal of excitement and energy in the beginning stages. It can be a relationship we have with a business partner, a friend, or a group.

We have all personally experienced coming back to reality after the honeymoon period. In actuality, we aren't coming back to "Reality" (i.e., to realization of the unbounded and eternal Self), but we are coming back to the negative patterns that were unconsciously limiting us before this meeting occurred. We have glimpsed into the realm of what is possible, of the way things are all the time in the awareness of Heaven on Earth, but we can't hold that level until we release the suppressed, unhealed energy from within. It has come to the surface to be released and healed. This is our opportunity. This is our gift.

When old patterns and limited ways of being surface within us, it feels like anything other than a gift, but if we continue to hold the intention to heal, to integrate, and to love, we can do the work and find ourselves back in that elevated level of awareness more consistently. This stored, unresolved energy in ourselves has been brought to the surface by the high vibration and energy of Love. If we fail to recognize it for what it is, and revert to a pattern of separation and judgment, we miss the opportunity.

Great love will bring to the surface that which is not of great love.

It surfaces to be healed. If we can have the humility to ask for help in these circumstances, to do projection work, to own what is ours and release it in order to further purify our hearts, we will find ourselves eventually living in that world we initially caught a glimpse of through those people or events.

The whole process, the whole of life, is designed for us to realize our True Nature. To realize that we are Love. Since our experience of the outer world is a reflection of our current state of consciousness, we begin hearing positive feedback more frequently when we treat ourselves in a more loving manner.

The clincher, the real irony, is that the positive feedback will be appreciated, but no longer hoped for or depended upon as it was when we were looking for it outside ourselves. We don't hope for and feel a need for what we know we already have an ample supply of.

Where is our supply?

At this moment, we probably have an abundance of water at our disposal. As we go throughout our day, we know that if we get thirsty we can get some water. We can go to the tap, to the well, to the drinking fountain, to the cooler, to our supply of bottled water, to the market, etc., where we know water is at our disposal if we are thirsty.

In the same respect, when we realize Love as our True Nature, we are freed from the illusion that there is a source we need to depend on in the world. We have learned to tap the spiritual well and no longer depend on the material world to fill us. We know that we can realize this Love within at any time, and we don't depend on a particular person, event, or substance to fill us in a particular way. We become clear about our supply and our source. We also become more and more aware of what we can do on a daily basis to tap that well consistently.

Imagine if we came to the conclusion that our water supply was dependent on another person? What if only one person could supply us with water? How much energy and attention might we try and give this person so they would supply us with what we think we need from them? How much of ourselves might we sacrifice in order to stay in good favor with this person, since we are under the impression (i.e., the illusion) that our very survival is dependent on continuing to get water from them? What might we try and hide about ourselves so that we might fit into this person's ideal? Into their idea of perfection? And not even this person's idea, but our idea of their idea of the ideal.

Is there a god we imagine to be outside ourselves that holds an ideal of what we are supposed to be? Do we imagine that we will become enlightened when we fit perfectly into this ideal? What ways might we be blocking the energy of our Heart in order to fit into a limited idea?

The truth is we don't need to compromise our Self in any way to be in Love. In fact, that's usually where the trouble starts.

While there are spiritual teachers committed to doing their own

226

work who can assist us in freeing ourselves of self-imposed limitations, we don't ever really need to go through any channels or "middlemen" to "get to" God. Most organized religion is not structured to enhance Self-realization, but to train people to abdicate to manmade laws. Buddha was not a Buddhist and Jesus was not a Christian. They are two examples of people who came into their own while living on the earth.

As fellow spiritual seekers, fellow soul initiates, this is what we are to do:

To come into our own.

Buddha and Jesus did not follow someone else's rules; they found their own. These people are our examples, not our rule-makers. Many times people believe they have to sacrifice who they are to get to Heaven or to have a relationship with God. But *You* never have to sacrifice who You are to know God; you have to *realize who You are.*

You have to realize You were not born in sin, but in Love. You have to realize that You are at Cause and not at effect. You have to realize that *You Are.* You need to sacrifice your limitations and excuses about why you can't live the life your Soul intended.

When we tap into the inner well, the well of our Soul, we realize that we don't need any person, institution, or rules to have a true communion with Spirit. We can also see that there are people, institutions, and rules that support us in our growth, our healing, and our exploration, who can help us stay centered in the joy of who We really are. At any true spiritual center or Heart-centered group, we become more and more aware that we, in our very essence, don't need a middleman to, because, in fact, *We Are.*

The Power of Love

When I was working at that bookstore a few years back, I had the good fortune of attracting a man who could not have been more angry and bitter. This might sound like sarcasm, but what transpired helped me experience the power of unconditional love firsthand, and it gave me something to remember when I become tempted to judge or give up on something or someone.

The man came over to the counter and asked me to search for a book. After a short while, it was apparent he didn't have a clear idea of the title, though he did have the author. I searched through a myriad of authors on the computer, then put keywords in for subject searches. Throughout this process, there was a steady grumble of insults from him being directed my way. I was able to see that these accusations and insults had nothing to do with me at all, and I remained unaffected during the ordeal. After exhausting every known resource, and after a good fifteen minutes, I told him I was sorry, but the book was not in the system. He was very upset and was about to leave when I told him to wait, that the book might be out of print and that I had the card of a used bookstore that specialized in out of print books. I remained calm, since it was obvious he was just having a rough time. His behavior had nothing to do with my service, and when I handed over the card, something happened. As I looked at him, all I could see was the perfection and sacredness of his Soul. He stood staring at me a little while. Then his whole demeanor began to change before my very eyes. It was as if he suddenly woke up and realized how he was behaving. His face and eyes softened, and he took my hand in his and said in a whisper, "Thank you." Tears came to both our eyes. In that moment, I felt the power of love. It was a power of its own volition. Its own agenda.

I realized later that I was never trying to be loving to this man. If I was, I probably would have eventually gotten upset because my love wasn't being returned in the way I thought it should have been. I saw that it wasn't my love at all; it was a love that was beyond me, acting through me, as me. It just sort of…happened. Since it wasn't a personal love, there wasn't a personal expectation. There wasn't a personal agenda.

No agenda. No conditions. No reasons for its existence. Just love. Pure. Potent.

Powerful beyond belief.

When we go beyond the tangled web of conditional love, beyond the "I love you because …" love, a whole new world awaits. When we stop approaching ourselves and others with this kind of love, it opens doors and windows to our psyche and our Soul. When there are no conditions or rules put on us, we have the freedom to explore who we really are, as opposed to continually exploring who we are supposed to be.

We have been trained to think, "When I accomplish this, then I will feel really good about myself" or "When I've got this area of my life more under control, then I'll love myself." Again, the problem with this way of thinking is letting something outside of Us (in this case, our performance or behavior) effect how we feel about ourselves. Stepping out in the world and taking risks, creating and completing projects, and being successful in the world, does give us a sense of fulfillment; but a lot of the time, because of a lack of belief in ourselves, we never start these projects. When we choose to love ourselves first, we can be free to take creative risks, since our performance isn't inextricably linked to our level of Self love. When we choose love over judgment on a consistent basis, we begin to tap into the well of Love that *We are*. We begin to find ourselves loving on levels we never before dreamed possible and living in worlds beyond our current beliefs or conditions.

One may be a little leery of this whole unconditional love thing for many reasons. We may point to past experience. Times of throwing ourselves wide open only to be burned, taken advantage of, or laughed at. Each time we allow our heart to open, a little wiser, a little more grounded, the more we learn about love, about life, and about how the conditioned mind may have had its hand in the deal. The path of the heart is never an easy path.

It is not for the faint of heart. It is not to be taken lightly. It is not expected to be easy.

Although living a lie or a life of quiet desperation is not easy either, it is at least familiar. There is a comfort in knowing, for the most part, what is coming next. It is somewhat predictable. There is a sense of wellbeing for the ego, but it is pretty much hell for the Soul. The path of the heart is one that creates a sense of wellbeing for the Soul, but is pretty much hell for the ego—especially at stages of great realization or growth.

When your heart has expanded to a new level, it is hell for the conditioned self. The path of the heart commands living in a world of flow, a world of continual change for the ego-self. In this scenario, the ego-self becomes the servant of the Soul and is only there to go along with the program. When our personality-self, the conditioned mind, begins to resist the change needed to move further into a more soulful expression of life, there will be great discomfort. *Great* discomfort.

The ego lives for control. It likes to have things its way in order to surround itself with the things it needs to be comfortable and to believe in a stable, fixed world.

There's only one problem. That world doesn't exist.

The physical world is in constant flux and calls for us to live within that flux. In that space, there is constant growth and change and endless new ideas and awareness.

We can choose to stay stuck in a fixed world of our own making, but in such a world we will never know true love, never experience the transforming effect of a true revelation, and never know the life of our Soul. We will only continually experience the contents of our conditioned mind and continue to live the same day over and over and over again.

If we allow ourselves to ride the wave of creation, we will eventually find a way to stay balanced through a regular practice. After some wipe-outs, we find out how to better hold the energy that is expressing through us and living as us. We find out that there are ways to get back up on the board and catch another wave. In hindsight, we understand the reason for the wipe-outs and learn ways to avoid or transcend them in the future.

We then may find ourselves riding bigger waves or treading water on unfamiliar shores where the old rules no longer apply. This usually results in more wipe-outs (i.e. more experience and wisdom). This type of wave riding is not the sport of choice for the ego. Thrill seeking for the sake of thrill seeking (or to prove something) may be, but riding the wave of true Living is not. Which brings us again to the point that Love is not for the ego.

Love is a fire that will ultimately burn alive the conditioned mind's sense of self-importance and its small ideas and judgments. It is not a fire of destruction, but a fire of Love, a fire that burns the overgrowth. The overgrowth of limited conditioning. The overgrowth of the old and dead realizations of time gone by. The only way for new growth to occur is for the overgrown and dead to be burned away. This analogy shows an aspect of love that does not fit in with being nice.

After more than thirty years, I had come to see how deeply I was living the saying, "If you can't say something nice, don't say anything at all." I learned to bury thoughts I didn't think were nice and allowed a lot of things to transpire because it wouldn't have been "nice" to say things against them. I had taken it to heart and ended up afraid of the fire that burned within. Afraid I might hurt someone's feelings,. Afraid of sharing my perspective.

The fire of Love is not a force of destruction, but a force of transformation. When used unconsciously (out of alignment with What Is and in an energy of fear and unhealed issues), it is a force of destruction and does not lead to positive change. When that same energy is used consciously, it can be an energy of profound transformation.

Healing through Love

Some may roll their eyes when they hear someone speak on the importance of Self-love, but it is at the very heart of our future existence. We are at a time in history where we have the technology to destroy the world many times over, and if we don't begin to clear ourselves of our resentments and misconceptions of Reality, the only logical outcome will be that we destroy each other. This is only a reflection of how we have come to destroy our Self, through denying our true greatness, our true Joy, our true Peace, our true Love.

As we begin to heal more of the false perceptions of ourselves, we realize that there are no inherently bad people out there. There are no beings who have come from the underworld or who are here from the dark side to make things hard for the light workers. On a Soul level, there are no people we need to watch out for. Such beliefs are a materialization of myths that are based on a lack of understanding of the Universal Whole. Remember that we can always prove our beliefs, since they prove themselves by manifesting as our experience. We can be right about anything if we have a personal investment in being right. It is a false teaching that there are some of us who are good and others of us who are bad.

We are all of God, of Love, of Life, and we are all made in the image and likeness of that One Power. There are not others who are natural demons, but only others less aware of who they really are. Those who are further away from the realization that the essence of Who they are is Love. Not yet awake to Love. Haven't yet realized that Heaven is here now.

We would not judge someone for sleepwalking. What we might want to do is to understand what factors may have caused them to sleepwalk in the first place in order to have compassion for them and to hold a space for them to wake up. We might also pray that in their sleep they do not hurt anyone, including themselves and continue to see the truth about them no matter how deeply they are sleeping. We may want to understand that if we had been born in the circumstances they had been born in, with their temperament, experiences, friendships, etc., we could very well be engaged in the same pattern of behavior they are.

This does not make them wrong, but actually it makes them right. They are right where they are supposed to be, doing the best they can with their current understanding and belief system. On a spiritual level, their behavior has nothing to do with us. If we are upset by their behavior, we can thank them for helping us to locate an area of self-judgment that resides within ourselves.

This work isn't just a nice way to pass the time or just a way to overcome self-defeating tendencies. It's not just to have a better life. It is at the heart of whether or not we as a species will survive. It is not a given that the human species will survive in physical reality indefinitely. We could very well kill ourselves off.

We are in a unique position, as we have a tremendous opportunity to evolve to our next level of awareness and way of being on the planet. Instead of being motivated by money, comfort, or safety, we must change. We must become motivated by Love.

When we reside in a consciousness of love, we will be able to see what is going on in the material, world and at the same time, we will acquire a sight that goes beyond physical sight alone. We will see everyone on the planet as our brother and sister, and we will see war for what it really is. Archaic and insane.

Once we have done deep and transformative forgiveness work with the parts of us we once judged archaic and insane, we will no longer find ourselves in a position of judgment, but discernment. Discernment leads one to action that is clear of unhealed energy. It leads to what the Buddhists call right action. Right action is not action motivated by our negative emotions or our romantic ideals, but by something completely different. By Real Love.

There is a whole other level of freedom that comes when we do what is right only because it is right, work only because we love to work, give only because we love to give. There are no conditions and no reasons for these behaviors. There are no strings, no personal agendas, no kickbacks. Everything is given freely and everything returns freely. Those who participate in this level of life are truly free. There is really no other way to live life, except unconditionally. Anything else is not real living, but real confinement. Confinement of the Spirit. Of the Soul. Of Life.

Most would argue the point that we are only human and can't be expected to live with such high standards. These are not human standards, but as a collective whole, we need to realize that we are more than human—more than what we believe ourselves to be. We are evolving into our next level of being. And if we do not work to realize our true Self, to know ourselves as Spirit at greater and greater capacities, we simply won't make it to that next level on this planet.

We are not sinners.

We are not mistakes.

We are Love.

The idea that being human equals weak and pathetic is ridiculous. The idea that human means lowly character, incapable of unconditional love, and only here to get through life without committing too many sins and without too much suffering is absurd. A lie.

That we have to play by other people's rule books to be saved. Asinine.

If you were conditioned to believe that you were a sinner and became afraid that you would be eternally damned if you did not frequent a particular church, hold a certain belief, give a certain amount of money, or do a certain amount of good for others, you would in fact not be living, you would be a pawn in someone else's game. You may not mind being a pawn, but you want to be Love's pawn, the Soul's pawn, not an organization's.

Whose pawn might you be at the moment? Where did you get your beliefs and what moves are you making as a result of those beliefs? What clothes are you wearing? What words are you speaking? What songs are you listening to? What car are you driving? Are you playing God's game, or someone else's?

Love does not ask anything of you other than to be yourself. It does not ask you to dress a certain way, believe a certain way, or act a certain way. It loves you no matter what, and in that energy, in that dynamic of freedom and peace, old ways of being that are no longer useful to the Soul, to the expression of genius, can be discarded.

No matter how much good you did, if you did it because you believed you should in order to be good or avoid punishment, you would be motivated by fear, not Love. The good would be given in an energy that is not of your true Self, but in an energy that is caught in the duality of good and evil, of crucifixions and pedestals, of saints and sinners. In truth there is only One Power. One Love.

In this sense, God did not create a world of suffering. Our current level of collective mental beliefs and awareness of the Truth creates the current physical world we experience. There is not a God flying in the ether cursing some and blessing others.

If we believe in a god that is conditional, that is the god we will experience. If we believe in a love that is conditional, that is the love we will experience. It is us flying around, cursing some and blessing others. That is not God, that is not Love, that is not Life. These are our own ideas that are revealing havoc or Heaven according to the energy behind them.

It is our lack of awareness of God, of Love, that leads to limiting behaviors and experiences. It is the understanding that there is someone out there doing something to you, as opposed to reflecting something back to you, that is the cause of your feelings of helplessness and confusion.

It, ultimately, it is the belief that you were born in sin as opposed to love.

The moment we can collectively, as a species, transcend that belief about who we really are is the moment our entire planet can transform into what it truly is: Heaven.

As we choose Love, Love chooses us. In this choice, all things are possible. As we speak, planet Earth is Heaven waiting to happen.

Heaven is calling.
it asks where I've been
"trolling around,
with this idea of sin"
"beating myself with old thoughts of defeat"
"covered in misery"
"lost in retreat"

234

Heaven keeps calling
it shouts from above

stop dreaming this nonsense
and wake up to Love
Love is your True Nature
your very birthright
You are my true love
You are my delight
Love is the answer to the question my dear
that question you ask:
"What am I doing here?"

Though love is the answer
you don't have to choose it
you can live in your misery
it's your choice to refuse it

Only you can decide
not someone from above
in what state you will live—
in fear
or in Love?

Knowing
Going Beyond Belief

Beyond opinions
that you hold
Beyond the lies
you have been told

Beyond time
Beyond space
Lies a life
of lasting grace

A life of peace
A life of cheer
lived in gratitude
of what is Here

A life so rich
A life sublime
beyond your goals
beyond your mind
beyond your pain
beyond your grief—
A life,
in fact,
beyond belief

There is an irony embedded in our perception of Life that helps to keep any sense of truth from ever being fully revealed. It is only by living comfortably within the paradox will we ever be able to transcend the apparently dualistic nature of life.

It is utterly fascinating that, in order to come into a state of complete knowing, one must spend so much time living in the unknown.

In order for the awareness of the "I Am" presence to reveal itself, the personal "I" must disappear.

In order for us to really truly know anything, we first have to realize that we know nothing.

On the one hand, we are powerful Creators, spinning webs of

excellence, beauty and genius, grace, compassion, and joy. On the other hand, without Love, we are nothing.

We have to be willing to stand in the full magnificence of *who We really are*. To be a solid expression of the Power that sent us. A messenger of Love. A gift from God.

And in the next moment be willing to fall to our knees in humility and gratitude.

The Master is actually the slave. A slave to his Soul. A slave to his Heart. A slave to God. He or She is but a drop in the ocean, but in being willing to be nothing more than a drop, has accessed the full presence and power of the entire ocean.

Until this knowing becomes a permanent state, the conditioned mind, personality, or ego has to be continually humbled, quieted, or just observed and seen through, so that Life can continue to express through us.

We come to realize that when we let go of a personal life, a personal opinion, or a personal agenda, we are free. When we don't personally possess anything, we have nothing to lose. By not having anything to lose, we live in the awareness that everything is already here. *Everything.* Everything worth living for (or living from), that is.

We are then free from the illusion of suffering and struggle. Free from the mind's idea of reality. In that awareness, we are truly free to choose. We are free to live life from a level of choice we never dreamed possible. The mind had tricked us into believing this life beyond belief was something that would come to us from the outside, that one day god or someone or something would grace us, give us a lucky break, and we would finally get the things we thought we always wanted. Living beyond belief has nothing to do with that. Living life beyond belief, beyond the conditioned mind, beyond the limitations of past history, is so completely radical, so completely different than most everything we have been taught about ourselves and about life, that most of us truly have no concept of what it really means or the implication of it.

It means we would recognize every being on the planet as our brother and sister. We would wake up to the fact that everything is alive and everything is a part of us. The implication is utter, complete, and unabashed freedom for yourself and everyone around you if they so choose. As more of us live in this state at greater and greater levels, we create the condition for the eventual awakening of the entire planet.

As long as we are in a state of unconscious creation, unaware of how our thoughts affect our experience of reality, unaware of the greater Reality, the Love, that surrounds us, *that Is Us* in every moment, and as long as we are unaware of the miscreations, or negative conditions, stemming from fear-based thoughts, we will remain stuck at our current level of awareness and our current level of creation. We will be subject to the continued experience of chaos and war. Of starvation and hunger for the majority of us on the planet. Of disease and discontent.

This awareness beyond the egocentric mind, beyond the historical mind, beyond the ten percent of the brain the average person has access to, is the key to our transformation on the planet.

Beyond Me and Mine

When I say "my" daughter, I don't imagine that I created her and that she is mine. The "my" does not demonstrate possession but simply distinction. The same goes for my house, my money, my book, my life. I don't see that these are things are mine. They have all been gifts from God, from God consciousness, manifested from a stream of endless possibilities of Love and Grace. Everything in this physical world is temporary. It is only the qualities of the Spirit that can be felt with the heart, only the eternal qualities that can't run out or be any more than they already are. Through our awareness and intentional activity, these eternal qualities can emanate through us as well as manifest as physical forms. To fall under the illusion that the form then is the Thing Itself though, is a misidentification of reality and a state of awareness that the average, and even "above average" human lives from.

Everything comes from God, everything goes to God, everything *is God*.

The manifest world has nothing for us, as in Reality *We* carry the infinite possibility of the un-manifest Good, the un-manifest Heaven within. We are not here on this planet to get anything. We are only here to allow this previously un-manifest Divine Good, these qualities of Heaven, to come though us. It doesn't matter if others are allowing Heaven to manifest through them; we need to do it as well, because no one can do what we have come to do. No one can be the unique potential that we are as individualized expressions of the One. We have come to do nothing more than allow this energy to come through and to be of service.

We are not here to serve in the way our egos have been conditioned to serve, but to serve in the way we are called to by the deepest Love within our Soul.

On my path, there have been times that I have done this terribly imperfectly. Terribly ungracefully. Terribly, embarrassingly, ridiculously, ineptly as I try to hang on to a limited idea of the calling and of myself. When I try to control the process, I have fallen under the illusion again and again that there is something here for me in this world, and that there is a good that exists outside of my Self.

As I try to put one foot back in this world to find some sense of security and balance, I realize again that from the Self level there is nothing to balance anything else against. It is an extremely radical state to be in, but one that is capable of accomplishing what "needs" to get done in the physical realm. I sometimes forget this and listen to those who tell me it is not possible. I fall again and again and again.

And, when all is said and done... *Who Cares??!!*

What does it matter how many times I have fallen? How many times I wanted to crawl under the table in embarrassment and shame? What does it matter how many times I have cried out in disappointment and pain, anger and regret? The truth is that self does not exist in the Mind of God. Those feelings, caused by a mistaken case of identity, by an extreme misunderstanding of who I really am and what Life really is, are completely unfounded and in the end make no difference to anything or anyone, including myself. The only thing that matters is that I get up again; that I return to my practice; that I say one more prayer, have one more sitting, follow one more calling of the heart, commit one more act of love and service, write one more page, speak one more word, and take one more risk on behalf of the Heart.

Temporarily forgetting who you are is nothing more than par for the course. Making mistakes, part of the process. To grow in anything, you have to be willing to do what it takes.

Whose Life Is It Anyway?

There is life. Then there is *Life*.

Many times we are living out our conditioned ideas of life and are under the illusion that we are really and truly Living. In real living we become aware of an indescribable essence of eternal and unbounded creation. This awareness cannot be perceived with our physical world senses and comes to us through the more subtle bodies, ones most people are not aware of and have not yet activated. When these more subtle bodies become activated, through activities such as our meditation practice, selfless service, and our pure and heartfelt intention, we don't lose the ability to process information which comes through our physical senses or our physical world sensibility. We begin to see through the illusion of it, though, and it doesn't hold as much clout as it used to.

What is happening is that we are actually acquiring a new sense. We are beginning to gain access to a different form of information, a different way of seeing, of hearing, of touching, and of knowing. After realizing the tremendous value of this other type of "information," or feeling or Life, we may temporarily choose to focus more on it and less on what may seem to be the more mundane, lower-vibrational, physical-world reality.

I've heard many say how they would love to be able to concentrate more on their spiritual growth, but they don't have the time. This is nothing more than a ploy of the ego. If one has the commitment and desire, and begins to make daily choices, begins to take five-minute meditation and prayer breaks throughout the day, they will definitely make progress on the path. The ego can make you think that you have to quit your entire life and join an ashram to awaken more fully to the truth of who you are. (Something you most likely will never do, and it can keep you right where it wants you.) The ego can trick you into thinking that a current circumstance has power over the creative power and Life within one's being. The truth is you always have choice. You always have choice to be yourself and to act on the calling of your heart. It can be expressed in an infinite number of ways.

My eleven-year marriage, much of which I spent in solitary due to the circumstances and controlling nature of our relationship, was actually a great blessing. If things had gone well for me according to my ego's point of view, I probably would not have had such a long period of focused attention and reflection. It was years before I was conscious enough to recognize it as a profound gift that allowed me to concentrate fully on my spiritual unfolding and awakening. I remember during that time, while I was working at the gas station, thinking that I should try to get a better job or go back to school again, but the gas station provided for a no-brainer environment to study and practice, even if it was more of an obsessive interest at that time rather than a focused practice.

We have to trust that every situation and event holds a gift and an opportunity for us. When things appear to not be going well according to our conditioned mind, we have to trust that there is something incredible—be it an inner opening, a greater awareness, a creative solution, maybe an entire life's work—that will potentially come out of these experiences. A mantra of sorts that I use now when I feel the illusion gaining some ground in my consciousness is "only Good can come from it." By saying this, one creates more space within their consciousness for creative ideas and new possibilities, while conditioning the mind to search for its idea of good. Even though the mind can only find a limited idea, at least it will be headed in another direction.

Some say that life can be anything we want it to be and that we are just making it up as we go along. This is true—and not true. It is true to the extent that we believe it is. It's the same thing as saying we can be anything we want and are just making up who we are as we go along. Again, as we believe it is.

This is one level of living.

To formulate an idea of who we would like to be and shuffle our ideas and behaviors so that we fit into the idea that we have created is a conscious way of living. Choosing our behaviors, our preferences, our agendas and using our willpower to change our circumstances— reinventing ourselves—is one level of creation. Living on this level is much more pleasing and fulfilling than living out unconscious negative ideas about ourselves and about life. But as long as the conditioned mind is the one making things happen—shaping and influencing it—it will be our personal mind's creation. We will experience it as our life, and we will be accurate in this description. It is "our life."

We have taken it back from the negative parental conditioning we were brought up with to a certain degree. Taken it back from the social conditioning and expectations that were placed on us. We have taken it from our own unconscious and limiting thought processes to a significant degree. We have done the work and our mind is our own now. Our life is our own. We look out and are pretty darn happy about the way things have turned out. We feel pretty good about what we have created. It's our life, and a life we don't mind taking credit for, since we have been conscious in its creation.

Our life.

Finally.

But then…

Now that we have it back in our control to a certain extent, something within us shifts, and if we haven't become too busy and obsessed with—or even addicted to—our personal creation, we begin to feel a deeper calling. We begin to see that there is something else completely. Just as we begin to feel we have mastered this whole belief/creation/manifesting thing to a certain extent, Life asks us once again to do the impossible: to give it all up for a new way of being.

We begin to see that there is more, far beyond what we could ever have imagined and materialized through the awareness of our conditioned mind. We get a glimpse of "God's game" and a level of playing that is beyond what we have known or thought possible.

When Jesus said, "Ye are Gods," the guy meant it. In Truth We are Divine. Our True Nature is Divine. We hold the key to Creation, just as any God does. At rock bottom, the True Self is the God Self, and there is no separation between the two. In this state there is no separation between Us and the Planet. Us and the Physical Realm. Us and Them. Us and Anything. We are One in the Same with All of Creation, and Manifestations can be instantaneous, as we realize We Are that which We Manifest.

During one level of creation, we may use the law to fulfill our ego's agenda. We work to mentally and emotionally align with ideas about material things, or behaviors, that we think will give our egos a boost and a greater sense of security. We use the law to align with things *we think* we want. We use this Power, as opposed to letting It use us as Its vehicle. When we allow It to use us, we become Gods of Divinity, as opposed to gods of our personal will.

Instead of being in alignment with Divine Will and claiming "I Am that I Am" from a space of inner alignment and complete surrender of the conditioned mind, in the beginning, our egos may get hold of the law of materialization—cause and effect—and claim: "i am that I Am."

The ego, the conditioned, rational mind, *is not God.*

There is nothing bad about this level of living; it's just that it will never be able to ultimately take us to where we need to go in consciousness on planet Earth in order for us to live on the physical plane without war and disease. This level of living cannot take us there because it is still operating at the level of the conditioned mind, which imagines itself to be separate from the One (even in its positive state); and it imagines it needs to create something other than what already *Is* (i.e. Love, Peace, Joy, Wisdom, Beauty).

There is a higher purpose and meaning to why we are here other than to fulfill desires of the conditioned mind. These will manifest organically as a result of being in alignment with the truth of our being, but no longer will they occur as a result of consciously using the law to materialize our personal will, and these things will no longer be able to give us the high they once did.

There is a life that is beyond our thought about it. There is a life that is only Good. We will someday come to realize we don't have to create it. We don't have to make it good anymore, because we come to realize that it is Good. It is *only* Good.

There is nothing else that Life really is or has ever, ever, *ever* been.

My Trip vs. God's Trip

Once I was in India with a group of about twenty people who were on a pilgrimage, traveling in the footsteps of the Buddha. A few days into the trip, my roommate and I were shopping in a crowded market, and as I reached into my bag to pull out my money, I discovered it was no longer there. All of my identification, credit cards, and every cent I had with me had been inside a smaller bag, which had been stolen.

It's in these moments that you find all of the inner work well worth any amount of effort that you may have felt. While we began to backtrack to see if we might find the bag, I became aware that all of this was happening for a Good reason. Along with this message—this inner knowing—came a remembering that Life is Good. It was that simple: *Life is Good.*

Oh my God, that's right! I thought.

This was the initial revelation that came with the awakening several years ago. I painted it, wrote it, sang it, couldn't get over it! Life is Good

—Really.

Who knew??!!!

This was another moment of remembering, another experience of awakening to the Truth: In Reality, there's only Good.

I realized that if there is only Good, this must be Good! If there is only Love, this must be Love! If there is only God, this must be God! Not what my mind would label a negative condition—*that* is not God. That is an illusion. But Good, God, Love exist within what the mind would label as the negative condition, resting within as a profound possibility, cloaked by appearance, as it were. It was there, always there. I just needed to recognize it.

In illness, perfect wholeness exists; it just needs to be recognized.

In times of war, peace exists; it just needs to be recognized.

In times of scarcity, abundance exists; it just needs to be recognized.

Realized.

Seen.

Felt.

Touched.

Tasted.

Embodied.

This wasn't a logical conclusion, but a total revelation—a conclusion that the conditioned mind will never, ever reach. In this higher awareness, there is no good and evil. There is no hierarchy. There is no dualism. There is absolutely nothing. In this awakened space, there is complete emptiness. Nothing.

And that leaves room for…absolutely *Everything.*

From this higher awareness we see can things as they really are: Full. Whole. Complete.

This, my friends, is prayer. True prayer has nothing to do with what a conditioned mind wants or doesn't want to experience. True prayer has nothing to do with circumstances or situations in the illusory world. It has to do with transcending the conditioned mind completely and tapping into the Truth of What Already Is. Prayer is not supplication. True prayer is Revelation.

In the physical world, opportunity always exists within what seem like crises. In fact, opportunity seems to exist in exact proportion. In other words: Big Seeming Crisis = Big Miracle Waiting to Happen.

Before the night was over, the loving bunch I was traveling with, the Sangha, had taken up a collection and I ended up with more cash than I started with—not a small amount by anyone's standards. Offers to pay for things or to loan me things continued throughout the trip. From the material perspective, it was nice to have the support and help, but on a deeper level it was even more significant as it was an opportunity for Us to participate in sharing and receiving and to participate in Love. Many other blessings came as well. I could probably fill a few pages with all of the blessings—miracles even—which came from that one event.

My ability to return to India was questionable without a passport, and since I was unable to cross into Nepal, a few of us stayed two nights near the border. We had the most amazing time in an old maharaja's hunting lodge that was built in the 1800s and had a full staff waiting on us hand and foot as we were the only one's there. The highlights included elephant rides and visits to neighboring villages. These times, as well as spending time sitting around the fire sharing stories and playing games with incredibly brilliant and fascinating women, turned out to be one of the most memorable parts of the entire trip.

Since the U.S. embassy took a few days to issue a replacement passport, when we got back to New Delhi, I missed my flight. For a while, it looked like I might not get back home for several weeks without buying a new ticket, since most flights were overbooked. My extended stay, which turned out to be about a week, was amazing. I saw the Taj Mahal, went to some incredible artisan markets, spent time visiting with wonderful people who lived in Delhi, and even dropped off some of this book to a publisher, who was a friend of one of the trip leaders—another whole story in itself! During this time, I stayed in one of the grandest hotels in Delhi.

God's idea of my trip was much grander than mine, indeed! Going beyond our beliefs about God, about Life, and coming to know *It Itself* is the most brilliant adventure imaginable. Unimaginable, actually.

It is so unimaginably Beautiful and Radiant. It is so pure and elegant. It is Self-aware and carries Its own agenda of Peace, of Joy, of Love that blows our little ideas of these things to dust.

We begin to see that it is only our beliefs of living in an enclosed mental idea or concept that keep us from living in this amazing world. It is our beliefs that keep us from realizing we are living in Heaven. It is our lack of trust that life is Good, just as it is. Right where We Are. Now. We just have to see it.

We may begin by using affirmations to "create reality," but in the end, we realize anything we could invent is nothing compared to what happens when we surrender to Love—not to the unknown or the ups and downs of a limited perspective, but to Love, to Reality, to what *Is*.

In this awareness, we realize that we haven't personally created anything; we have only aligned with the Truth. We *are* beautiful. Life *is* good. We *are* whole and complete. We *are* free. All of our needs *are* met. We *are* living in Heaven now. There is *nothing else* going on in Reality.

The only reason conditions of scarcity and fear continue to appear on earth is because people are still dreaming the nightmare of a God outside of themselves, continuing to believe in the lie of an inherently sinful nature, and trying to influence a world that does not exist.

The Real Real *World*

One might wonder why a world of love and peace and joy is the "real" world and not just a "different" world. What would make one real and the other an illusion?

When you learn something on the mental level, like how to speak a language, how to do a math equation, or how to tell time, there are certain functions involved in that learning. You have to take in information and learn to put it together in a specific way, and when you do, there is a certain sense of it fitting together and it being right. What makes it feel right is that there has been a collective agreement in consciousness that it is, in fact, right. There has been an agreement that a certain word symbolizes a certain action or thing, or that a specific number symbolizes a particular amount, day, or time. If you are sensitive to the process you can feel it all coming together. In a sense, you are not learning something new, but aligning with a concept that is already whole and complete.

When you are learning a language, you begin by learning specific words, then by conjugating verbs and putting sentences together. When you do, you may feel a mental "aha" of sorts.

The same process happens when you begin to experience Life and your Self. The only difference is that real Life and the Self are not ideas created by man which exist in space and time. Time, language, and numbers were all created by humans for the purpose of living together effectively. By our agreement of what certain sounds mean, we are able to communicate more efficiently in our current state of awareness. By creating measuring systems, such as numbers and time, we are able to live together more effectively from a mental realm. We use these concepts to create efficient mental systems of living. These creations help give us a collective base to make sense of the world around us and to better understand our place in it.

The problem comes when people begin to imagine that these creations are the real ones and forget that they are only creations of the mind. When you come into deeper understandings of systems of thought, you are coming into deeper levels of ideas or concepts that were created by the mind. When you come into deeper realizations of Life, you are not coming into deeper understandings of mental ideas, but a deeper understanding and experience of the original source of those ideas themselves.

You come to see what is *Real* as opposed to what has been previously agreed upon by others as real. In this space, you become a candidate for original thought, since you have found your way to the origin of thought itself. To the well. To the non-local space beyond mental conception. There is no history in this space. There is no time. No boundaries or dimensions. The mind cannot "go there," so to speak, but you come to see that you are more than your mind and can experience it with a different dimension of yourself. With your Soul. With your Heart.

In this experience, you go beyond understanding and come into knowing. It is a different way of being informed. As opposed to being informed by outer sources, you have truly been *in*-formed. You have seen your true form from the inner dimensions of your Soul. You have seen the formless unlimited potential of your being. You have been informed by your Self. You have found your way to what is in fact Real, and in that finding you are forever changed.

You still see and experience things in physical reality that have been created with the mind, but you are no longer under the illusion they are Real. Even though the physical senses would convince you they are solid, fixed, and real, you know that they're not. You can appreciate them, be delighted by them—even love them—but at the same time be completely aware that what you are really loving is all part of the same thing. It's the Only Thing. The One Life, the Beauty, the Reality behind what is showing up in the physical world.

You realize it is from this source that true Life is manifested on earth. You see that Life is not just a regurgitation or reorganization of existing theories or thoughts, but a dimension of unlimited potential. If you act on the ideas from this Source rather than the ones based on your personal history or the history of others, you won't be living *your* life anymore, you will be living Life itself.

One day while visiting my mom, I found myself standing in the middle of the bedroom I had grown up in. Years ago when I would visit, I would sometimes feel a deep sadness, a longing, or a myriad of other emotions. They had lessened through the years, but there was usually a sense of remorse, even if it was very subtle. When I stood in my old bedroom that day, I began to realize that not only was there no remorse, I had never gone through any of the things I had formerly remembered going through. It's not that I had forgiven enough so that it no longer hurt; it's that it actually hadn't happened. In Reality none of it had ever really even happened.

When you begin to see glimpses of what Life really is, when you begin to tap the mystical well of understanding, it takes you beyond what you may have formerly experienced as a mental "aha." It takes you to a different realm of consciousness. A place beyond words or thought to another world you may have formerly suspected, believed in, and even hoped for, but until that moment never really, truly *knew*. Your outer life will become a demonstration of this connection.

True knowledge is knowing something, not just memorizing theories. Not just thinking or talking about it, but consciously knowing it.

Rumors vs. the Truth

We can talk about things as if we know them when in fact we only know *of* them, just as we can think and talk about a person without actually knowing them. We may have heard rumors about a certain person, such as a celebrity, and maybe we even engaged in conversation about them as if we knew them. If we go by what another person has told us about them, without really knowing them ourselves, we would only be passing on someone else's interpretation of who this person is, and we would only know them through someone else's experience. We wouldn't *actually* know them.

What we have heard about them may not even have been true, if the source of the information was coming from someone with a personal agenda, or if it had been filtered through a personal belief system, or especially if it had provoked an unresolved issue.

Instead of listening to gossip and getting secondhand information, we could choose to have a personal relationship with the celebrity and cut out the middle man altogether. A part of us might not even attempt this, believing it would never be possible for us to get to know someone so revered and special. A part of us might not feel deserving enough to attempt a meeting. This is not a call to begin stalking your favorite celebrity, but an invitation to come to know your own Soul. It is a metaphor demonstrating the kind of determination and worthiness one needs to even entertain a real and substantial relationship with God.

It's very hard to believe you are worthy of knowing some "one" who you see as all-powerful and omnipresent when it has been drilled into your consciousness that you are sinful and undeserving of such a relationship. On the other side of the coin, if we have bought into the collective, underlying agreement that we are lowly, sinful beings, how motivated are we going to be to even want to know our Creator and our Selves on deeper levels? Why would we even want to get to know someone who had created something so inherently flawed? Why would we really want to get to know ourselves on deeper levels if we believed that we would find more weakness and sin?

If we turn this celebrity analogy to ourselves, we may find that we have been listening to gossip about ourselves all our lives—what our parents thought of us, what our teachers thought of us, what our lovers and employers thought of us.

When we begin to delve into the landscape of our Soul, we realize that most of the gossip was, in fact, just rumor. These negative rumors don't have anything to do with who we really are. Behaviors may have formed because of many different reasons, including events that were traumatic to our psyche, but We, in essence, are not our behaviors.

We Are Not Our Past

Different labels may have been put on us by others, by their projections, by their misinterpretation of situations or events, and/or by a misunderstanding of the difference between a behavior and a being. But when we come to know who we really are, we see that anyone's idea of who we are is not actually who we are at all. We're not even our own idea of ourselves!

If we turn this analogy back to God, we can see that most of what we actually know of God may only be gossip. We may think we know God without ever even having met "Him" other than through the words of others, and we may talk about "Him" without having any actual interaction in the world. We may think we know our Selves when in fact we have only known ourselves through the interpretations of others and their observations of who we are.

When we come to see that God is everywhere, all the time, we come to see that the miracle of Life is everywhere all the time. We may have harbored a secret fear or distrust of God because we have heard rumors of what a vengeful, spiteful character "He" is. When we really come to know the true source of Life, though, we see that It is only Love. Everything else was just a rumor, spread by others who had most likely never, ever met "Him" at all. For women, this opening can be especially powerful as we come to see that God is not a man at all, as well. We come to understand that many sacred texts were written in times where men lived in fear of the sacred mysteries of women. Out of this fear myths were created that would cause her to mistrust and even fear herself and would keep the patriarchal rule intact. In a true meeting of Divinity, any unconscious feelings of inferiority and shame around being a woman, or around any other perceived sense of limitation, can be instantaneously healed.

We may be so incredibly blown away by the initial meeting that we may not know what to do with ourselves. Our old paradigm of life begins to look a little silly, and the things that once seemed so important may not matter much at all anymore. If you knew that nothing you did could ever make you bad, that you were abundantly supplied with everything you needed in this moment, and that you were never going to die, what would you do with yourself? What would you do with your life then?

Now that would be the thing to do!

We may argue that we couldn't do such a thing because we're not abundantly supported by the Universe in this moment, but we must come to understand that We are. Our ego may not feel abundantly supported by the Universe because it only has an idea of what it needs in order to fit into its idea of life, and only has access to the physical senses for its assessment of reality. It has no knowledge of what Real Life is; it only has an *idea* of it.

Shaken Awake by Love

When we realize our True Nature and the true nature of Life, we see that we are always supported by the Universe, and that we always have been. We see there was never one moment in our lives that we were not supported by this benevolent and loving Universe. There may have been times in the past when we felt unsupported by the Universe, felt abandoned and unloved, but we eventually come to know the Truth because we come to know our Self.

The truth is, the Universe does not support our ego, our limited conditioned mind, or our idea of how things should be. True Life does not support the ego in staying satisfied and comfortable in its little limited world. It supports Itself. It supports growth and expansiveness. It supports our Soul. It supports Spiritual evolution. It supports our Soul in realizing Itself, in realizing Life, in realizing Love, in realizing the eternal, never-ending, never-beginning Goodness of Life and the eternal never-ending, never-beginning Goodness of our Selves. It does not necessarily support us in our unconscious sleep.

When you begin asking questions as to the nature of your true being, things can get really wild for a time, especially if you're a deep sleeper. A nice little beep on an alarm clock may not do it. You might have to be shaken awake.

Being shaken awake is not a pleasant experience by anyone's standards. In the end, though, we realize that the Universe did not shake us awake in order for us to go to a job we had no interest in or passion for, but one that we will find ourselves Living for. In a good way.

We have been shaken *AWAKE*.

Awake to Truth. Awake to Love. Awake to Heaven on Earth. Awake to true Living.

It is a different life in that it is sourced by the One, the Heart, the Soul, rather than our personal ideas and beliefs about the way it should be or the way that is nice and convenient for us.

It is sourced by Freedom rather than shoulds.

It is sourced by Abundance rather than schemes to make money.

It is sourced by Guidance rather than goal-setting.

It is sourced by Knowledge rather than belief.

When we begin to really pay attention, we see that there is a Self-aware Universe, and that this Universe is Good. We see that True Life is not a belief we churn over and over in our minds and hope to materialize in our experience of the world. It is a perfect and complete—beyond what we can conceive—organic process that proceeds at Its own rate, with Its own agenda, Its own Idea. When we allow ourselves to Live, we come to see what is *Really* Here.

We see what the prophets and sages have seen: that Heaven is here Now. That Life operates independent of our limiting thoughts and beliefs. It even operates beyond our positive thoughts and beliefs. It is actually completely independent of what we think of as thought.

When we begin to become aware of the conditioned thoughts, through meditation or other mindful activity, we can begin to identify the difference between conditioned, historical, mass consciousness thoughts and Life's thoughts. We see that we can "think Its thoughts" and "see what It sees." When we act on these intuitions, on this Thought beyond thought, we become the Gods—not Gods of our personal creation, but the Gods of Creation itself. The ego may be appalled by the seeming arrogance of calling oneself a god, only because from its limited perception, it is arrogance! From a state of separation, it is definitely arrogant and a little nuts. From a state of knowing the Truth of your Being, it is not arrogance; it is a simple fact.

AKA: Living on a Need-to-Know Basis

Many times life has been described as a game. We might sometimes feel that we are pawns in some kind of universal game of chess. If the game was being played from our unconscious beliefs about the way things are, then we would be the pawns of those belief systems. We would only be able to move in reaction to others' moves. We would be limited in our positive influence on the world, since our entire understanding of the game would be that we had no real power to affect our moves and we would be playing a victim in life. We would be the pawn of others' expectations and rules, of our personal history and our genes—even our birth date—and in that game our moves would be severely limited.

When we begin to understand that we have an effect on our experience and can make up our own rules to a degree (by means of conscious direction of thought), we move to a higher level and find ourselves playing a game more of our own making. In this game, we call the shots. We use the intelligence of the world, what we have been taught, to move the pieces in our lives and can become quite good at the game through practice.

After a time though, we begin to get glimpses of the game being played an entirely different way with an entirely different result. At this level of understanding, we begin to play "God's game." For this game, we have to give up doing things our way and once again become a pawn. Only instead of being moved by our unconscious beliefs, as in the beginning of the game, we are now being moved by our super-conscious thoughts. By our intuitive Self and a Self-aware Universe. By a power beyond the mind's comprehension. In a dimension beyond the physical world. By the voice of our Soul.

As we begin to allow this still, small voice to override our belief systems, instead of moving where we believe we should (based on our beliefs about life), we move to where our Soul wants us to move, which may be quite out of range with what we might think is a good move at all. These moves aren't based on mental strategy but on the intuitive guidance of Life Itself. Our moves don't come from our mind but from our Heart. Rather than being a pawn for our idea of life, we end up becoming a pawn for real Life. We end up becoming a pawn for Love and, in the playing, Love itself. And, as in any game, the more you practice, the more you play, the better you get.

About a year after my initial awakening, I was playing chess one night with a friend. I had only played a few times in my life, and he had to remind me of the different moves each piece could make. When I won the game, he became quite frustrated, asking me "What are you, one of those idiot savants?" We played again, and I won again. A few days later, he called and said he and a friend of his had come to the conclusion that I must have been lying. He was sure that I was really an accomplished chess player, since none of his friends had been able to beat him at chess for some time. He hadn't told me any of this before, but I remember it didn't surprise me too much. I had been quite aware that I was in a state of flow while we were playing. I was coming to get more and more familiar with being in that flow and had found that when I was in that state I could do just about anything. Especially things I had little or no prior knowledge of. I also have to say that at the time of this writing, I have been playing chess nightly with my eleven-year-old daughter and find it impossible to win. I don't know why I suddenly became a chess master of sorts for that brief period, other than, when you're in the flow, you're in the flow.

A lot of the time, living the life your Soul intended is like living on a need-to-know basis. For instance, as large-scale covert operations are carried out in the CIA, each person may only be privy to their particular role and may not be told of the larger plan so they don't become a security risk. They may not really have a clue as to what is going on in the bigger picture, but since they have committed to serve the government, they trust that what they are being told to do is serving their country. It's the same way when you begin to have the intention to live the life your Soul intended. Except that when you are serving your Soul, you are serving Us All, the One, not certain people at the expense of others. But the process is the same. When you get an order from the "commanding officer," from your intuition, from your Higher Self, you follow it. Period. No questions asked. You are fully committed to your Soul, to your Life, and you know that in some way you are involved in a much bigger plan.

Of course, things are a little different working for God.

There is no actual person physically giving you the orders. It takes a lot of practice to discern between the orders that have been given by the "commanding officer," the Higher Self, and the ones being given by the "commanding ego," the personal self. This scenario has the potential to make you feel pretty weird on many different levels, for many different reasons.

But there are perks.

Before I had found my way to the school for spiritual psychology, I was seriously considering quitting school entirely. The classes I had taken at a community college had opened my eyes to just how severely limiting traditional "education" was. By that time I had taken my daughter out of school, and after being out of that system I began to ask a very basic question I hadn't really ever thought of before, "What is learning?"

After taking some classes, I thought, I'm not sure what it is, but it's definitely not that.

After continually coming into contact with another dimension of life, another dimension of myself, I saw that there was an element of Reality that traditional schooling completely ignored. It was like an ingredient being left out of a recipe. Iit wasn't a small ingredient that one could afford to leave out, but the main one! Without that ingredient, it was all just empty calories.

In an epistemology class, we talked about body and mind, but not of Spirit. There were some religious references, but as a means of knowing, Spirit, or intuition, was noticeably absent. In a neuroscience class, we spoke of the brain as if it were the thing itself that kept us conscious. In that paradigm, if our brain goes, we go. Hence, we are our biology. In a Psych 101 class, the professor made a comment one day to the few hundred students in the lecture hall that made me really wonder what I was doing there. He said that love was only a delusional state. Not that "some people believe that love is a delusional state and others believe it is our natural state," but that it was, in fact, a delusional state. It had to be true. Hell, it was on the test.

It became harder and harder to mark these answers on a test, but to argue would have been futile. Not only was it on the test, it was in the textbook. God himself may as well have written it.

A point I did make one day in the epistemology class was that new ideas are always ridiculed, or worse, and that the only way to move ahead as a people, as a species, was to try out new things. Experiment with altering theories. Most people thought Columbus was nuts, that

Galileo was a heretic, and many of the cutting-edge ideas we think are silly today will become common wisdom tomorrow. Some theories may eventually be proven wrong, and the professor talked at length about Timothy Leary's group experimentation with LSD to prove her point.

I had become a little disenchanted with the educational system, to say the least. Recycling and regurgitating chosen theories did nothing more than swaddle a person in the current paradigm. It did nothing to help one actually learn to think. It did nothing to help one truly learn about themselves and how they fit into the larger design of things. It did help tremendously to keep one in check and to keep them from participating in the very things it was touted as doing: thinking and learning. I began to have serious doubts about whether I wanted to continue to participate in school. I wasn't going for a degree. Initially I thought I wanted to be a psychologist but could never picture myself sitting in an office as the "expert" on someone else's "problems," which was how it was sitting in my mind at the time. The only educational program I knew of that included the things I had experienced was the program in spiritual psychology I had begun attending. I decided that I didn't need to complete my Bachelor's degree after all. I would just go through this program for personal enrichment as opposed to going for a Master's degree.

That was my decision. Yep. It turns out that was my decision, but not my Soul's decision. It seemed as if school just would not leave me alone.

I began to ask the Universe within if I was in fact "supposed" to go to school and get my degree. If it was indeed part of the Plan. Answers seemed to pour in from every channel. In my mailbox, there were fliers from local and national schools and learning centers.

In conversations, everyone seemed to be talking about education in one way or another. Just about every time I struck up a conversation with a stranger, it turned out they were a teacher. It was an obvious answer. All the same, this was something I was having a severe resistance to. I didn't understand why I should have to go through an experience I saw no real value in and was actually personally opposed to. It seemed silly. But it would not go away.

One Sunday morning I was in meditation at a local spiritual center that had become like a second home of sorts. I found myself

258

engaged in a "heated" inner conversation. This was it. I promised that if I got a message this time, I would absolutely go back to school, no questions asked. But it had to be clear. Unmistakable.

After the meditation, the reverend said they were going to do something special that morning as people began making their way up to the stage. As it turned out they were all being honored for recently graduating from high school or college. Simultaneously cursing under my breath and nearly laughing out loud, I made a commitment that day to complete my degree.

Through a series of serendipitous events, I was enrolled in a college where credits were banked, and tests were taken at local testing centers to accumulate credits. At first I was very intimidated by the three-hour exams and was sure I wouldn't be able to pass. When I called to schedule my first test, I found the testing center was booked solid for weeks. The only alternative was to come in the very next morning and take the test. The test was on world population, and while I had the books to study, I had only spent a few hours going through all the information. I figured the worst that could happen was I might fail, so I said I would be there the next morning.

With much reservation, I went to the testing center and took the exam. I got to the end and knew I had failed. Miserably. A feeling of shame and embarrassment came over me, which suddenly turned to anger. Wait a minute, I thought. I'm not even the one who wanted to take the stupid test in the first place. If You want me to go to school so much, You take the test!

At that point, I went back to the beginning of the test and began to go through and change some answers. After a while I got into a flow and began to change answers without even really looking at the questions.

"Oh, that's not C, that's A." I knew without knowing why. Much less how. For a time, there was only the sound of the clicking of the mouse, and even though I was only halfway through the 160 questions, I was suddenly so tired and dizzy I didn't care whether I passed the test or not. I was done.

I went out and informed the person at the desk that I had finished and went to get my things out of the locker. I came back to the desk and the woman handed me a paper. There on the corner of the paper was a handwritten letter that to this day still surprises me. According to my paradigm of what is possible, it should have been an F. In fact, it was an A. This scenario continued for months. Just about every time, I would walk out of that room expecting an F, but what I would see was an A. I'm sure it was beyond a statistical probability, but I will probably never know, as statistics was the one test I did manage to fail. Interestingly enough, though, in the Master's program we had to use statistics in an actual scientific experiment, so I eventually did end up learning how to interpret data statistically.

Even the failed statistics test was a victory in the sense that the defeat didn't slow me down. In the past, it would have been grounds to begin questioning my path, to begin doubting. But it was obvious there was something else at work here, and I was as curious as I was compelled to see how in the world it was all going to turn out.

After about seven months, I had completed most of the three years' worth of credits I needed. When others have wanted to complete their Bachelor's degree and have asked me how I managed to do it in that time, I don't have an answer. This has probably been one of the more frustrating aspects of the journey: not knowing *how*; just knowing. I find that most of the time I can't instruct on specific steps. I mean, really, how would I advise someone on completing their Bachelor's degree?

"Well, first you have to be very resistant to the whole idea. Then you have to get a message from God to proceed. Then you have to be fairly lazy and resistant to most of the work involved, and then all you have to do is remember that you're not the one who wanted to do it in the first place and tell whoever did want it done to do it themselves."

This advice is of no value to anyone. But there is advice that is of value: Know thy Self. To thine own Self be true. Follow your own path, no matter where it leads. Even when—and, perhaps, especially when—it leads you to places that are not of your own choosing.

How would one go about doing that?

Become as a child, incorporate a sense of wonder and play.

Be willing to let die what needs to die.

Be willing to birth what needs to be born.

Understand that you have come here to fulfill a Divine Purpose.

Be willing to be initiated by Life in order to realize what is Real.

Understand the power of your beliefs, and that you are an "at cause," not an "at effect."

Use your negative emotions not as an excuse to vent or judge, but to identify unhealed areas in your own psyche and to move to new levels in awareness.

Get clear on the underlying intention you are holding for your life and allow your personal intention to align with the intention of your Soul.

Have patience in order to see God's Plan, in order to align with the creative inspiration of the Soul, rather than trying to force a limited idea into existence.

Integrate all of the dimensions of your being and all of your insights into your awareness and daily life.

Practice unconditional love until you realize it as yourself, then practice it some more.

Go beyond believing in something, and through your intention, dedication, and practice, come to know it.

We can hold great amounts of information in our minds, great understanding of how things work, but if we don't practice what we supposedly know, we will not ever really know it. We'll just know about it.

Teaching What You Know

One can either teach through projection or through knowledge. In teaching through projection, the students are seen as "needing instruction," since the teaching is originating from a state of separation. In that paradigm, students are experienced as lacking in knowledge, and the teachers experiences themselves as the providers of the knowledge the students need in order to progress.

Teaching through knowledge is different in that, instead of having a set agenda to teach a specific lesson, the agenda is created by the underlying Soul intentions of the particular person or group of participants. Rather than instructing, such teachers are *Being*. Rather than teaching, they are *Sharing*. Rather than working, they are *Loving*.

These teachers may follow a general outline, but just as any great speaker never lets his topic get in the way of his speech, a great teacher never lets the curriculum get in the way of the lesson. The lesson doesn't come from a system of "shoulds," it comes from inspiration. The teachings are flexible because the source is not a mental understanding of a mental system, but is the eternal moment. The source is the Source.

In the second model, the teacher does not see the students as lacking in knowledge, but instead as whole and complete. He or she sees all of the wisdom, or answers, within her students. The teacher then taps into the wisdom of the moment to allow Life to instruct. This model of instruction goes light years beyond merely passing along information. We have so much information, we don't even know what to do with it. We have information coming out of our ears. What we need is the wisdom to put the information together in a way that supports our planet and everyone on the planet, which simply isn't possible from our current paradigm of reality. This tremendous feat is only possible through an awareness of Love and in doing what we are moved to do from that awareness.

We really do need to "teach" that everyone is a unique contribution to the planet and that life is sacred, but we don't teach this by showing flip charts of various countries around the world and having people memorize their names and customs. We do it by making the people in the room feel that way about themselves.

If we know our own lives to be sacred, we know that all life is sacred. If we know we are more than our cultural rules and beliefs, we will know that others are not limited by their cultural rules and beliefs. If we have been able to step out of our cultural box, while appreciating and sharing the wisdom and benefits we find inside it, we will attract others who have been able to do the same. Instead of building more rules, more walls, and more resentments, we will build bridges.

In the beginning of our lives, we trusted openly, loved openly, gave everything we had to the moment and to Life.

We weren't afraid of living.

In one way or another, we were taught not how to Live, but how to conform. Not how to Trust, but how to fear.

Ironically, to live the life your Soul intended, you have to unlearn more than you have to learn. You have to remember an inherent truth more than you have to learn something new. You have to trust completely, outrageously, in Life. In your Self.

In the end, you find yourself back at the beginning. You know this beginning for the first time, though, because in your journeys you have discovered more of who you are. You have participated on the physical plane and, in turn, have become a different person through that participation. At the end of this journey, you come to know, once again, a place in yourself that existed before you sold out to a set system of beliefs, a set system of love, a set system of life. A place where there is never really anywhere to "get to," since there is no personal idea to adhere to and no personal plan to follow, and since, in Reality, the journey never, ever ends. Nor would you want it to.

A place where, once again, everything becomes possible.

So when did you forget?
The game isn't over yet
When did you stop playing?
If you choose to stifle
and keep your Self bridled,
it's only joy you're delaying.

The wise ones all know
to possess that glow,
one must become like a child.
It's somewhat tragic
to cut off the magic
that remains within all the while

So just let yourself go
and always know
that heaven is at hand.
When you can smile
and just play a while
Life becomes more than you planned

About the Author

Jaia Lee is an inspirational poet, writer, and singer/songwriter who, as a teacher and healer, is dedicated to personal and global healing and transformation. She is a spiritual life coach, a certified firewalk instructor, and holds a Master's degree in Spiritual Psychology. She makes her home in Santa Monica with her teenage daughter Ariel, the kitty Lord Cid, and an exuberant Pomeranian named Scooter.

Living Beyond Belief *is a soul-charging book, one that opens up new dimensions in human possibilities.*
-- Dr. Jean Houston